Reframing

Neuro-Linguistic Programming™
and
the Transformation of Meaning

by
Richard Bandler
and
John Grinder

edited by
Steve Andreas
and
Connirae Andreas

Real People Press
Box F
Moab, Utah, 84532

ISBN: 0-911226-24-9 clothbound $9.00
ISBN: 0-911226-25-7 paperbound $5.50

Cover Artwork by Rene Eisenbart

Library of Congress Cataloging in Publication Data:

Bandler, Richard.
Reframing : neuro-linguistic programming and the transformation of meaning.

Includes index.
1. Attitude change. 2. Meaning (Psychology) 3. Negotiation. 4. Psychotherapy. I. Grinder, John. II. Andreas, Steve. III. Andreas, Connirae. IV. Title.
BF323.C5B36 1982 616.89'14 82-16609
ISBN 0-911226-24-9
ISBN 0-911226-25-7 (pbk.)

The name *Real People Press* indicates our purpose; to publish ideas and ways that a person can use independently or with others to become more *real*—to further your own growth as a human being and to develop your relationships and communication with others.

2 3 4 5 6 7 8 9 10 Printing 85 84 83

Contents

Introduction

A very old Chinese Taoist story describes a farmer in a poor country village. He was considered very well-to-do, because he owned a horse which he used for plowing and for transportation. One day his horse ran away. All his neighbors exclaimed how terrible this was, but the farmer simply said "Maybe."

A few days later the horse returned and brought two wild horses with it. The neighbors all rejoiced at his good fortune, but the farmer just said "Maybe."

The next day the farmer's son tried to ride one of the wild horses; the horse threw him and broke his leg. The neighbors all offered their sympathy for his misfortune, but the farmer again said "Maybe."

The next week conscription officers came to the village to take young men for the army. They rejected the farmer's son because of his broken leg. When the neighbors told him how lucky he was, the farmer replied "Maybe." . . .

The meaning that any event has depends upon the "frame" in which we perceive it. When we change the frame, we change the meaning. Having two wild horses is a good thing until it is seen in the context of the son's broken leg. The broken leg seems to be bad in the context of peaceful village life; but in the context of conscription and war, it suddenly becomes good.

This is called reframing: changing the frame in which a person perceives events in order to change the meaning. When the meaning changes, the person's responses and behaviors also change.

Reframing is not new. Many fables and fairy tales include behaviors or events that change their meaning when the frames around them change. The different-looking chick seems to be an ugly duckling, but he turns out to be a swan—more beautiful than the ducks he has been comparing himself to. Reindeer Rudolf's funny-looking red nose becomes useful for guiding Santa's sleigh on a foggy night.

Reframing also appears in almost every joke. What seems to be one thing, suddenly shifts and becomes something else.

1) "What's green all over and has wheels?"

2) "What do Alexander the Great and Smokey the Bear have in common?"

(Answers appear at the end of this introduction.)

Reframing is also the pivotal element in the creative process: it is the ability to put a commonplace event in a new frame that is useful or enjoyable. A friend of physicist Donald Glaser pointed to a glass of beer and jokingly said "Why don't you use *that* to catch your subatomic particles?" Glaser looked at the bubbles forming in the beer, and went back to his lab to invent the "bubble chamber," similar to the Wilson cloud chamber, for detecting the paths of particles in high-energy physics experiments. Arthur Koestler, in *The Act of Creation,* calls this process "bisociation": the ability to simultaneously associate an event in two very separate and different contexts.

In general communication theory there is a basic axiom that a signal only has meaning in terms of the frame or context in which it appears. The sound of a squeaky shoe on a busy sidewalk has little meaning; the same sound outside your window when you are alone in bed means something else altogether. A light in a church belfry is simply that. But to Paul Revere it meant that the British were coming, and also how they were coming: "one if by land, and two if by sea." The light only has meaning in terms of the previous instructions that established a frame—an internal context that creates meaning.

Reframing appears widely in the therapeutic context. When a therapist tries to get a client to "think about things differently" or "see a new point of view" or to "take other factors into consideration," these are attempts to reframe events in order to get the client to respond differently to them.

Explicit conceptualizations of reframing have been used by a number of therapists who understand that "problem behavior" only makes sense when it is viewed in the context in which it occurs. These include a number of therapists with a family or systems orientation, notably Paul Watzlawick and the Mental Research Institute group in Palo Alto, and Jay Haley and Salvador Minuchin and the group at the Philadelphia Child Guidance Clinic. These therapists generally use what is described in Chapter I as "content reframing."

They nave designed specific reframing interventions such as "prescribing the symptom," and "paradoxical injunction," which effectively reframe behavior in order to change it. They also use techniques of directly intervening to change the actual external physical context in which the behavior occurs.

Virginia Satir uses a great deal of reframing in her work, from simple redefinitions to more elaborate reframing via psychodrama in her "parts parties" and "family reconstructions."

Carl Whitaker reframes with nearly everything he says to the families that he works with. Symptoms become reframed as accomplishments or skills, "sanity" becomes craziness, and "craziness" becomes sanity.

A more elaborate and "all-purpose" method of reframing, called "six-step" reframing, was developed by Bandler and Grinder, and already appears in print in *Frogs into Princes.* This book presupposes that you are already familiar with that basic six-step model of reframing; much of the book will make sense to you only if you have some prior knowledge of, and experience with, that kind of reframing. You can find an excellent description and discussion of six-step reframing (as well as other basic NLP patterns) in the third chapter of *Frogs into Princes.*

What is new in this book is an explicit description of the basic structure of reframing, and the presentation of several additional models of reframing. This book presents specific step-by-step techniques to implement these models, as well as ways to determine which model is most appropriate for a particular problem situation.

This is a book about "advanced" reframing. The first three chapters present several distinct alternative models of reframing that are useful in certain contexts, and for specific kinds of problems. Following that are chapters about building flexibility in doing six-step reframing (Chapter IV), reframing with couples, families, and other larger systems such as businesses (Chapter V), reframing with alcoholics and other examples of dissociated states (Chapter VI).

Reframing is a very powerful communication tool. This book takes it from the realm of a hit-and-miss art to a set of predictable and systematic interventions for achieving behavioral change.

This book has been edited from transcriptions of a number of different workshops and training seminars presented by Bandler and Grinder, and is presented here as if it were a single three-day workshop. No distinction is made between when Richard is speaking and when

John is speaking, and the names of most participants have been changed.

As you read this book, keep in mind that Bandler and Grinder are usually *doing* what they're talking about. The astute reader will find much more in the text than is overtly commented upon.

Connirae Andreas
Steve Andreas

Answers to jokes:
1) "Grass . . . I lied about the wheels!"
2) "They have the same middle name."

(If you haven't yet seen the unicorn on the front cover, look again. This is another example of reframing: seeing something that was there all along, but previously unrecognized.)

I

Content Reframing: Changing Meaning or Context

You have all learned the six-step reframing model. In that model you establish communication with a part, determine its positive intention, and then create three alternative behaviors to satisfy that intention. It's an excellent all-purpose model that will work for a great many things. It's got future-pacing and an ecological check built into it, so you can hardly go wrong if you follow the procedure congruently and with sensory experience.

However, that's only *one* model of reframing. There are several other models that we don't usually get around to teaching in workshops, mostly due to lack of time. One of them, called "content reframing," is the most common way that reframing is done in therapy. We call it content reframing because, unlike six-step reframing, you need to know specific content in order to make the reframe. There are two kinds of content reframing, and I'm going to give you an example of each. One of my favorite examples is this: one day in a workshop, Leslie Cameron-Bandler was working with a woman who had a compulsive behavior—she was a clean-freak. She was a person who even dusted light bulbs! The rest of her family could function pretty well with everything the mother did except for her attempts to care for the carpet. She spent a lot of her time trying to get people not to walk on it, because they left footprints—not mud and dirt, just dents in the pile of the rug.

When I grew up, I had relatives who bought carpet and then put plastic walkways across it, and people weren't allowed to step off the plastic walkways. They were the ones who bought a piano and then locked it so that no one could play it, because they didn't want to have to clean the keys. They should have just lived in a photograph. They could have stood in the house, taken the photograph, died, and hung the picture where the house should have been. It would have been a lot easier.

When this particular woman looked down at the carpet and saw a footprint in it, her response was an intense negative kinesthetic gut reaction. She would rush off to get the vacuum cleaner and vacuum the carpet immediately. She was a professional housewife. She actually vacuumed the carpet three to seven times a day. She spent a tremendous amount of time trying to get people to come in the back door, and nagging at them if they didn't, or getting them to take their shoes off and walk lightly. Have you ever tried to walk without any weight on your feet? The only person I've ever seen do it is the guy at the beginning of that old TV program, *Kung Fu,* where they roll out the rice paper, and he walks down it without leaving footprints. When you can do that, you can marry this woman and live in her house.

This family, by the way, didn't have any juvenile delinquents or overt drug addicts. There were three children, all of whom were there rooting for Leslie. The family seemed to get along fine if they were not at home. If they went out to dinner, they had no problems. If they went on vacation, there were no problems. But at home everybody referred to the mother as being a nag, because she nagged them about this, and nagged them about that. Her nagging centered mainly around the carpet.

What Leslie did with this woman is this: she said "I want you to close your eyes and see your carpet, and see that there is not a single footprint on it anywhere. It's clean and fluffy—not a mark anywhere." This woman closed her eyes, and she was in seventh heaven, just smiling away. Then Leslie said *"And realize fully that that means you are totally alone, and that the people you care for and love are nowhere around."* The woman's expression shifted radically, and she felt terrible! Then Leslie said "Now, put a few footprints there and look at those footprints and know that the people you care most about in the world are nearby." And then, of course, she felt good again.

You can call that intervention "trade feelings" if you like. You can call it a change of strategy. You can call it anchoring. You can call it lots of things, but one useful way to think about it is as reframing. In this particular kind of reframing the stimulus in the world doesn't actually change, but its *meaning* changes. You can use this kind of reframing any time you decide that the stimulus for a problem behavior doesn't really need to change—that there's nothing inherently bad about it.

The other choice, of course, would have been to attack the rest of the family and get them all to shape up and not leave footprints. This woman's mother tried that; it didn't work very well.

If people have a sensory experience that they don't like, what they don't like is their *response* to it. One way of changing the response is to understand that the response itself is not based on what's going on in sensory experience. If you change what the experience *means* to them, their response will change.

What we know about the woman who kept everything clean is that she engages some strategy that allows her to decide when it's time to feel bad. She doesn't feel bad on vacations, or in a restaurant. My guess is that when she walks into somebody *else's* house and it's messy, she doesn't feel bad, because her response has to do with ownership. Her home is *her* territory; she only feels bad within certain limits. She may not consider the garage or the backyard to be in her territory. Some people keep their houses spotless, but they don't consider their children's rooms to be part of the house, so they don't feel bad about them when they're dirty.

These are all people, of course, who use negative motivation strategies. As they walk into the kitchen and see dirty dishes everywhere, they go "Ugh!" In order to make the bad feeling go away, they have to wash all the dishes. Then they can stand back and go "Ahhhh!" When they walk into a clean hotel room, they don't go "Ahhh!" because it's not *theirs.* So there's some kind of a decision strategy at work.

One way to help this family would be to alter this woman's strategy. Her strategy has some other characteristics which are unpleasant for her. But to solve the immediate problem and achieve a very limited therapeutic gain, all you need to do is to get her to have a positive feeling about one thing: the carpet. That is not a pervasive change, but it's something you should be able to do. This is *especially* true for those of you engaged in the business world, because content reframing is the essence of sales.

Some people call this "redefining" or "relabeling." Whatever you call it, what you are doing is attaching a new response to some sensory experience. You leave the content the same and put another piece of meaning around it—the same *kind* of meaning that the person has already made. The clean-freak mother makes a judgement that when she sees this sensory experience, it means something important enough to feel bad about. If you can define the footprints as being something important enough to feel good about, then her response will change.

To get a change, it's very essential that you have congruent supporting nonverbal analogues as you deliver the reframe. You have to do it with a serious facial expression and tone of voice.

Virginia Satir is one of the people to study if you want to learn about content reframing. She is a master at it. One of Virginia's main maneuvers to anchor new responses in the family is to do content reframing. Let me give you an example of one I saw her do. I almost blew it for her, because I cracked up when she did it. That's not appropriate in a family therapy situation, so I began coughing. That's always a good cover: when you laugh, you can go into coughing right away, and no one will notice.

Virginia was working with a family. The father was a banker who was professionally stuffy. He must have had a degree in it. He wasn't a bad guy; he was very well-intentioned. He took good care of his family, and he was concerned enough to go to therapy. But basically he was a stuffy guy. The wife was an extreme placater in Virginia's terminology. For those of you who are not familiar with that, a placater is a person who will agree with anything and apologize for everything. When you say "It's a *beautiful* day!" the placater says "Yes, I'm sorry!"

The daughter was an interesting combination of the parents. She thought her father was the bad person and her mother was the groovy person, so she always sided with her mother. However, she *acted* like her father.

The father's repeated complaint in the session was that the mother hadn't done a very good job of raising the daughter, because the daughter was so stubborn. At one time when he made this complaint, Virginia interrupted what was going on. She turned around and looked at the father and said "You're a man who has gotten ahead in your life. Is this true?"

"Yes."

"Was all that you have, just given to you? Did your father own the bank and just say 'Here, you're president of the bank'?"

"No, no. I worked my way up."

"So you have some tenacity, don't you?"

"Yes."

"Well, there is a part of you that has allowed you to be able to get where you are, and to be a good banker. And sometimes you have to refuse people things that you would like to be able to give them, because you know if you did, something bad would happen later on."

"Yes."

"Well, there's a part of you that's been stubborn enough to really protect yourself in very important ways."

"Well, yes. But, you know, you can't let this kind of thing get out of control."

"Now I want you to turn and look at your daughter, and to realize beyond a doubt that you've taught her how to be stubborn and how to stand up for herself, and that that is something priceless. This gift that you've given to her is something that can't be bought, and it's something that may save her life. Imagine how valuable that will be when your daughter goes out on a date with a man who has bad intentions."

I don't know if you begin to hear a pattern in this. *Every experience in the world, and every behavior is appropriate, given some context, some frame.*

There are two kinds of content reframing. I've given you an example of each. Can you tell the difference between them? Can you hear an essential difference between the two examples I just gave you?

Man: One changed the context, and one changed the meaning.

Yes, exactly. In the last example, Virginia changed the context. Being stubborn is judged to be bad in the context of the family. It becomes good in the context of banking and in the context of a man trying to take advantage of the daughter on a date.

Bill: So you're really changing the context that the father uses to evaluate the daughter's behavior.

Right. Her behavior of being stubborn with him will no longer be seen as her fighting with him. It will be seen as a personal achievement: he has taught her to protect herself from men with bad intentions.

Bill: So you switch contexts in imagination and get a different response "there," and then bring that response back to the present context. You get him to respond to what is not going on.

Well, he's already responding to "what is not going on." You get him to respond to something *different* which is not going on. Most of the behavior that puzzles you about your clients is a demonstration that the majority of their context is internal, and you don't have access to it yet. When a husband says to his wife "I love you," and she says "You son of a bitch," that's a pretty good sign that she's operating out of a unique internal context. If you explore, you may find out that the last time a man said that to her, he then turned around, walked out the door, and never came back. A lot of your ability to establish and maintain rapport with your clients is your ability to appreciate that what looks and sounds and feels really weird and inappropriate to you, is simply a statement about your failure to appreciate the context from which that behavior is being generated.

Rather than imposing a new context, you can use the client's own resources to find a new context. Your client says "I want to stop X-ing." You ask "Is there some place in your life where behavior X is useful and appropriate?" If the client answers "Yes, there are *some* places, but in other places X is just a disaster," then you know where that behavior belongs. You just contextualize that behavior, and substitute a new pattern of behavior in the contexts where X was a disaster.

If the client says "No, it's not appropriate anywhere," you can assist him in finding appropriate contexts by giving him specific representational system instructions. "See yourself performing that behavior and listen to it. . . . Now, where did that happen?"

"Oh, it happened in church. I stood up and yelled 'God dammit' and then they came and dragged me out."

"All right. You know that standing up in the middle of a group of people in church and yelling 'God dammit' didn't work out very well for you, and you don't want that to happen again. Let's find a place where it would be useful for that behavior to happen. You can see and hear yourself doing it in church. Now I want you to change that background—the pews and the altar and the interior of the church—to something else. I want you to keep substituting other backgrounds for that same behavior, until you find one in which if you stood up and said 'God dammit!' every part of you would agree that that is an appropriate response, and you can see, by looking at the faces of the people around you, that others also consider it appropriate. As soon as you find a context like that, then go inside and ask the part of you that makes you stand up and yell 'God dammit' if it would be willing to be your primary resource in *just* that context."

That's using a visual lead, of course. You have to tailor the search for a new context to the person's actual internal processes in terms of representational systems. For some people it would be more appropriate to search auditorily or kinesthetically.

Another way of approaching this more formally and more generally would be to do the following: identify a behavior that you want to change. I want all of you to pick a behavior in yourself that you don't like. You don't have to say anything out loud; just pick one. . . .

Now, rather than contacting the part that generates that behavior directly, just go inside and ask if *any* part of you whatsoever can figure out *any* situation in which you *want* to be capable of generating that exact same behavior. . . .

Now, go inside and ask the part of you that has you do that behavior if it would be willing to be the most important part of you in that situation, and to generate that behavior exquisitely and congruently *only* in that context. . . .

Those are variations on the theme of context reframing. All the reframing models that we use are based on some kind of content reframing. In the stubbornness example we left the meaning of the behavior the same and put it in a new *context.*

Now, what did we alter in the first example I gave of the woman and the footprints? . . . We left the context the same and changed the *meaning* of the behavior in that same context. Everything remained constant except what the behavior *implied.*

For another example, let's say that someone had a part of themselves that was greedy, and they believed it was bad to have a greedy part. One way to alter that would be to have him conceive of a context or situation in which being greedy would be very important—perhaps after an atomic war, or being greedy about learning new things. You can always come up with some change of context that will change the significance of the behavior.

Another choice is to find out what behavior they generate that they name "being greedy" and give the behavior itself a new name with a new meaning. "Greed" has negative connotations, but if you give the behavior another label with positive connotations, such as "being able to meet your needs," you can change the meaning of the behavior.

A Virginia Satir "parts party" is nothing more than doing this over and over and over again, in lots of different ways. If you have a part of you that is devious and malicious, it later becomes renamed "your ability to be creatively constructive" or something else. It doesn't matter what name you come up with, as long as it has positive connotations. You're saying "Look, every part of you is a valuable part and does positive things for you. If you organize your parts in some way so that they operate cooperatively, and so that what they are trying to do for you becomes more apparent, then they'll function better."

In the case of the stubborn daughter, "stubbornness" in the father's experience changes from being something that works against him to being something that he feels good about when he sees it occur, because he knows that this behavior is something that she will need to survive in the world. That changes his internal response.

In the other example, when the mother looked at the footprints on the carpet, she took them as a comment about her being a bad housewife—that she hadn't finished doing the things she was supposed to do. If you change the meaning of the footprints to "You're around the people you love" then her experience changes. *That change in experience is really the only essential piece of any reframing model.* That is what reframing is all about.

Man: When you change the meaning, aren't you installing a complex equivalence?

Yes. Actually, you're not installing a complex equivalence, you are just altering the one that's already there. You're really trading. She already has one complex equivalence. She is saying "Footprints on the carpet mean bad housewife, therefore feel bad." You are saying "Well, since you are so good at complex equivalence, try this one. This one is a lot groovier: footprints on the carpet mean that the people you love are around, therefore feel good."

In order to make reframing work, sometimes it's better to begin with the reverse case. Leslie could have just looked at this woman and said "Well, no, no, no. You see, you're all wrong. When you see footprints, it just means that the people you care about are there." That would not have had an impact; it would not have changed her internal experience or her response. So of course the sequencing of your delivery and your expressiveness are *very* important.

"You see the carpet there and it's *spotless!* You've cleaned it *perfectly.* It's fluffy. You can see the white fibers." This is pacing: she is responding to the complex equivalence. Then you lead: "And then suddenly you realize that that means you are *all alone.*" That is something she had never considered before. If you think about it, that is not necessarily true. The whole family might be in the next room. However, it *sounds* so meaningful in that context that you can use it to influence behavior. Then you switch back: "Now put a few footprints there, and realize that those you love are near."

Which kind of reframing is more appropriate if somebody says to you "I can't take notes. I'm so stupid!" They'll both work, but which one is more immediate? When you hear a complex equivalence as in this example, it tells you something about meaning. If I say that I don't like something, especially about others, typically it has to do with meaning. If I say "Well, Byron has never been really interested in my groups; he sits in the back corner," that's a statement about the *meaning* of a behavior.

If you make the statement "It annoys me when X happens," which kind of reframing is going to be most appropriate? . . . Meaning reframing will be. What kinds of statements will tell you that context reframing is more appropriate?

Woman: "I'm not happy when I'm sitting in this room."

Which kind of reframing is going to be most immediate for that: context or meaning? She's essentially saying "I don't like what this means," so it's meaning again.

What happens if I say something like "I'm too tyrannical"? . . . That tells you something about context. Too tyrannical for *what?* . . . or for *whom?*

Now, what's the difference between the two forms? Each of them is a kind of generalization. Can you tell the difference between those kinds of generalizations? If you can identify form, that will tell you which kind of reframing is more *immediate* to use.

No behavior in and of itself is useful or not useful. Every behavior will be useful somewhere; identifying *where* is context reframing. And no behavior means anything in and of itself, so you *can* make it mean anything: that's meaning reframing. Doing it is simply a matter of your ability to describe *how* that's the case, which is purely a function of your creativity and expressiveness.

Now let's play with this a little. Give me some complaints, and I'll reframe them.

Woman: There's no more coffee in the evening, and I don't like that.

Have you been sleeping well?

Man: There are too many sessions scheduled at once. I decide to be in one workshop, and then I want to be in another. I can't switch and go over to another session in the afternoon, because it's already progressed too far.

Yeah, I understand. I really do sympathize. And one of the nice things about arranging the workshop that way is that it gives you extra practice in decision-making processes.

Woman: I don't see the reframing there.

Well, I placed his remark in a frame in which it has a function other than the one he consciously recognized: it gives him practice in decision-making.

Man: My wife takes forever to decide on things. She has to look at every dress in the store and compare them all before she selects one.

So she's very careful about decisions. Isn't it a tremendous compliment that out of all the men in the world, she chose you!

Man: I don't want to tell my wife what I want sexually, because that would force her to limit herself.

But you *are* willing to limit her ability to please you when she wants to, by not telling her what you like?

Woman: My children yell and run around too much.

When they are playing outdoors or at sporting events, it must give you great satisfaction to see how uninhibited your children are, and how well you and your husband have preserved their natural exuberance.

Now I'll give you some complaints, and you reframe them. "I feel terrible because my boss always criticizes me."

Man: He must really notice the work that you do, and like you enough to want to help you improve it.

OK. Fine. "I'm too easy-going."

Woman: Well, I'm thinking of many of my friends who are getting heart attacks because they react so strongly when someone asks them to do something they don't want to do.

Exercise

I want you all to practice meaning and context reframing for twenty minutes. Get together with two other people. One of you will be a client, one of you will be a programmer, and one of you will be an observer. Switch roles periodically.

The client's job is to come up with a complaint. You could role-play a client of yours and state some really powerful complaint that you typically get from clients in your practice. Or you could pretend to role-play a client but come up with a complaint that might be relevant for some part of your own personal evolution. I want you to state your complaints in a particular form to make it easier for your partner. The form of the complaint will tell the other person which kind of reframing is most appropriate.

1) Present your complaint as a complex equivalence that links a response to a class of events: "I feel X when Y happens" or,

2) Present the complaint as a comparative generalization about yourself or someone else, with the context deleted: "I'm too Z" or "He's too Q."

The programmer's job is to find a way of reframing the problem, and then to deliver the reframe in such a way that it has an impact. This is a training seminar, so don't force yourself to respond immediately. Let me give you a strategy to generate reframes. First you identify the form of the complaint that your client has presented so that you know which kind of reframe to go for. With a complex equivalence you do a *meaning* reframe, and with a comparative generalization you do a *context* reframe. The next step is to create an internal representation of the complaint that you have received from the other person: either make a picture of it visually, feel what it would be like kinesthetically, or describe it auditorily.

For a context reframe, ask yourself "In what context would this particular behavior that the person is complaining about have value?" Think of different contexts until you find one that changes the evaluation of the behavior.

For a meaning reframe, ask yourself "Is there a larger or different frame in which this behavior would have a positive value?" "What other aspect of this same situation that isn't apparent to this person could provide a different meaning frame?" or simply "What else could this behavior mean?" or "How else could I describe this same situation?"

When you have found a new frame for the behavior, take a moment or two to think of alternative ways of delivering the reframe, and then select the one that you think will get the maximum response. Pacing and leading will be extremely important in doing this. If you have difficulty, take the observer aside for a moment and use her as a resource.

When you have thought of a reframe, ask the client to repeat the complaint, and then deliver your reframe. Carefully observe the nonverbal changes in the client as he considers what you have said.

The observer and the programmer both have the job of getting a sensory-based description of the nonverbal changes that occur in the client as he makes the transition from complaining about a behavior to at least a partial appreciation of how the behavior has value for him within a different frame.

Do you have any questions?

Woman: What is the purpose of pausing before you reframe?

I want you to take the time to employ one of the specific strategies I offered you to come up with a verbal content reframe. If you are practiced in content reframing, and you have an immediate response, fine. Go ahead and make it. But if you have any hesitation, I want you to drop out. Go into internal experience and check all representational systems to figure out visually, auditorily, or kinesthetically how you could verbally reframe the content of the complaint.

If you are practiced in reframing, it will be to your advantage to take a little time to figure out what your own typical strategy for verbal content reframing is, and use any *other* one, so that you increase your flexibility. If you usually lead visually and search for alternate contexts visually, try doing it kinesthetically or auditorily.

Come back to me with a successful example of each kind of content reframe, and with a specific sensory-based description of the changes that you saw in the client. We'll compare the descriptions to find out how we can generalize about the things that you observed. Any other questions about this exercise? . . . OK. Go ahead.

* * * * *

Discussion

Woman: I had a lot of difficulty reframing the problem that my partner presented. It was an interaction with his wife, and when she does something that she—

Did he give you one sentence?

Woman: Yes. He wants to stop making so many visual side trips when he's talking to his wife.

That doesn't fit one of the two forms that I asked him to express the statement in, so it has nothing to do with what we are doing here today, *unless* he rephrases it for you, or *unless* you question him until you get a statement which fits those forms. I want you to use the two forms that we demonstrated earlier, so that you have some control over your language and your sense of expression. I said "Describe a problem in one of these two forms." He did it in some other form, so it has nothing to do with what's going on here. If you were to Meta-Model him, eventually it would come out in one of these two forms. You weren't the only one who did that, by the way. A lot of people came up and asked "What do you do with this sentence?" And I said "Nothing. It has nothing to do with what we are doing here."

An important part of being successful in NLP is knowing what kind of problem your procedure works on. If you know that, you can do successful demonstrations any time you want to. You just ask for volunteers who have exactly what your procedure works on. You say "Who has a problem like this: you go into a context and you want to have a certain feeling, but instead you have a completely different feeling, and it happens every time?" If you have a therapeutic model like reanchoring which is designed to deal with that, you can't lose.

People often come up to us after seminars and say "You guys do therapy *so fast!*" It's fast because we ask for problems that fit the form of what we want to demonstrate. As soon as somebody raises his hand, we're done.

Being able to identify these forms and ask for them is very important. If you have a client who comes in and says "Well, you know, I have all kinds of problems" then you can say "Do you have anything like this?" And he'll say "Yeah, I have a couple of those. I've got these two." You can fix those, and then you can describe another form and ask "Well, have you got any of these?" It's a very different mental set for doing therapy. If you've got certain things you do that work, being able to describe the kind of problem that they work on is very important.

If you take one of these two reframing models and use it where it's inappropriate, it won't work. That would be like taking the phobia cure and using it for something else. It just won't have an impact, because it's not designed to do something else. One man who was in a workshop we did in Chicago phoned me about a month later and said "You worked with a woman who had a phobia of birds, and it worked really well, but I've been doing that with all my clients and it doesn't work." I asked "Well, do they have phobias?" He answered "No, I don't have any clients with phobias." He came right out and said that! I said "Well, why are you using that technique then?" And he said "Well, it *worked!*" He really understood the seminar!

In essence that's the biggest mistake that has been made in therapy all along. Somebody did something and it worked. Then he thought "It worked! Good! We'll use it for *everything!* And we'll call it a new school of therapy." And then he went out and tried that one thing with everybody. It worked with some people and not with others, and he couldn't figure out why.

It's really quite simple. The structure of what he did was appropriate for accomplishing certain goals and not others. Since those specific goals were not described, people didn't know how to look for them and find them. I am hoping that you will come to realize that there are appropriate and inappropriate times to use these tools. It's important that you know what your tools do, and what they don't do. Otherwise you have to find out by trial and error.

Jim: I'm interested in getting others' reactions to a reframe that I did. My partner role-played a patient who had attempted suicide several times. She said to me "You people profess to know a lot about human behavior. I don't like it when all you do is continue to lock me up instead of letting me kill myself."

Marie: Well, there was something else that I said: "I really know I want to kill myself." His response to that was "Good! I'm really glad you know what you want." Then I responded "Well, if you appreciate that, why do you lock me up here? I don't like it that you send the police for me when I swallow pills."

OK. That's the complaint. All of you take a moment to figure out a content reframe you might make to that input, and then Jim can tell us what he did. . . . OK, now go ahead, Jim.

Jim: I said to her "You know, I have never really understood suicide before. We really don't know what goes on with people like you, and you are offering me an unprecedented opportunity to learn. What I would like to do is cooperate with you, but what you have proposed is too simple, and I won't learn enough. What I would like to do is make your death more complex, so that I can really learn about it."

She was obviously very surprised by what I said. She just went "Tchew!" and inhaled suddenly, and her stomach sucked in.

Marie: When he said that, I got the feeling that he is as crazy as I am!

Cathy: When Marie was talking about suicide I thought about how fantastic it is to have something in life that's worth dying for. So it would be important to search for *the* thing that would really be worth giving your life for, and to take the time to do that.

Marie: I would go along with that; I would feel good about it. The question is "What can I do with that next?" I'm really hoping that you can tell me what to do after that.

The important thing about the responses that Cathy and Jim made is that they both accept the idea of suicide. It's a good pace, and establishes rapport. And now since they've accepted that she is going to kill herself, they move on to *when* and *how*. Cathy's response is really a natural extension of the *how* part. "If you are going to do this, you may as well do it *well*. It's far too precious a thing to do just on the spur of the moment." With this kind of patient, the outcome of exploring what she's going to die for is that you will get to the intent behind the suicidal behavior. Typically the suicidal patient will never give you a positive statement. They can't. They are committing suicide out of desperation: they would rather be dead than continue living with the kinds of experiences they are presently having.

What Cathy and Jim have suggested is a kind of shock treatment to gain rapport. You follow that with a statement presupposing that the only justifiable way to die is *for* something which is positive. What you will end up getting is some positive intent behind the suicide, and then you can approach that intent in a variety of ways. That sequence is particularly nice.

Bunny: I did that with a client who was talking about a part of her that wanted to die. I said "How wonderful that you are looking for heaven on earth." Then we went into what heaven on earth would be for her, and she was much less depressed after that.

"Heaven on earth" of course, is a way of defining a very general secondary outcome: the positive intention that suicide will achieve. You are essentially relabeling "suicide" as "trying to achieve heaven on earth." Any time your relabeling can include an idiom like "heaven on earth," it will have an extra force to it, because it appeals to both brain hemispheres simultaneously. It is one of the few language forms computed in both hemispheres, so it has an extra power to it. Her complex equivalence for "heaven on earth" will be essentially the goals which you can now work toward in other ways than having her commit suicide. That's a really nice way to lead into a situation which is appropriate for the six-step model of reframing.

Man: When your client talks about committing suicide, how about saying *"Wonderful!"*?

Again, that's fine as a first step, particularly if all your nonverbal analogues support what you say. One way to interrupt a client's pattern is to do something totally unexpected. One of the least expected responses to suicide in this culture is to compliment him and agree and approve of such a statement. Agreeing will interrupt him, and it will also get immediate rapport with the part of him that made the statement. This is not a complete maneuver, but it's a good way to change the focus of what's going on. You don't want to stop there, especially when you are dealing with life and death matters. You need to go on immediately to utilize this opening to explore outcomes. "Who would you like to find your body?" "Have you composed your suicide note? Would you like to have me edit it for you?" These are ways of specifying the outcome that this part of him is trying to gain for him by suicide.

So these are only first steps in a complete therapeutic intervention. They are simply ways of interrupting and changing the frame in which the person understands his behavior, giving you a lot more freedom to maneuver. That's the whole point of reframing, anyway: creating freedom to maneuver. If a person has behavior X, it's a very specific behavior. It has actual sensory components: seeing, feeling, and hearing. If you try to change that piece of behavior directly, it will be very difficult. However, if that piece of behavior, with all its specificity, is suddenly seen or felt or heard to be in a larger context, a larger frame, you can discover that what you are really committed to is not the specific piece of behavior, but to the *outcome* that behavior is supposed to lead to in your world-model. Then suddenly you have a lot of room to maneuver. You hold the outcome—the goal that you are trying to achieve—constant, and recognize that this particular pattern of behavior is only *one* way to achieve it. There are many other ways to achieve "heaven on earth."

Let me remind you that we almost never take a response away, except temporarily. There may be a context in which even murder, suicide, etc. is a good choice. I'm not willing to play God to the extent of removing any choices from a person; I simply want to add additional alternatives which are somehow more congruent with the person's conscious understanding of what he wants to achieve. I don't want to take away the ability to engage in the "inappropriate behavior" because it may become appropriate at some other time in some other context.

However, with a suicidal client it's quite appropriate to *temporarily* take away the choice of suicide. I recommend that you be very explicit at the beginning of your work with her. "I agree that it is better for you to die than continue living the way you are. I believe that I can assist you in changing your life in ways that make life worth living. I will accept you as a client *only* if you give up the possibility of suicide for three months. At the end of that time, if you still believe that suicide is appropriate, I'll even help you do it. Do you agree to that?"

That's what I do verbally. As I do that, I read the client's nonverbal responses, to be sure that I have full unconscious agreement. Anybody who tries to commit suicide is dissociated enough that she wouldn't consciously know whether she was going to commit suicide anyway or not.

After using NLP for three months the situation will be so different that the issue of suicide probably won't even come up again. I will bring it up myself, just to make sure, and because I've made an agreement.

Milton Erickson often used a contract like that. He would then point out that since she has been planning suicide anyway, she may as well go out in style. "How much money do you have in the bank?" "Oh, $5,000." "Good. By Wednesday you will have consulted a hair specialist, and someone who is competent to teach you to dress appropriately.

You look gross! You will also consult someone who can teach you how to walk and talk and meet people, both in social settings and in interviews." She can't object to spending money, because soon she will be dead, so it won't matter. He uses her planning to be dead as *leverage* to move her into new behaviors that he knows will make suicide unnecessary.

Man: What if you decided that suicide was an appropriate choice, because the person was very old, incapacitated, and in great pain, or something like that?

Then I would do essentially the same thing that I do when both members of a couple have decided to end a relationship. I help them really complete the ending of the relationship so that they can go on cleanly and congruently. When a person ends a relationship, typically he carries lots of "unfinished business" with him and leaves a lot of messes behind him. This is also true of suicide.

Let me give you a specific ritual that I have used to accomplish this. I ask the person to select a place in the outdoors that is very special to him, preferably a high place where he can look out over the world. "In your imagination, go to that place, and gather around you all the people who have been important in your life. Take one of them by the hand, look her in the eye, and tell her of your decision to suicide. There may be other things you want to tell this person so that you can be fully satisfied with the way you are ending this relationship. If there are, tell her now. Think about any messages left unsaid or activities left undone, and as you do this, watch and listen to her response, to know if you are completing this relationship in a manner that is satisfactory to you. Take as much time as you need to do this thoroughly until you feel complete with this person. . . .

"Then I want you and this person to look into the future together to see how present events will develop without you. As you do this, I want you to consider if there is anything you want to do now before you go, to influence those future events. . . .

"Now take the time to do the same with each and every one of those people you have gathered around you."

If the person is truly ready to die, it can alert him to the things he needs to do first so that his death has the most constructive impact on his friends and relatives. If the person is not congruently ready to die, this ritual will give you lots of information about the outcomes behind his decision to suicide, and you can use this information to develop other ways of satisfying them. You will also learn a lot about the people and events that still have meaning for him, and you can use this as leverage to help accomplish the changes you want to make.

Now let's get back to the exercise and talk about the other part of it. Somebody give me a sensory-grounded description of what you could see, hear, or feel—if you were making tactile contact—that seemed to be an indication that you just did a successful reframe. What did you observe when there was a reorganization of the person's understanding unconsciously—and usually also partially at the conscious level—that indicated that you succeeded in the reframe?

Ben: There was a loosening of the body, especially in the chest. The muscle tension in the face and shoulders softened.

Does anyone have any counter-examples to that? Did anybody tighten up in that area when the reframe worked?

Man: The initial surprise seemed to make them tighten up . . . and then they relaxed.

Becky: I experienced what I perceived to be a slight epileptic seizure internally, and then I relaxed.

OK. Did it show up externally?

Becky's Partner: Yes. I also noticed another thing. When Becky was considering something, she would "chew it over" metaphorically. She was also literally chewing. It was very visible in her jaw movements.

OK, and what happened when she made a decision on whether or not she was going to swallow it?

Becky's Partner: Her jaws relaxed, and there were major skin color changes. Each time I made the reframing statement, there was a visible pink flush in her cheeks and forehead.

OK, so there was an increase in blood flow to the skin. Are there any counter-examples to that?

Woman: Along with the tightening there was some whitening, and then the flush came with the relaxation.

What we are describing now are some of the visible signs of the functioning of the autonomic nervous system. There are two parts to the autonomic nervous system: the sympathetic and parasympathetic nervous systems. The two tend to balance each other through opposite effects.

Sympathetic activation results in increased muscle tension and a readiness to respond physically to some threat. There is more adrenalin, and the skin whitens as the blood vessels and pupils constrict. Parasympathetic activation results in muscle relaxation, flushing of the skin, dilation of blood vessels, dilation of the pupils, etc.

These are some very general visible characteristics of those two systems. What we have been describing is that people tend to have sympathetic activation when presenting a complaint and considering the reframe. Then they shift to parasympathetic activation when the reframe works, which is what you would expect to occur. If the reframing works, what was perceived as a problem to cope with becomes not a problem at all. What other changes did you observe?

Ken: I saw accessing changes. Typically when the client was presenting her complaint, she would be in one mode of accessing. Usually the ones we saw were high-intensity kinesthetic. As we presented the reframe, her accessing switched into a visual or auditory pattern. Then when we went back and talked about the problem situation, she accessed in the second pattern.

Excellent. That's a really elegant nonverbal test to find out if the reframe continues to work after you first introduce it. Your client may accept your reframe at the time that you make it. Later, she may reject it because of objections that arise. However, if later you mention some other dimension of the same presenting problem, and you see that she goes through the accessing sequence which was characteristic of the reframe and not the accessing sequence that was there before the reframe, then you know that the reframe is integrated into her experience of the problem area.

Woman: That's what happened with Bob. His eyes went to visual construct when he made the complaint. When the reframing took place, his eyes became defocused and he stared straight ahead. Then when I mentioned the complaint again, he went through that same defocusing process.

Great. As far as I'm concerned, the generalization is this: one indicator that the reframe works *at the moment* is that you get a different accessing sequence when the person considers the same problem area. You observe some new strategy. Perhaps rather than being locked into kinesthetic feelings, the person is able to take a new perspective. Or you may observe the same accessing sequence, but with a different response. You recognize that by observing the autonomic cues that we mentioned earlier: skin color changes, breathing changes, muscle tension changes, etc.

Then you go on to other material, or have the client practice some new behavior to be wired in, so that she has lots of choices in the context that you reframed. Then later, at the end of the session, you can use what you observed earlier to test whether the reframe has endured. You might ask "By the way, does so-and-so—who is part of the original presenting problem—have a moustache?" If you see the same changes that were characteristic of the reframe moment, then you know you've got integration for that material. If not—if she goes back directly to the original pattern—then you might suspect that you need to do some more work. Any other examples or comments?

Woman: My client was playing a blind person, and she said "You people just don't understand what it is like to be blind." I said "Gee, we must be missing a lot." Her whole body jerked, and her eyes opened up.

Great! What you said *reversed* the presupposition of her statement. She's complaining "You don't understand what it's like to be blind and miss so much." Your response is "*We're* the ones who are missing out."

This is a typical pattern that Carl Whitaker uses. Let me give you an example. Carl is working with a family and the father says "Nobody in this family has ever supported me by taking care of me. I always have to do it all myself. No one is ever solicitous or takes care of me, and it's been like this my whole life." His supporting nonverbal behavior is "Isn't it terrible that I should have to live through this!" Whitaker watches and listens very attentively. When the man finishes, Whitaker pauses meaningfully while the man is waiting for some supporting remark like "Oh, that's really too bad. Maybe we can make changes in the family." Then Carl looks over at him and says "Thank God!"

The outcome of that maneuver is 1) pattern interruption, because Carl's response is so unexpected, 2) the father will go inside and search for some way of figuring out how he could possibly be glad about that behavior, and 3) it honors the part of the father that has organized his behavior in such a way that nobody ever supports him in an overt way by taking care of him.

If you think about the message that is being offered, it's actually a conscious-mind complaint about his own behavior. He has behaved in such a way that no one has ever formed a relationship in which they take care of him. The response that Carl offers is a validation of the part that put him in that position of not having people take care of him. He is essentially saying "I'm sure glad that this part of you established those kinds of relationships with your family members and caused those behaviors to occur."

That is a meaning reframe. It's fast and it can be very effective. Carl is presupposing that there really is something good about that behavior, and that the father will be able to come to a recognition, at least unconsciously, of the point of Carl's comment "Thank God!"

However, that is making an assumption which, strictly speaking, isn't warranted. It's possible—though not very likely—that there isn't anything good about that behavior. I trust Carl as a communicator, having had the opportunity to watch and listen to him. If he were to make that intervention, and the father's response was incongruent with the outcome Carl was working towards, I trust him to have enough sensory experience and flexibility to go on to try something more appropriate. Carl has finesse, so he wouldn't go back and talk about it, he would simply go on to another reframe or some other intervention that would help the person make the change.

The thing I don't trust is formulas. For instance, there is a formula in gestalt therapy that guilt is really resentment, and beneath that is anger, and below that is a demand. That could be a useful formula for some people. If you want to use a formula, of course it's another choice that you ought to have available to you. If you engage in content reframing, then you need to take the responsibility of being very sensitive perceptually to any incongruencies in response to your intervention, to know whether your reframes work. If they don't, you are imposing content on that person and probably doing him a disservice. If you know via feedback that a reframe has worked, that indicates that you made a guess which resonates and is congruent with an unconscious set of patterns in that person.

One way of thinking about content reframing is that it can be used as a temporary measure to loosen a person's perceptual frame. The client is fixed on the fact that some particular thing is the issue. She has riveted her conscious attention on the fact that X is the case, and you point out that it is "really" Y, or also Z. When you have succeeded in shaking up her perceptual frame, it will be much easier to go on to do other things.

For instance, there's a man in California who does a single content reframe that works with anorexics. He has an 80% cure rate with anorexia, which is a tough problem for most therapists. He brings the whole family into a room with a one-way mirror. There's a table in the room with a big pot of hot dogs on it. He walks in and says "I'm Dr. So-and-So; you have fifteen minutes to get this young woman to eat. I'll be back." Then he walks out.

The family does all kinds of things to try to get the anorexic to eat. Some of them physically pin the girl down and start stuffing food in her mouth. They do their usual inadequate best to try to get her to eat. At the end of fifteen minutes he walks back in and says to the family "You failed miserably. Get out!" He throws everyone out but the anorexic. Then he turns to the anorexic and says "Now, how long have you been using this as a way of getting your family's attention?"

That's a gross imposition of content on the anorexic, but it works. Four out of five times the anorexia cycle is now broken and the anorexic can move into more healthy states. I don't argue with success like that.

Woman: I do something similar when I want to change the way the family members view the "problem" child. In a family session I'll say to the child "Don't stop getting into trouble. You're doing something really important with this behavior. Until you get the attention of these fools, or until you find a better way to get their attention, you keep on doing what you're doing."

Excellent. There are actually two reframes in that intervention: 1) describing the problem behavior as a useful way to get attention, and 2) characterizing the symptomatic problem behavior as being under conscious control. That can be very useful. Any time you relabel another person's behavior like that, you are imposing your own beliefs and your own values. You are hallucinating freely and projecting your hallucination. There's nothing wrong with that, as long as you know what you are doing and realize the consequences of doing it.

Let me give you another example from Virginia Satir's work. She's working with a couple and the husband is yelling at the wife "You stupid bitch, blah, blah, blah." When he pauses, Virginia says to him "I want to tell you, Jim, that I know that you are angry. You look angry and you sound angry, and I just want to tell you that one of the most important things for *any* individual in a family is that he feels the feelings he has, and that he can express them. I hope everyone in this family has the ability to express anger as congruently as Jim has."

That's pacing: she builds a frame that says "That's good! That's really wonderful." The husband isn't yelling anymore; he's listening to this appreciative message about his yelling and screaming—which is the last thing he expected!

Then Virginia moves in and gets really close to the husband. She places her hand gently on his stomach, and says in a soft, low tone of voice "And I'm wondering if you would be willing to tell me about those feelings of aloneness, hurt, and isolation underneath that anger?"

Whether or not there were any feelings of isolation, aloneness and hurt *before* she said that, there are *now!* The father isn't yelling, and he isn't even angry. Now Virginia can go on to build more useful patterns of interaction in the family.

Some people who have been exposed to Satir's powerful work simply copy the content of something she said that worked. You will never succeed in being an effective communicator if you base your responses solely on the content, because content will vary infinitely. Every one of us represents another unique human possibility in terms of content. However, we all seem to use the same kinds of processes or strategies to create our experience. So you do yourself a favor as a professional communicator if you focus on, get in touch with, and listen carefully to the kinds of messages that are offered which identify process as opposed to content. This is one of the advantages of using the six-step reframing model. It's more complex, but it safeguards the integrity of the client because it is a pure process model that stays out of content. . . .

Do you all understand the statement that is written up here?

THERE WILL BE TIMES WHEN DINNER IS NOT SERVED.

Man: Is it true?

It's true right now, isn't it?

Woman: It made me wonder.

Man: It's true even when we're eating dinner.

Depending upon how persnickety you are, of course. Do you all understand, now, that this is a true statement at this moment in time? Does it make sense to you?

It seems like a cheap trick, and it is. The point of writing it up here is that when you make statements, and they *sound* meaningful, people will assign all the necessary connotations to make them meaningful. Let's say I walked out and left this sentence here. Some people would walk into the room and say "What do you mean there's not going to be any dinner?!" People pay very little attention to the preciseness of meaning. When I wrote it up here, several people looked up and gasped "Ohhhh! I *paid* for meals!" The statement is a perfectly true statement. The only thing that gives it meaning is the context in which it's presented.

When Leslie made the reframe that I described earlier in the context of therapy, the outcome was very powerful, even though what she said was actually irrelevant. "The fact that your carpet is clean means that no one is around" *does not have anything to do with being lonely.*

Delivery is *very* important. Saying "The fact that your carpet is clean means that nobody's home right now" will have much less impact than saying "And you see that your carpet is clean, and you *realize* that this means that you are *all alone!*" Those two statements have very different connotations, although the meaning could be identical.

Man: You are firing off anchors with your tone of voice and emphasis.

That's right. The connotation of what you are saying is as important as the words you use to describe it. All the patterns for building connotation are the patterns of hypnosis, what we call the "Milton-model": ambiguity, nominalization, all of that good stuff. For the most part people don't consciously notice all those linguistic forms because language goes by too quickly to process all the exact words. People read "There will be times when dinner is not served." *"No dinner!"* It doesn't say that there's not going to be dinner. It doesn't say anything about that. If I say "You realize you are all alone," that doesn't mean that nobody is coming later. However, the fact that the statement is uttered *implies* that.

If I look at you and say "Are *you* here *again* in the front row?" it's just a question, but the tonal emphasis gives a few additional implications. "You *again?*" "Do you have *another* question?" I cannot emphasize enough the importance of what we call "congruence" and "expressiveness." That is always going to be a very important part of the context in which the reframe occurs.

The actual physical context is also very important. It is very, very different to be in a doctor's office and see the doctor glance at you and look uncomfortable, than to see the same thing at a hotel registration desk. Those are two *entirely* different experiences, although the sensory experience has some similarities. I want you to keep the context in mind when you do reframing. That will help you to have the impact you want to have.

The frame that you put around a proposed new behavior will also have a strong impact on whether, or how, a person will consider it. Once for a demonstration someone brought in a client who was "frigid." She was a school teacher with three children. Her husband wanted more sexually than she was able to offer, and she also congruently wanted more than she had been able to offer.

I established rapport quickly, and then said "Now, think of one thing that you can do sexually with comfort and ease. Don't tell me about it."

Her slight body movements as she thought about it were ample evidence for me of what the content was, but she was unaware of that.

Then I said "And now think of one thing that lies just on the boundary of what is acceptable for you consciously as far as sexual behavior is concerned." I asked her to consider actually engaging in some sexual behavior with her husband that wasn't quite acceptable: something that was a bit tantalizing and interesting, that she wasn't quite sure she could pull off, but that she thought some day she probably could. This was asking her to imagine doing something that was on the edge of the limits of her model of the world.

When I asked for that, I got a very strong polarity response. She wouldn't do it. No way. My understanding is that the part of her that had an objection to that kind of behavior was afraid that she might actually try it, so it stopped her from even *considering* it.

When I observed her polarity response, I shifted my own analogues and asked her to think of one of the most outrageous sexual behaviors that she could engage in with her husband—something that she knew for sure that she would *never ever* have the audacity to actually do. She was able to do that comfortably. She accessed, and went through a sequence of implicit muscle movements.

Later her therapist told me that the following day she sent her children off to school and her husband off to work, and told him to be sure to come home for lunch. When he came home for lunch, she was wrapped in cellophane with a big red ribbon—exactly the behavior that was so outrageous she would never consider actually doing it.

If the proposed new behavior is perceived as being somewhere within a person's model of what she might do, she may resist even considering it. But if you go far enough outside her model, you'll get a dissociation that allows her to consider it. Since the new behavior is framed as being totally beyond what this woman would consider doing, the part that objects has nothing to object to, and it's safe to allow her to think about it. Thinking about it allowed her to contemplate fully what it would be like to do the new behavior, thereby setting up the internal programs to do it at some future time. Considering the behavior fully, in context, is actually a future-pace—the same as step five of the six-step reframing.

Man: Why wouldn't the part object to the behavior as it is future-paced?

Well, what this particular part objected to was her *considering* doing the behavior, not the behavior itself. Once she actually considered the behavior, the part didn't object. If a part had objected to the behavior, she wouldn't have done it.

Many people limit themselves by never even considering certain behaviors. If they actually considered the behaviors, they would often find them acceptable. But some part objects to their even *considering* the behavior. The part assumes, with very little evidence, that doing the behavior would be bad, and it also may assume that if you consider a behavior you have to go ahead and do it.

One of the greatest favors you can do for many of your clients is to get them to make a distinction between considering a behavior and doing it. If they can do that, they can fully consider what it would be like to do *anything*. As they consider it, they can find out in internal experience what it would be like to do it, and they can discover whether or not they think it would be worthwhile—in terms of their values and goals—to actually do it in external experience.

Man: So reframing—whether it's a small belief or a larger presupposition—is simply taking the concern about something and making it into something positive.

No. Be careful with the "positive" stuff. You reframe in a way that is *useful,* in some *context.* You have to be careful about this "positive-negative" stuff. It's *positive* to be *useful.* That's a reframe, by the way.

So far we have talked exclusively about reframing something "bad" into something good, and in therapy that's usually the way it's most useful. But reframing isn't just for taking things that have negative connotations and changing them to have positive connotations. Sometimes it's useful to reframe the other way. For instance, think of somebody who really believes in himself, but is incompetent. He needs to have his confidence reframed to *over*confidence.

I saw Frank Farrelly do an interesting "negative" reframe once. Frank was working with a man at a conference where I was supposed to model his behavior. The man was telling Frank about how he couldn't seem to get a zing out of his wife, basically. And Frank, in his inevitable form, was badgering the guy so fast he couldn't keep track of what he was saying.

Frank: "Well, do you ever kind of give other women the eye, you know?"

Man: "Well, yeah, sometimes."

Frank: "But you get with your wife and nothing happens?"

Man: "Well, yeah, I just kind of stiffen up."

Frank: "Well, *where* do you stiffen up? *This is very important!*"

Man: "Well, you know, all over."

Frank: "And when you're with other women, do you stiffen up all over?"

Man: "Well, no, no. You know, I've had lots of interactions with other women and ah--"

Frank: "*Interactions?* Is that like fucking?" Frank is very subtle.

Man: "Well, ah . . . yes."

Frank: "Does your wife know about this?"

Man: "No."

Frank: "Well, does your wife have 'interactions,' too?"

Man: "Well, ah, no."

Frank: "How do you know?"

Man: "Well, you know, I just feel that--"

Frank: "Ah! The intensity of your feelings is *not* the test of reality!"

Now that's a reframe of sorts. If you think of reframing as only being useful for taking something unpleasant and making it nice, then you should probably find a new profession. Many people need to have a more accurate view of themselves and the world, and that's not always nice.

The man Frank Farrelly worked with *assumed* that his wife didn't have "interactions" with other men, and that she didn't know that he was seeing other women. He also assumed something even more dramatic: that she was not important to him. He is the one who will come to therapy when his wife drops him like a hot potato. Suddenly no other woman in the world will do. I call people like him "pinies." They come in pining away for their lost loves. And if they had had more sensory experience to begin with, they might never have lost them.

Let's say I'm a therapist from the Midwest, and I became a therapist without knowing exactly how I got to be one. I was going through school, and chemistry was too hard; I didn't really like mathematics, and I found history boring. All my friends were going to be teachers, but I didn't want to do that, because I wanted a new crowd. I felt inadequate, and when I got into therapy, I saw that people always compliment each other in groups, and I thought that was really groovy. So I became a therapist and got a license, but I still have strong feelings of inadequacy, and this causes me trouble. If I generalize my own problems to the rest of the world, there are going to be a lot of people I can't help, because some people do not have problems with feeling inadequate. In fact, if some of them felt inadequate, they'd be a lot better off.

There are many people in the world who do not know how to use sensory experience to test and find out what they do and don't do well. What they really need is a good strong dose of self-doubt. When they get too sure of themselves, they often do something that results in their getting hurt. However, they don't use that as the basis for becoming less sure of themselves in a way that's useful. They go through cycles almost like a manic-depressive: competence, *competence,* COMPETENCE, failure! I often meet people like that. One of the things that you can do to help them is to stick your foot out and trip them just as they are feeling really competent—before they fall too hard. Then you can begin to assist them in building the kinds of sensory feedback that will give them valid information about themselves.

So don't think of reframing as being appropriate only in a context where you take something negative and make it positive. Sometimes a good stiff dose of fear or incompetence or uncertainty or suspicion can be very useful.

Woman: You sound like the devil.

You're not the first one who has said that, I'll tell you! There was a cute little social worker who came up to me in a workshop I did in the Midwest—

Woman: A man or a woman?

Does it matter? Are you a sexist? How's that for reversing a presupposition! The comment this person made to me as it came up and coyly looked at me was "Are you telling me that it's OK to be tricky?" I said "Yes, that's what I'm telling you." And it said "Oh, I was *so good* at that when I was young, and I haven't been able to do it for years. Will it be manipulative?" And I said "Yes." Now, I think that's an example of where reframing is really needed.

Virginia Satir does "parts parties," which are reframes done through psychodrama. Everyone gets to be one of somebody else's parts. If you don't like the person, it's a great time to get revenge. For some reason I was always a bad part. I never got to be Little Bo Peep or any part like that. I always had to be Machiavelli. And I was always the *last* one to get reframed! In one of these parts parties, I got to be somebody's ability to be manipulative. I don't know why; type-casting, I guess. Suddenly in the course of the parts party, this person stopped and said "I *like* that part! I never really thought about it, but my ability to be manipulative has gotten me *a lot* of good things." And if you think about it, it's really true.

However, a content reframe has been done in the field of humanistic psychology: "manipulating is bad." If you look in the dictionary, the first definition of manipulation is "To work or operate with the hand or hands; to handle or use, especially with skill; to manage or control artfully." That doesn't have anything to do with good or bad. It has to do with being able to do something *effectively*.

If your frame is that "Anyone who manipulates is bad" it limits you from doing many things. If you believe, as Sidney Jourard said, that "Anyone who is good is transparent" that means you have to go out of your way to say unpleasant things to people. If you go to Humanistic Psychology conferences, people come up to you and say "Hi, you look awful today." "I don't really feel good, but I'm going to tell you that I do anyway." When you are caught inside of any frame like that, it limits your choice. Whether the frame is a "good" one or a "bad" one doesn't really matter.

As a communicator you want to have the ability to shift the frames that people put around anything. If a person believes that something is bad, the question is "When, where, how, and for whom?" Reframing is a different way of doing the same things you do with all the Meta-Model questions. Rather than asking the question "for whom?" you just change it. If somebody says "Stupidity is inherently bad; it is bad to be stupid" you say "Some people use stupidity as a way to learn a tremendous amount. Some people use stupidity as a way to get people to do things for them. That's pretty smart."

Typically people think that success is good and confusion is bad. In our workshops we're always telling you that success is the most dangerous human experience, because it keeps you from noticing other things and learning other ways of doing things. That also means that any time you fail, there's an unprecedented opportunity for you to learn something that you wouldn't otherwise notice. Confusion is the doorway to reorganizing your perceptions and learning something new. If you were never confused, that would mean that everything that happened to you fit your expectations, your model of the world, perfectly. Life would simply be one boring, repetitive experience after another. Confusion is a signal that something doesn't fit, and that you have a chance to learn something new.

The phrase "unprecedented opportunity" is a reframe in itself, because it directs you to search for the opportunities that always exist, even in the worst disaster.

Another reframe we're always making is *"The meaning of your communication is the response that you get."* Most people don't think that way at all. They believe that they know what the meaning of their communication is, and that if somebody else doesn't realize it, it's the other person's fault. If you really believe that the meaning of your communication is the response that you get, there is no way that you can blame others. You simply keep communicating until you get the response that you want. A world without blame is a very altered state for most people!

Ben: People's beliefs, or presuppositions, often give them a lot of trouble. My question is how do you pull out a pin on someone's belief system, and will you give me an illustration of it?

Why would you want to? Let me ask you that, first. . . . How do you know someone will be better off without a particular belief? You're asking for a model without having an outcome. . . .

I only pull the pins out of someone's reality when I believe that it will take somebody somewhere useful. I don't agree that doing that with everyone in this seminar is going to be useful. There are people here whose pins I am not going to touch. That's a decision which I make, based on my sensory experience. The only basis on which I can make that decision is knowing what the ramifications of pulling that pin are going to be. Let's say we have somebody in here who bases eighty percent of her experience on certain religious beliefs. What happens if I pull the pin about good and evil? I have no way of knowing what I will end up with! And if I don't *know* what I am going to end up with, I don't pull pins!

Ben: Well, I'd still like to know what it's like.

Woman: I think you would certainly be safe doing it with Ben, because he is asking for it.

I still won't do it. I don't care what his conscious mind wants. Conscious minds are dumb.

Woman: What if his unconscious mind wanted you to?

Unconscious minds can be *just* as stupid. I don't want to pick out anybody's in particular, either!

Ben: Well, let's say a man comes to you and you listen to him and it becomes obvious to you that he believes that women are *intrinsically* out to control his behavior. His mother always controlled him, and now he's thirty-six years old and has never been married because of this limiting belief. It would certainly be useful for him to generalize his belief and realize that *all* people attempt to control the behavior of others.

Yes, of course. But that's going to be a *final* step. What I would do *first* is to metaphorically describe how much it delights me to have a woman try to control my behavior—what a compliment that is. Because if she didn't try to control me, it meant that she wasn't interested in me in any way whatsoever. That's a meaning reframe.

Woman: I assume that this man has been around men who have been trying to control him for a long time and it hasn't bothered him. That's why it doesn't seem as if that is the essential thing to reframe. I don't think he minds being controlled by a man.

Of course not.

Woman: So even if you reframe that it is good to be controlled he still might say "Well, OK, it's good to be controlled and I think I'll choose to be controlled by a man."

Well, you give people much more credit than I do. I don't think people can usually make those kinds of distinctions. First, I doubt seriously that he would admit that men are out to control women and each other nearly as much—and it would always be *as much*—as women are.

Woman: But he's been experiencing that and tolerating it and not *seeing* it.

Yes, but that's just a lack of sensory experience. His lack of sensory experience is going to be based upon all the presuppositions in his behavior. It's like eye accessing cues: if you know about them, you are much more apt to see them. He *knows* that women are controlling, so he's more apt to notice it when a woman is manipulating. However, a man will be able to control his behavior like crazy, because he won't notice it.

All I want to change is his internal response. Now his response to being controlled by a woman is negative. If I can change that to a positive response, *then* it will be possible for me to do what I want, which is to get him to control people and to do so gracefully and expressively.

Man: Last night I was really glad I watched a show about the feminist movement. If I hadn't watched that show, I wouldn't have realized how well women can control men.

Well, I find that the more women get into the feminist movement, the *less* they can control men. That has been my experience. It's one of the disservices that the feminist movement has done to women. I think we're now going through a phase where women are going to keep some of the benefits that they got out of the feminist movement, like more money when they work and not having to go through certain rituals that they don't want to go through. But women are going to get back into some of the groovy stuff, like fancy clothes. They had a fashion show on television the other morning, showing all the new fashions. Women's clothes are really becoming women's clothes again—great things with capes hanging down, and feathers, and all kinds of long trailing things. Feminists *can't* wear those.

Now, who's limited? Whenever you say "We will not do this," then you lose. If you say "I'm going to do it when I feel like it, and when I don't feel like it, I'm not going to do it," *then* you've got choice and you've got some basis on which to be in control.

Man: With the man who believes that women want to control him, would it be an appropriate strategy to get him to notice the ways in which *he* was controlling people, even though he is a man?

No. Absolutely not. Your question is "Would it be appropriate to get this man to consciously see or feel that he is in fact controlling people, *without knowing about it.* So perhaps women don't know about it either." And my answer is "Absolutely not, that's the wrong approach." This is a choice about the syntax, the *order* in which you do things. If you do things in the wrong order, you make it really difficult for yourself. *If* you succeeded in doing it, what would be the result of convincing him that for years he had been controlling people without knowing about it?

Man: Probably guilt. He's just like his mother.

Right! Guilt. He'd go straight to a psychiatrist.

Man: Then you could reframe his belief about guilt.

You could do that. *But if you change the meaning of control ahead of time, it's much easier.* If you *first* make controlling into something *good,* then he'll never have to feel guilty. And it will be a lot easier to reframe controlling if it's not him doing it. If you reframe so that he begins to notice that the women who are trying to control him are after his body, then controlling becomes something that's worth having. Then later you say "By the way, this counts for you, too." The syntax, the *order* of what you do makes it easy for him, and it makes it easy for you.

Frank: You said earlier that content reframing was the essence of sales. Can you give us some examples?

Sure. Let's say someone comes in to buy an expensive car. He is looking at one model, and he says "I can't see myself driving a car like this; it's kind of racy and frivolous." First you can say something like "Well, I certainly couldn't see myself in one that had racing stripes on it, or something gaudy like that" to pace his objection. Then you go on to say "But having the quick acceleration and power that this car has is more than just a frivolous thing: it's really the safety of being able to get out of somebody's way quickly. This car handles better and performs better on wet and winding roads, and I certainly don't consider my safety to be frivolous."

You first give him something to object to that isn't on the car anyway, like racing stripes. Then you go on to reframe the implication of the content. The fact that it's a fast sports car doesn't mean that it's frivolous; it means that it's *safe.*

Of course you first have to gather enough information to know that safety will appeal to this particular person. Safety doesn't mean a thing to some people. To do an effective content reframe you have to know at least a little bit about what criteria are important to the person that you're talking to. Then you take whatever elements he objects to, and find a way that those elements can satisfy other criteria that he has. You go for saving money, saving time, prestige, or whatever is important to this particular person.

If somebody says "It's too racy; I want something more conservative," then you go for redefining the car as being truly conservative: the safety, the speed, the good repair record all conserve your investment as well as your life.

If he agrees but says that other people won't realize it, you can reframe that. "Doing what *you* know is best is the earmark of a true conservative. It's really conservative to be willing to drive a car like this even though other people don't know that you're being conservative." With your emphasis and tonal shifts you imply that it is a question of appearance in contrast to the car's real function.

You can also utilize his concern about appearances and what other people think. You can use this concern to propel him into going ahead and buying a car. "You know, a lot of people come in here and really don't care what other people think of them. They just decide what is appropriate for *them* and go ahead! Of course those are the people who are pleased with their decisions later." Now he is in a dilemma, because he is faced with "what people think" on both sides of the argument. On one side some people may think it's too racy; on the other side you are saying "You're too concerned with what other people think of you." So you utilize his concern about others' opinions to move him in the direction of deciding for himself.

One thing that all salespeople need is to be able to reframe objections about price. "Well, this car definitely costs a lot more than a Chevy Chevette or something similar. In fact, it's twice the price, but if you think about buying a car just in terms of the short run, then you are better off buying a more expensive car, because you can finance it over a longer period of time and keep your monthly payments down lower. You would actually be spending less money per month to drive a better car. It takes a lot longer to own it, but in the long run when you finally do own it, you end up owning something that you can still drive, instead of a pile of junk that has no equity."

I typically look at the customer and say "Do you think all those doctors and lawyers drive cars like this just because they are ostentatious? They do it because they know about money. If you think it's cheaper to pay $220 a month for three years to buy a Datsun as opposed to $220 a month for five years to buy a BMW, look at a five-year-old Datsun and compare it with a five-year-old BMW. Check their value and the kind of shape they are in, and notice which one is still running. You will discover that it's really much too frivolous and expensive to go out and buy a cheap car. You can't *afford* to do it. While you may be saving a few dollars in down payment and perhaps a few dollars a month right now, three years later you're just going to have to buy another new car all over again."

Five years from now the person who bought the expensive car will actually look at it and say "I've still got a car that's holding together. It runs well and it's still worth money." Your job as a salesperson is to create that experience for the customer *now,* so that he can take that into consideration as he decides which car to buy.

The really critical element in doing successful reframing is to find out enough about a person's world-model so that you know what kind of reframe will fit for him. You can gather information directly, and you also need to listen very carefully to objections. Every objection will tell you about his important criteria. The more you know about his world-model, the more appropriately you can reframe. Simple information-gathering is where most salespeople fail miserably. Most salespeople are terrible at pacing, too. They tend to jump in with a standard sales pitch that may be completely inappropriate, instead of pacing and gathering information about *this* particular customer's criteria.

A lot of salespeople think they should try to sell everything to everybody. That is a situation in which *they* need to be reframed, because they need to understand that sometimes they make more money *not* selling something. When you find out that the product you have is really inappropriate for a particular customer, you're much better off *not* making a sale. If your product is as good as what somebody else has, or if there is no way of making the distinction, it doesn't matter. But if you really are convinced that something else would be better, then you're much better off if you convince the customer of that, so she can go somewhere else and be happy with her purchase.

If you sell someone something that doesn't fit her criteria, sooner or later she will have what salespeople call "buyer's remorse." People tell their friends about unsatisfying purchases, and typically they blame it on the salesperson. That's the kind of advertising you don't need.

Satisfied customers also tell their friends, and satisfied customers aren't necessarily people to whom you actually sold something. If they were satisfied with the experience they had with you, they will send you their friends even if they themselves didn't buy anything.

I know a realtor who is very good at information-gathering. She is able to select the few houses that actually might appeal to a particular customer. If those aren't appropriate, she doesn't try to show them anything else. She just says "I know what you want. That's all there is right now that might interest you. I'll let you know when something else comes onto the market." Almost all her sales are referrals from people to whom she *didn't* sell, but who liked the way she treated them.

There's a great little book about this, called *Miracle on 34th Street*. A guy is hired to play Santa Claus for a large New York department store. He starts sending parents to other stores whenever he knows they can get better deals on toys elsewhere. The store manager finds out about this, and is about to fire him. Just then a flood of people come into the store, because they've heard that this store has a Santa who won't just try to con them into buying junk. And of course they sell out the store completely. Most salespeople are shortsighted, and never consider the long-term benefits of recognizing when there isn't a valid way to make a match between product and buyer.

The problem that reframing addresses is the way that people generalize. Some people don't ever consider that they will be in the same position three years from now if they buy a car that won't last. Or they buy a used car because it's cheaper, and they don't think about things like not being able to depend on it, having to rent a car while it's being fixed, and so on. When they are buying a car and they look at prices, they see the difference in total price, but they don't ask the question "*When?*" Something that's cheaper now may be *much* more expensive in the long run.

This is exactly the same situation as the father who says to his daughter "Don't ever be stubborn," rather than realizing "She's hard to control, and it's a bother; I want to find a way around it, but this same behavior is going to pay off for me in other situations later on." There's no utilization in the process by which most people generalize. Reframing is saying "You can look at it that way, or you can look at it this way, or you can look at it this other way. The meaning that you attach is not the 'real' meaning. *All* of these meanings are well-formed within your way of understanding the world."

Think of the clean-freak mother that Leslie worked with. When Leslie had the woman visualize the clean carpet and said to her "And realize this means you are alone!" the old meaning was "You are a good mother and housecleaner" and the new one was "The people you love aren't around you!"

Leslie just changed *one* response in that mother, but that radically changed the entire family. Before, the mother would see footprints, feel bad, and then nag the family for being so careless and inconsiderate. Afterwards, she would see the footprints, feel good that the people she loved were nearby, and then do something nice for them. *She became just as good at appreciating her family as she had been at nagging them!* After a few weeks of that, the family was *completely* different.

Broadening people's views through reframing doesn't force them to do something. It will only get them to do it *if* the new view makes more sense to them than what they have been thinking, and is an undeniably valid way of looking at the world.

When people think of buying something, they usually make up their minds ahead of time, and don't even consider alternatives. They don't realize that they can buy a car over three years or five years, or they can lease it or pay cash. There are always variables like that which *they have never considered.* Those variables are the bases for making the product fit into the way they think about themselves. If someone comes into a Mercedes showroom, they already want the car. It's just a matter of making it possible for that desire to fit in with all their other criteria.

Of course, no one's understanding will ever completely match the world out there. You can't ever know whether a car is going to last. You can always get a "lemon." Or you might buy a crummy car that later turns out to be one of those priceless used cars that lasts forever. People who bought Edsels thought they got burned, but look how much they're worth now!

If you call up a woman and say "I sell pots and pans door-to-door. I want to come over to your house" and she says "Come on over," at that moment you know that there is at least a part of her that's interested in pots and pans. There's a part of her that wants to buy them, and there are probably other parts that can't yet fit buying them into her well-formedness conditions for her to actually buy something. If you don't take those other parts into consideration when you make a sale, you get what's called "buyer's remorse."

I think buyer's remorse isn't regret. Buyer's remorse simply means that the product was not adequately sold, and that the decision to buy it was not fully made. In other words, the product wasn't shaped into something that met all the person's standards. Then later when one of these standards is violated, the buyer says "I should have known better," and that wrecks everything. From then on, the product is an anchor for unpleasant feelings.

We once worked with some people who sold china door-to-door. Their problems stemmed from the fact that door-to-door salesmen are the lowest on the prestige ladder. People assume that door-to-door salesmen will try to fast-talk them into buying overpriced goods. Their china was good and reasonably priced; their customers really wanted the china and bought it. Then when the customers went to work the next day, their friends said *"Oh! You fell for a door-to-door routine?"* and then they felt cheated.

My proposal was for the salespeople to future-pace that problem away. Immediately after writing up a contract, I would have them say this to their clients: "Look. I've got this contract here and I'll rip it up right now if you want me to. I know that people are going to say 'You bought something from a door-to-door salesman? You got *burned.*' You either want something or you don't. If you don't want the china, I'll tear up the contract." At that point you can tear the top of the contract a little bit to give them a thrill. You just look at them and say "A lot of door-to-door people sell overpriced goods. If you want to go out and look around and compare, that's fine. I need to know that you want to buy, and that you are *sure* you want to. I don't want you to come back to me dissatisfied later on. I want customers to send me other people because they're satisfied with what they bought. I know that some people are going to say that you were cheated, and if that creates doubt in you, it's bad for me. I need for you to be sure enough that you won't spoil my reputation."

That effectively reframes something that is going to happen in the future. When it does happen, it will now elicit a different response. Rather than "Oh, I'm just another sucker" the person responds "Oh, he told me this was going to happen." That makes the person even *more* confident, because the salesperson knew what was going to happen in advance.

When I proposed that idea to the china salesmen, they were scared to death. They thought that they would lose a lot of sales. But that proposal is not only protecting the salesperson, it is protecting the client. If you don't do that for your client, you deserve all the customer dissatisfaction you get.

A lot of salespeople think of themselves as taking advantage of people, but their real job is to protect people. I think that should be an industry-wide reframe. The salespeople who operate that way make much more money with a lot less work, because they get so many referrals. They don't have to try to force people into anything. Many salespeople act like bulldozers, and there are a certain number of people who can be bulldozed. But you get a lot of buyer's remorse from that, and you end up having to work a lot harder.

Reframes are not con-jobs. What makes a reframe work is that it adheres to the well-formedness conditions of a particular person's needs. It's not a deceptive device. It's actually accurate. The best reframes are the ones which are *as* valid a way of looking at the world as the way the person sees things now. Reframes don't necessarily need to be more valid, but they really can't be less valid.

When the father says "Oh, my daughter's just too stubborn" and you say "Aren't you proud that she can say 'no' to men with bad intentions?" that's a really valid way of looking at that situation. At another time and place, that father would actually look at it that way and be proud of her, but he didn't think about it until you brought it up.

You can't reframe anything to anything else. It has to be something which fits that person's experience. Saying to that father "You should like your daughter's being stubborn because that means she's a liberated woman" probably isn't going to work with him. You have to find a valid set of perceptions in terms of that particular person's model of the world.

What reframing does is to say "Look, this external thing occurs and it elicits this response in you, so you assume that you know what the meaning is. But if you thought about it this other way, then you would have a different response. Being able to think about things in a variety of ways builds a spectrum of understanding. None of these ways are "really" true, though. They are simply statements about a person's understanding.

II

Negotiating Between Parts

The six-step model of reframing makes the assumption that there's a part of you making you do what you don't want to do, or a part stopping you from doing what you want to do. That's a big presupposition. However, that's one way of describing a difficulty, and usually you can organize your experience in that way. You can *make* any difficulty fit the six-step model. That description can always be taken as accurate, because *something* is producing the difficulty.

Sometimes it's more convenient to start out making completely different assumptions. You can act as if the difficulty is that two or more parts are in conflict. Each part has a valid function and a valid way of accomplishing its function, but they step on each other's toes. So it's not that one part is "making you do it"; it's that two parts are each doing something useful, but the ways that they are doing it conflict with each other.

For example, have any of you ever tried to work and not been able to? Is the following experience familiar? You sit down to write a term paper, fill out your insurance forms, or whatever work you have to do. Your work is in front of you, and you have congruently decided that you're going to do it during the next hour. You pick up the pen and you look at the paper. You begin to write and a little voice comes in and says "Hey, baby, want a beer?" "I wonder what's on television?" "Nice day outside; it's *sunny*."

Now, the question is, do we describe this situation of not being able to accomplish something as a result of *a* part that stops you? Or do we describe it as a situation in which you have *two* parts: one that wants to go out and play, and one that wants to work?

Work and play are both valid functions, and most people also have valid ways to achieve those functions. But if both parts go about doing their jobs at the same time, neither of them can function well. Neither can do their job as well as they could if they had some way of jointly organizing their behavior to get the outcomes that they both want.

Describing it in this way can be much more useful than to assume that the problem is the result of a single part. Either description can lead you to the same outcome. It's a question of efficiency. Sometimes you can get good results more expediently and more quickly if you presuppose two parts.

One indication of there being *two* parts to reframe is if the inverse of the problem also occurs. How many of you have gone out to play for the day and suddenly a little voice inside said "Your taxes aren't done." "The house isn't clean." "You should have written that paper first." This lets you know that each part interferes with the other.

Deciding which model to use is only a question of when you're going to tell which lie. I'm serious about that. If I look meaningfully at somebody in a session and say "Now, look, there's a part of you that finds this a little scary and I can understand that," that's a huge lie. "Part of *what?*" I don't know what that means. Or we can say "Now, you have a strategy, and your difficulty is a byproduct of this strategy." These are all just ways of talking about things, and those words are not grounded in reality. *These descriptions are just useful ways of organizing experience.*

It's not that one way of talking approximates reality more closely than the other one. Whenever you start trying to decide that, you're gone. People who try to approximate reality fall into what we call "losing quotes." For example, once I was reading a Tolkien book out loud to some kids. One of the characters in the book, Strider, said to Frodo "Close the door," and one of the kids I was reading to got up and shut the door. That's losing quotes.

The biggest losing quotes of all is what we call the "lost performative" in the Meta-Model. The most dangerous, and I think the most lethal, is losing quotes on yourself and believing that your thoughts *are* reality: believing that people really *are* "visual," "kinesthetic," or "auditory"; believing that people really are "placators," "super-reasonables," or *anything*. Believing that you actually have a "parent," "child," and "adult" is psychotic! It's one thing to use those constructs to do good work—to organize someone's behavior. It's quite another thing to lose quotes and believe that that's reality. So when you say "Well, this lie approximates what's 'really' going on more than the other one" be *very* careful, because you are on dangerous terrain. You might become a guru if you do that.

Somebody like Werner Erhard is in a dangerous situation. If he loses quotes on his own ideas, then he's going to go into a very strange loop. If somebody who goes to EST loses quotes, typically they'll fall out of EST after a while, so the consequences aren't too bad. However, if the guy that *runs* EST loses quotes, then it's all over.

I don't know which model of reframing is more real. I would never admit it if I thought one was more real than the other. More important, it doesn't *matter* if one is more real.

Man: One is more real for me and yet neither of them is real.

Well, you can get by with that one. Whichever lie works, it's important that you understand that they are all lies. They are only ways of organizing your experience to go somewhere new. That's the only part that counts. We're going to assume that the other lie, the six-step model, is antiquated because it's been around too long. That is always a good policy. That model, presupposing that one part is responsible for negative behavior, has been around for several years now.

So we're going to take another lie for a while and assume that the problem is not inherently that some part generates behavior that you don't want. We're going to assume that the problem behavior is the result of the *interaction* of two or more parts, and the solution will come from negotiating between them.

So let's say somebody comes in and says "I can't study. I sit down and I try to study, and I can't concentrate. I think about going skiing." With the old model we'd say "There is a part that interrupts your concentration." Rather than doing that, with this model we say "Look you've got lots and lots of parts inside of you. You've got all kinds of parts running around doing different jobs. You have the ability to study. You have the ability to go out and play. When you sit down to study, some other part is active in trying to carry out *its* function."

In order to negotiate a solution, I need to identify each part, get communication with each part, and get the positive intention of each part. I might start by going for the part that interferes with studying. So I say "I'd like you to go inside and ask if the part of you that really wants to study knows which other part is annoying it so that it can't concentrate fully." Then I have you go to this interfering part and ask "What is your function?" That's a quick way to find out what the intention behind the behavior is. "What do you do for this person?"

"Well, I get him to go out and play."

Then I want to find out if the interference goes both ways. I ask this part, "When you want to get the person to go out and play, do other parts get in *your* way? Does this work part ever come in and say 'Hey, you should be studying'?" If you get a positive answer, you've got it cinched, because then both parts want something from the other, and all you've got to do is make a trade.

Bill: I don't even understand how you get that part to say what its function is.

You don't? There's no way in the world that you could possibly do that.

Bill: Well, I want to keep listening to you.

Is that the only option you have? Do you ever have trouble listening at a lecture? Have you ever had trouble doing that?

Bill: Sometimes.

Would you go inside and ask if the part of you that likes to listen to lectures knows which part interrupts it from time to time . . . ?

Bill: Umhm. It knows one of the parts.

OK. Did it give you a name?

Bill: Yeah. The part that worries about business and financial matters. The part that worries about things—the worry part.

The "worry part." Listen to that name! Which of the two types of content reframing is really appropriate right now? . . . Meaning. This is very important. If you define a part as "The Old Worry Part" you'll have much more difficulty getting to its positive function.

So there's some part of you that has grave concerns about things, and gets labeled your "worry part." I'm wondering if you could go inside and ask "Will the part of me that gets labeled the 'worry part' tell me what your function is for me? What is it that you do for me?" . . . OK, did it tell you?

Bill: Umhm.

Do you agree that this function is something positive?

Bill: Yes, it is positive under some circumstances. The worry part overdoes it, I think.

Well, if I was your worry part, I would, too. That's all I've got to say!

Bill: It keeps me behaving responsibly, and keeps me paying my bills; it keeps me out of jail.

OK. The point is that it interrupts you sometimes when you want to concentrate on something else. Now go back and address the part of you that concerns itself with your well-being, which you like to call your "worry part"—a little meaning reframe there! Ask that part the following: when it's trying to do what it does for you in terms of adequate planning and motivating you to take care of business and that sort of thing, is it ever interrupted by the part of you that would rather be just paying attention to a lecture, listening to a tape, or doing something else that part does? Go inside and ask it if it ever gets interrupted by that particular part.

Bill: I just scanned a whole lot of interruptions, and when I came back out, I noticed my head was bobbing up and down.

That "well-being" part has a tendency to be more visual, that's true. It makes sense.

Bill: Umhm. It's always on the lookout for possible dangers.

Now, ask that "well-being" part this: if it was not interrupted when it was spending time organizing your behavior in the activity that you call 'worry'—what I call 'preparation'—would it be willing to allow you to listen to lectures without interrupting? Ask if that's a trade it would be willing to make, *if* it had a way of being sure that the other part wouldn't interrupt it. . . . (Bill nods.)

OK. Now, go to the part that likes to listen to lectures. Ask if that part thinks it's important for you to pay attention during lectures, and not to let your mind wander into things which are not important at that particular time. . . . (Bill nods.)

Now, ask if it thinks it's *important enough* to pay attention during lectures, that it would be willing not to interrupt the "well-being" part when it spends time preparing to do things. Even though the "listen to lectures" part may not enjoy the process of having to pay bills, ask if it thinks paying attention when you go to lectures is important enough that it would be willing not to interrupt the other part in exchange. . . .

Bill: Umhm.

Now, if we think about this in terms of the six-step reframing model, where are we?

Man: Just short of the ecological check.

How much short? Is it the next step? Have we done step four—giving the part three new ways? . . . Do we need to get three new ways? . . .

No. In negotiating we don't need to get three alternatives. Both parts already have appropriate behaviors. All we need is for them not to interfere with each other. That is the new choice, so step four is out of the way.

Have we gotten both of these parts to accept the responsibility for not interrupting each other? . . . Have they agreed to do it? . . .

No, they haven't agreed to do it. They said they *would* agree. Remember, this process is always broken into two parts: First, in step four, the part *agrees* that the new choices are better and more effective than the one it's using now. Second, in step five, you ask *"Will it be responsible for actually using these new choices?"* Many people leave that step out. As any of you who have children know, agreeing that a task is worth doing and agreeing to do it are very different things.

So now we want to say "Look, I want to get these two parts together and find out if they will make an agreement not to interfere with one another and to test this agreement for the next six weeks. The part of you that is in charge of worrying and taking care of business will not interrupt while you are listening to a lecture or doing the activities that this other part does. And that part will not interrupt the planner when it is taking care of business." Get them both to agree that they'll try it out for six weeks and find out how it works. If either one becomes dissatisfied during this time, then they will notify you, so that you can negotiate further.

There may be other parts involved, and of course things change, so you always want to provide the person with a next step. The last time I went to Dallas, a therapist said to me "I was in your seminar a year ago and I did reframing with a woman about her weight. She went on a diet and she lost tons of weight and she's been thin for almost a year. Then about a month ago she started to gain weight, and I want to know what I did wrong." What did the therapist do wrong? . . . She assumed that there was some relationship between eleven months ago and now! People change all the time. How many changes could that woman have gone through in eleven months that could have gotten in the way of keeping her weight down? The point is that nothing lasts forever. However, if something goes wrong, you can always go back and modify what you did, to take the new changes into account.

Now, what's left to do? What about step six, the ecological check? What do we need to do to have an ecological check in the negotiation model?

Man: Ask for any objections. "Is there some way in which this may not work?"

Who's going to object?

Man: The other parts.

The other parts haven't agreed to do anything, so what would they object to?

Bill: Other parts still might object to agreements that have been made that might interfere with them in some way.

How? Give me an example. Other parts haven't agreed not to interrupt.

Woman: What if there's another part that interrupts things?

Well, that part has not made any agreements yet.

Bill: If there's some part that uses the interruption as a signal to do its thing, then we're taking away its ability to take action. For example, in another seminar you talked about a woman who wanted to stop smoking. It turned out that another part used smoking as a cue that it was time to talk to her husband. Every evening she sat down to have a cigarette with her husband and they used that time to talk. The part that wanted her to talk to her husband had not agreed to anything, but the opportunity for it to perform its function had been taken away.

OK. In your case you are "worrying" and you have a part that comes in and says "Hey, let's go do something else." That interrupts the part that "worries." Do you think there's another part that could get something from that interruption? Is that what you're saying?

Bill: That's possible.

OK. Give me an example.

Bill: I haven't got one. I'd have to generate one.

Good, generate one.

Bill: I'm worrying, and a part interrupts to play. Some of my play also has a very definite physical health motivation. For example, I label jogging as play, but it also has to do with my physical health. So if I were worrying and my play part didn't interrupt my worry part for a long time, the part that watches out for my physical health would get left out.

Are you saying that part can't interrupt on its own?

Bill: No, it can interrupt on its own, and it probably would. So why don't we ask to see if it is going to interrupt, or if it has any objection to what has been agreed to here?

Well, is there any need to do that? . . .

There's another way to think about this, which is what I am leading up to. What happens if we ask "Does any part object to these two parts making the agreement?" If we get a "No" do we learn anything? . . .

No. We learn nothing. So it's a stupid question to ask.

Man: But if we get a "Yes" we have learned something.

Right. However, can we ask a question which will get the information we want; can we ask a question that will get any possible "Yes" answers, *and* something else?

Man: Do any of the other parts have any suggestions?

OK. "Are there any other parts involved in this?" "Are there any other parts that interrupt this part or utilize those interruptions?" "Are there any other parts that might interrupt either of the two of you?" That kind of question is going to get us the information we want.

Man: Also if we have been completely off base in identifying these two parts, that will get us back on the track of finding the parts that are involved in this problem.

Right. That kind of question also does something else that is very important: it can give you relevant information about how this person's parts are organized. In your example you have a "work" part and a "play" part. Some people's play part has within it a part that says "This is how we're going to stay healthy." Some people's play part only plays poker and smokes cigars, while somebody else's goes out and jogs on the beach. It depends upon how you organize your parts.

Jogging is a great example of a reframe, by the way. Anybody who can jog six miles a day and call it "play" is already a master of reframing as far as I'm concerned. It's a good reframe to have. If you're going to do reframing, you might as well do it in places where it is useful. Some people even decide "It's *cool* to be a jogger." You get to wear special shorts and shoes and other running gear. It's become *fashionable.* What a *great* reframe. I think that's marvelous. Let's all be healthy because it's groovy. If some people could reframe sugar to taste bad, think how much their lives would change. If you can redefine fun as being something that's healthy, I think that's really slick. When I was growing up, "fun" was beating each other up, and sitting around in drive-ins eating hamburgers and french fries and smoking cigarettes.

Kit: I'm suddenly having a lot of trouble taking notes. I just noticed that I wrote "jiggling" instead of "jogging." Can I talk to you about that now, . . . or later?

You could! That's a pretty good presupposition you've got there. What you're talking about might fit this negotiation model. There certainly are at least two parts. As long as we are messing around with reframing, let's play a little. Go inside and ask if there's some part of you that is interrupting your usual process of note-taking. . . .

Kit: Yes.

OK. Ask it if it's willing to tell you what it's trying to do for you right now by messing up your note-taking, something which you normally do smoothly and evenly. That's a yes/no question, by the way. Is it willing to tell you? . . .

Kit: Umhm.

OK. If it is, tell it to go ahead and tell you. . . .

Now, do you agree that that is something you want to have a part of you do?

Kit: At times. The behavior that I see it doing for me is good at times, but not in this particular situation.

OK. Ask what it is trying to do for you by doing it *here.* It might know something that we don't know. . . .

Kit: I just hear the words "Be here now."

Oh, sensory experience.

Kit: The feeling that I have is that when I'm listening to you I'm experiencing you, and that's how I gather information. So I need to kind of dissociate from that dissociation, or, um—

OK. Well, go inside and ask if this part of you objects to your taking notes at this moment.

Kit: The only thing that I would need is to be able to be in two places at once.

Have you ever done that? . . . Ask if there is any part that knows how to be in two places at once. . . .

Kit: Umhm.

OK. Ask it if it would be willing to have you be in two places at once right now. . . . What was its response?

Kit: That this isn't a good setting to be in two places at once.

OK. There's obviously another part involved in this. There's a part that believes you should be taking notes: that this is somehow relevant and important to your education. Would you go inside and ask *that* part if it would be willing to tell you what it is doing for you by taking notes. . . .

Kit: It's just an anchor.

It's an anchor for? . . .

Kit: A state of mind.

OK. Now, ask it if it can think of some other anchor you could use for the next two hours. . . . (She nods.) Good. Tell it to go ahead and use that.

Now, part of what I just did has to do with the negotiation model, and I mixed it up with some other things. Was one of the two kinds of content reframing incorporated into what I just did with her?

Woman: Oh, the context. "This is OK at one time or in one situation and not in another."

Certainly. So there was a piece of context reframing. I also included the basic element of the standard six-step reframing model, asking "What's the purpose?" and finding an alternative way. The purpose of the note-taking part is to provide an anchor. "Well, good. Can we use something *else* as an anchor?" So I included a piece of the six-step reframing model, and also a piece of switching the context. These different models are all closely interrelated, and if you know the six-step reframing model, you already have all the tools that you need for negotiation. If you know all the reframing models, you can then mix them together whenever that's appropriate.

The important thing with the negotiation model is to find out which parts are interrupting each other, and then to find out what their functions are—not why they are interrupting one another, but what their functions are. Is it a part that amuses you? Is it a part that takes care of responsibility? Is it a part that gets you to church on time? What part is it and what does it do? When you have this information, then you make a deal. Whatever deal you make is OK, as long as the deal provides the outcome that both parts want.

One of our students frequently finds himself feeling very sleepy when he's driving late at night. He uses this model to negotiate between the sleepy part and the part that wants him to get home in one piece. Sometimes he trades an extra hour of alertness for a promise to sleep later the next morning, and other times the sleepy part demands a half-hour at the side of the road first.

Where else is this negotiation model going to be most appropriate? For what kinds of experiences is this multiple-part reframing model going to be more appropriate than the six-step model?

Man: Critical and placating parts.

Give me an example in experience. If you try to study and you can't concentrate, that's a very concrete example. That is what I want.

Man: You are trying to go to sleep and your mind is off on some other matter.

Insomnia is a marvelous example. You can tell it's a good one, because the rest of the people in the room sigh when you say it. Give me some more like that.

Woman: Trying to save money and finding yourself spending it.

That's a good one.

Man: Being disorganized.

That *can* be. If you can fit it more into the form like she did, it'll be better.

Woman: Constipation.

Constipation is an elegant example. The more you can find the problems that fit this form, the more you'll know when this model is appropriate as opposed to some other model.

Woman: Someone who has trouble getting himself to go to bed? Someone who never quite gets around to going to bed?

. . . Or someone who never quite gets around to getting up? Yes, this model is appropriate for people who have trouble changing from one context to another. If they are in a restaurant, they can never quite leave. Anyone who has been a waiter knows about those people.

Man: Spending time alone and being with groups.

You're saying "this versus that." That's something else. I want you to identify things that have the same form as insomnia. Insomnia happens when you try to go to sleep and you wake up.

Man: It sounds like any behavior that's compulsive.

Yes, but I don't want you to generalize yet. I want you to give me some *specific examples.*

Man: Getting really nervous before you make a presentation.

Yeah, stage fright can be a great one. The more you try to relax, the more you get tense.

Man: What about procrastinating?

Procrastinating can be a great one.

Man: Impotence.

Impotence can be a classic example.

Man: Anything with the form of "The more you try to do one thing, the more you get the opposite."

Yes. The more you try to stop yourself from preventing the fact that you're denying that it's time to pair up and go outside and try this model with each other, the more you *will.*

Now.

(An outline of this chapter appears on the following page.)

Negotiating Between Parts: Outline

1) Ask the part that is being interrupted (part X) the following questions:
   a) What is your positive function?
   b) Which part(s) is (are) interrupting you? (Part Y)
2) Ask the same questions of part Y:
   a) What is your positive function?
   b) Does X ever interfere with your carrying out your function?
3) If both parts interrupt each other at times, you are now ready to negotiate an agreement. (If not, this model is not appropriate, so switch to another reframing model. If Y interferes with X, but X doesn't interfere with Y, six-step reframing with Y may be most appropriate.)
   a) Ask Y if its function is important enough that Y would be willing to not interrupt X so that it could receive the same treatment in return.
   b) Ask X if it was not interrupted by Y, would it be willing to not interrupt Y?
4) Ask each part if it will actually agree to *do* the above for a specified amount of time. If either part becomes dissatisfied for any reason, it is to signal the person that there is a need to renegotiate.
5) Ecological check: "Are there any other parts involved in this?" "Are there any other parts that interrupt this part, or that utilize these interruptions?" If so, renegotiate.

III

Creating a New Part

One of the questions that we have asked over and over again since the beginning of our dealings with the field of psychology is "What is it about an experience that makes it therapeutic or not therapeutic?" Every school of therapy has within it certain elements which lead to change when used by some people, and don't lead to change when used by others. When used by a third group, those elements lead to change which is not profoundly useful. As far as I can tell, the ways you change people into behaviors which are *not* useful are not really different from the ways you go about changing them into behaviors which *are* useful. The kinds of techniques that are used by well-intentioned parents, probation officers, and teachers, to lead people into behaviors which will actually cripple them for the rest of their lives, are powerful and effective mechanisms of change.

This morning we want to teach you a third model of reframing: how to create a new part. Parents, educators and well-meaning psychotherapists don't create new parts as explicitly as I'm going to teach you to do. They mix the pieces up, and they do it over a longer period of time. However, those of you who are therapists will recognize the elements readily. This model has more steps to it than the six-step reframing model, and it's designed to accomplish something entirely different.

The presupposition of the six-step reframing model is that somebody has a part that deliberately stops her from doing a behavior, or a part that makes her do a behavior.

Yesterday afternoon we dealt with a second logical possibility: that there are two or more parts, and each of them is doing exactly what it is supposed to be doing. Their intentions are positive and their behaviors are appropriate, but when those behaviors overlap, they produce an unwanted condition such as insomnia. You have a part that takes care of business and methodically plans out everything, and you have a part that wants to go to sleep. When one part of you starts to go to sleep, then the other part goes "Oops! You forgot about X! What's going to happen if you don't do this?" The other part says "Don't worry about it now. Let's sleep." However, you didn't find a solution, so as you begin to drop off to sleep, the other part says "But if you don't, Y will happen." The negotiation model is adequate to deal with situations like that. You negotiate between the parts so that they work more cooperatively.

This morning we want to explore a third logical possibility: somebody doesn't do something simply because there isn't any part of her that's organized to do that behavior. There is no part actively stopping a behavior, and there aren't two parts interfering with each other. She has lots of other parts that work. Consciously she desires a particular outcome; however *unconsciously* she really doesn't have a part that can carry out that particular behavior.

All the other reframing models change a response, and that new response triggers a different sequence of behavior. For example, in verbal content reframing you just change the response and assume that it will fire off more useful behaviors. Of course you need to check to be sure that assumption is correct.

In six-step reframing, you change the response, *and* you ask the client's creative part to go on an internal search to find specific alternative behaviors. You anchor those behaviors into the appropriate context by future-pacing, and do an ecological check. When you negotiate between parts you assume both parts have appropriate behaviors already, and you just need to provide a way for them to sequence *when* they do their behaviors, so that they don't interfere with each other.

Content reframing, the negotiation model, and six-step reframing all presuppose that either 1) alternative behaviors already exist, or 2) some part can easily organize itself to carry out behaviors that will be appropriate. Those are very useful presuppositions, but they aren't always true. If I put one of you alone in the cockpit of a Concorde SST, you could be perfectly calm and alert with no parts interfering with your behavior, and still not know how to fly the plane. You just don't have the appropriate behaviors organized to do that. You need to go through some kind of learning process to organize and sequence those skills. That is the kind of situation in which you have to create a new part to do a specific behavior, and that is what most education and training is supposed to do.

A few years ago we were doing a workshop up in the Northwest, and one woman in the seminar had a phobia of driving on freeways. Rather than treating it as a phobia, which would have been much more elegant, we did a standard six-step reframing. We don't recommend that you use reframing with phobias, because usually your clients will get the phobic response as a signal. Once they've collapsed into the phobic response, it's very difficult to do anything else with them. However, we were demonstrating reframing at the time, and decided to demonstrate that it's possible to do reframing with phobias.

We said to this woman "Look, you have a part that's scaring the pants off you when you go near freeways. Go inside and reassure this part that we know it's doing something of importance, and then ask if this part is willing to communicate with you." The woman got a very strong positive response, so we said "Now, go inside and ask the part if it would be willing to let you know what it's trying to do for you by scaring the pants off you when you go near freeways." The woman went inside, and she reported "Well, the part said 'No, I'm not willing to tell you.'"

Rather than go to unconscious reframing, we did something which may sound curious but it's something I do from time to time when I have suspicions, or what other people call intuitions. We had her go inside and ask if the part *knew* what it was doing for her. When she came back outside, she said "Well, I . . . I don't . . . I don't believe what it said." We said "Oh, yeah? Well, go ask if it's telling the truth." She went inside and then said again "I don't want to believe what it said." We asked "Well, what did it say?" She said "It said it *forgot!*"

Now, as amusing as that sounds, I've always thought that was a *great* response. In some ways it makes sense. You are alive for a long time. If a part organizes its behavior to do something and you really resist it and fight against it, the part can get so caught up in the fight that it forgets why it organized its behavior that way in the first place. That's a real possibility. I don't know how many of you have ever gotten in an argument, and in the middle of it forgot what you intended to do in the first place. Misers are like that. They've forgotten that money is only useful if you spend it now and then. Parts, like people, don't always remember about outcomes.

Rather than going through a lot of rigamarole at that point, we said "Look, this is a very powerful part of you. Did you ever think of how powerful this part is? Every single time you go near a freeway, this part is capable of scaring the pants off you. That's pretty amazing, you know. How would you like to have a part like that on your side? The woman said "Wow! I don't have any parts like that on my side!" So we said "Go inside and ask that part if it would like to do something that it could be appreciated for, that would be worthwhile, and that would be worthy of its talents." Of course the part went "Oh, yeah!" So we said "Now go inside and ask that part if it would be willing to be responsible for being sure that you are comfortable, alert, cautious, breathing regularly and smoothly, and *in sensory experience* when you go on a freeway entrance ramp." The part went "Yeah, yeah. I'll do that." We then had her fantasize a couple of freeway situations. Previously she had been incapable of doing that; she would go into a terror state, because even the fantasy of being near a freeway was too much for her. When she imagined it this time, she did it adequately. We put her in a car, sent her out to the freeway, and she did fine. She drove happily for three hours and ran out of gas on the freeway.

Now this made me curious. I thought "If you can have a part hanging around that's not doing much, and you can give it some other job, you can probably build a part from scratch!" When I thought about it, I realized that's what Transactional Analysis does. TA goes through a rather laborious procedure to build three parts—parent, adult, and child. The Michigan TA people build nine parts. If you can build nine, you can probably build any number. If you can build a "critical parent" to torture you all the time, you ought to be able to build just about anything.

When you start thinking about it, most therapies teach you how to have your parts organized. Gestalt builds a topdog and an underdog. Psychosynthesis is a little bit more creative about it: They've got a big circle, and you get to have a whole bunch of parts inside. However, they all have to be famous people; there are no unknown parts.

Most of the time when parts are described, they are described not in terms of *what* they do—their function—but in terms of *how* they do it—their behavior. If you have studied the psychosynthesis model or the TA model, you know that people usually describe, isolate, and create parts in terms of *how* the parts behave. So for example, if you go through a Satir parts party, you might have a "stupid" part—a part that makes you act stupid. At the end of the party, rather than being a "stupid" part, it would become your "ability to learn at your own rate" or your "ability to ask questions" or some other positive behavior. The behavior goes from being something negative to being something positive. *However, it is still a behavior that is not clearly tied to an outcome.* This is a *very* important difference. We build parts to achieve *outcomes.* The parts that are created through the random processes that people use in therapy usually achieve behaviors rather than outcomes.

Every therapy I've ever studied has within it some way of building parts. Some people don't have an unconscious mind until they go into hypnosis. If you believe that the "unconscious mind" exists *a priori,* then one day you're going to hypnotize somebody and when her conscious mind is gone, you're going to be *all alone!* That has happened to me. You can't assume that everything is there. Sometimes a person has all her marbles in her conscious mind. Sometimes a person doesn't have much going on in her conscious mind, but has a very well-developed unconscious entity that is a single organized unit. Sometimes that has happened through therapy and sometimes through experience.

No matter how parts are created, people have a tendency to describe how a part behaves, rather than to describe the behavior in relationship to outcomes—what that behavior does for them. At one of my first workshops for TA people, I said I believed that *every* part of *every* person is a valuable resource. One woman said "That's the stupidest thing I ever heard!"

"Well, I didn't say it was true. I said if you believe that as a therapist, you'll get a lot farther."

"Well, that's totally ridiculous."

"What leads you to believe that that's ridiculous?"

"I've got parts that are totally useless. All they do is get in my way."

"Well, name one that's useless."

"No matter what I decide to do, I have a part that tells me that I can't ever do it, and that I'm going to fail. It makes everything twice as hard as it needs to be."

"I'd like to speak to that part directly." That always gets a TA person, by the way. Talking directly to a part isn't in the TA model. Then if you look over her left shoulder while you talk to that part, it really drives her nuts. It's also a very effective anchoring mechanism. From that time on, every time you look over her left shoulder, that part knows you're speaking to it.

So I said "I know that that part of you does something *very* important and is *very* sneaky about how it does it. And even if *you* don't appreciate it, *I do.* Now, I'd like to tell that part that if it were willing to inform your conscious mind about what it's doing for you, then perhaps it could get some of the appreciation that it deserves." Then I had her go inside and ask that part what it does for her that is positive. It came right out and said "I was motivating you." When she told me that, she added "I think that's weird." So I said "Well, you know, I don't think it would be possible for you, right now at this moment, to come up here and work in front of this entire group." She immediately stood up defiantly, walked up to the front of the room and sat down.

Those of you who have studied strategies know that this was a demonstration of the phenomenon that we call a "polarity response." This part of her was simply a Neuro-Linguistic Programmer who understood utilization. It knew that if it said "Aw, you can go to college; you can do it," she'd respond "No, I can't do it." However, if it said to her "You're not going to be able to cut the grade," then she would say "Oh, yeah?!" and she would go out and do it.

I began to discover that no matter how you organize yourself, or what parts you build, if the model that you use to think of parts is tied to how they *behave,* then 1) You don't do them justice, and 2) You might be right, which would be dangerous. If you really had a part that didn't have a positive function—it was just critical or destructive—then what can you do? Exorcism?

There is a guy in Santa Cruz who exorcises parts. The exorcism is terrible; it takes a long, long time, and has some unfortunate consequences. This man has "discovered" an epidemic of multiple personalities in this country that no one else has noticed! He doesn't even begin to suspect that he is creating them.

I wouldn't recommend exorcism as an approach. I would rather tie parts to outcomes, whether or not they were tied together originally. If you *act* as if they are, they will be. Once you have an outcome, you no longer need to exorcise a part. You simply give it new behaviors.

If someone doesn't have a part to do something, you can create one, but you need to be sure that the part is designed to achieve a *specific outcome.* If you are not able to open doors, you can create a part that opens doors. It sounds simple; it's actually somewhat complicated. However, it's something that you do all the time. All of you have parts which you managed to make somehow or other. *All* the things we do explicitly with parts and reframing are things that people do anyway. These are all naturally occurring processes.

I think there's a tendency for human beings to organize themselves in terms of outcomes that are contextual. A man behaves differently with his wife than with his colleagues at work; he has an entirely different set of analogue behaviors in order to get different outcomes. That used to be called "role theory," and I think role theory was on the right track in some ways. However, therapists got stuck trying to prove that that's all there was.

Many of B. F. Skinner's students have gotten stuck in the same way. They said that since Skinner didn't look in the "black box," there wasn't anything in there anyway. Skinner didn't say "There's nothing in the black box"; he said "I'm not going to open it." Those are two very different statements. Skinner's students took the connotations of his statement to mean there was nothing in there anyway. That is not the case, and I do not think, from reading his writing, that Skinner intended that. However, we all know how some people are: if they don't see something, it doesn't exist.

In order to build a part to achieve a specific outcome, the first consideration is to identify a "need."

Woman: Could you distinguish need from outcome? I don't understand what you mean by need in this context.

Well, that's why I put it in quotes. What *you're* going to do is find an outcome. What your client is going to tell you is that she has a "need."

The tricky part about this is to build a part that won't interfere with the rest of the person's outcomes. If there really is a part that *stops* her from doing something, and you build a part to *do* it, guess what's going to happen? *WAR.* To prevent this, we have built into the model that all the parts of the person that don't want you to build the new part become allies during the design process.

The first thing you do is identify whatever "need" it is that you are going to build the part for. For example, a woman might come in and say "Well, you know, I've been on lots and lots of diets and I never seem to lose weight. I'm just much too heavy, so I want you to put me in a trance and make food taste bad." If she really wants that, I would recommend that you send her to one of those Schick clinics, where they will put big cakes in front of her and shock her. If she smokes, they will put her in a room full of cigarette butts and make her drink ashes, and all kinds of wonderful things.

That's a way of building a part that *stops* you from doing certain things. However, it doesn't take into account the secondary gain—the outcome of the problem behavior. That makes it a very difficult way to stop behaviors. It is an experiential way of going about it, and it will work insofar as it's reinforced. Sometimes after a period of time, when the part that you have developed discovers that you're not going to get shocked any more, then it won't care if you smoke. So you might have to go back at a later time and repeat the procedure or do something else. That's a problem with building parts in that particular way. However, don't underestimate that approach, because it works. It seems a little severe and it doesn't work with everybody, but it does work; that's an important consideration. It's important to understand what goes on when people change, and to make up a metaphor or a lie to describe it that enables us to be able to make changes more elegantly.

Let's go back to our overweight client. Her expressed need is to "lose weight." However, if you build a part whose job it is to *lose weight,* what's going to happen when she loses weight? She will lose some *more!* She may become an anorexic! So if you opened up a weight clinic and built parts to lose weight, you would end up needing another clinic down the street for anorexics. There you could build eating parts, and you could have the client switch back and forth every six months. There's nothing in her stated outcome that has anything to do with stabilizing weight.

Most people really don't understand *substituting* symptoms. There's one school of thought that says "Well, if you use hypnosis, then you will get symptom substitution." My response is "*Bravo! Let's deliberately substitute something and have it be something useful.*"

Years ago a man wrote an article in which he described making cigarettes taste like the worst thing he could think of—cod liver oil. The client he did this with quit smoking, but he became a cod liver oil junkie! He carried a bottle of cod liver oil in his coat all day. I guess that's better than smoking. I don't know the ramifications of overdosing on fish oil. It sounds disgusting to me. I prefer to substitute symptoms that are positive.

So the really important question is "What is it that you are going to do in terms of an outcome?" If somebody comes in and says "I want to quit smoking" and you make the outcome *no cigarettes,* then the way you organize that person's resources to suppress that activity can have lots and lots of *other* outcomes that are not positive.

The question is "How can you conceptualize change work so that you avoid undesirable side effects?" When somebody comes in with a weight problem, what part are you going to build? In other words, what is going to be the outcome of the part that you build? At the moment, her need is to lose weight. But how can you do that and not have her end up an anorexic?

Ann: You could set a specified weight that she wants to weigh, and not let that part function when she gets under that weight.

Well, yes. We can put semantic conditions on when the part is to be active and when it's not. You could have the part begin to respond every time she weighs more than a certain amount. However, parts don't like to be inactive.

Man: You could get all parts to agree on the same outcome.

Try it some time! I'm serious. If somebody comes in and wants to lose weight, you try to get the part that likes candy to agree to that. His parts may all say "Well, that's a groovy outcome." But if you get all his parts to agree that it's a great outcome, it still won't take him there. What the parts object to is the *process* of getting there.

Man: Could they generate alternatives?

You can have them do that, but then you're using a different reframing model. Then you're saying that the problem is a result of the interaction of the parts you have now. You could use the six-step model to do that. However, it's not very elegant, because then you have to go in and deal with a huge number of parts. The question is simply one of expedience: if you were only going to build one part, what would it do? I want you to make a distinction between the outcome—what you want to be sure happens—and the behaviors or procedures that the part uses to get the outcome. They are both important, but now I want you to specify outcomes.

Man: You need to make it more versatile, so that it can do more than one thing.

OK, but what *is* it going to do? What is its job?

I don't want to get you off the track. If we build a part whose function is to have somebody weigh a hundred and five pounds, that will work. That's great. That's a well-formed outcome. Now I want to ask "What are *other* outcomes that will work equally well?" There are *lots* of right answers to this question. The important thing is that you learn how to conceptualize them. Ann was on the right track. She said "These are what we don't want; this is what we do want. This is one way of getting *only* what we want." The key question you have to ask yourself is *"Will this give us ONLY what we want?"*

Man: You could put the part in charge of "health" or "attractiveness" or some superordinate structure that includes weight.

Woman: How about a "central eating control" that takes all those factors into account in the process of deciding how much she should weigh?

Woman: I think you have to take all those needs which that part intends to gratify, and satisfy those needs in different ways.

Well, that's all true. The question I'm asking is *"What is the part going to do?"* If we have a part whose job is to be in charge of overall health, and we include maintaining a certain weight in that, then will we do *only* that? The magic word is "*only.*" Sometimes it may be advisable to do a lot more than the client requested. But right now let's talk about limited therapeutic change. Your answer is an accurate answer, and may be a better answer in experience, when you are treating clients. However, *each job that a part has makes it harder to install that part.* I want you to keep that in mind. Every extra outcome that a part has makes it more complicated for that part to function. *The more limited its outcome, the easier it is to install a part.* Sometimes it is better to make the extra effort to install a more complicated part in order to get a better result in the end. A part that keeps someone at a certain weight is going to be a lot easier to install than the kind of central coordinator that you're talking about, because the coordinator will have to have a lot of knowledge about what it means to be healthy, etc. It will also have a lot more behaviors, so you're more apt to get objections from other parts.

Man: How about installing a semantic cue for eating, and a motivation strategy to get her to eat only then?

Well, you will always be doing that. Ann suggested that the semantic cue be a particular weight. However, I want you to talk about it differently today. Part of the game we play is how you can change how you talk about experience so that you can make changes in different ways. You're still playing the strategy game. There's no such thing as a strategy, and there's no such thing as a part. The question is "How can we talk about it differently and be able to do different things?" If you forget that, then I recommend that you build a part that reminds you. "The map is not the territory" and that's not true, either.

Man: How about changing the extra weight to happiness?

I beg your pardon? A part whose job it is to dissolve weight and turn it into happiness?

Man: As long as we're dreaming.

Sure. OK, but is that going to do *only* what the person wants? You see, there's a big danger in what you are suggesting: six months later this thirty-pound person is going to walk in the door smiling and saying "You're the best therapist I ever had!" Either that or she's going to come in with both arms gone, and she's still going to be fat. She'll say "I feel great . . . but I've got this small problem. . . ."

I want you to listen very carefully to your definition of a new part, because in experience, that's the kind of thing that will actually happen. I think that anorexics are made by well-intentioned people, although not necessarily by therapists. Parents often give a young woman lots and lots of messages that make food such a negative anchor that she throws up when she tries to eat. Through the positive intentions of parents, the daughter ends up becoming anorexic.

I'm recommending that as a therapist you be *very* cautious about specifying outcomes. The more carefully you specify exactly what a part is going to do, the less you'll get objections from other parts about having it exist, and the better it will actually be able to function. If a new part is poorly designed, the other parts will be more likely to wipe it out. If we build a part that is going to take weight and turn it into happiness, that part's going to get annihilated! All the other parts are going to do an exorcism. What about the part that likes to eat candy? It's going to pull out its samurai sword, sst—whacko, and that's it. I'm asking you to conceptualize definitions for the purpose of making installation easy, effective, and useful.

Man: How about a traffic control?

You'd better be more specific than that. This is not a metaphor seminar.

Man: A part that would sequentially direct other parts to do their thing to get the desired outcome. Most overweight people know how to gain weight and lose weight. Maintaining it is the difficulty.

So you would have a part that's in charge of maintenance, for example?

Man: It would provide directions for other parts, and say "Now you do this, and you do this, and then you do this, and now it's your turn."

OK. That's certainly a possibility. What other outcome could you specify for a part that you could build to take care of this problem?

Bill: I'm thinking about a client of mine who eats mainly in the evening when she's alone and bored. I want to build in a part so that whenever she is alone and begins to feel bored she will immediately generate several interesting activities she can engage in, so that she'll do those instead of eating.

OK. That's a strong possibility, *assuming* that your information is accurate, namely, that eating at that time produces the unwanted weight. Then the first question you have to ask is "Does she already have a part whose job it is to entertain her when she gets bored?" She might have one already, and the *way* it does that is by stuffing candy down her mouth. Then all that part needs is three other ways to entertain her. The six-step model would be adequate to do that. That is one possibility. Or it may be that she doesn't have a part to entertain herself, and it would be appropriate to build one.

Bill: She has had a lobotomy, which raises some interesting problems.

It could. I don't think parts get cut out that way, though. I think they become *subdued.*

Bill: But it does raise some anchors in her mind about what she is incapable of doing or thinking.

Well, all you have to do is produce research which proves that it's possible to make the changes you want to make. I'm sure you can come up with lots of studies and dates.

Bill: I've just remembered a whole volume.

Yeah. It's known as "instant research." For some clients it's very, very valuable.

Let me give you another problem. Let's say you are using the six-step reframing model. You ask "Do you have a part of yourself you consider your creative part?" And the person says "I don't know." And you say "Well, go inside and ask if there is a part of you that can do things creatively." She goes inside, and then she comes out and says "Nothing happened." And from your outside observation, nothing happened. There are two choices at that point about how you create a creative part. One is to act as if you received messages from one that was there. If you congruently convince them of this, they'll build one on their own. The other choice is to officially build them a part because they don't yet have one that can perform that function.

What other kinds of contexts would be appropriate for *building* parts, rather than reframing ones that are already there? Give me some examples of when building a part could be more useful than messing around with the parts that already exist.

Man: Some kind of a history that the person has never had, never experienced in his life?

That's not an example. Examples are content-specific, so that when you name them, people can go "Oh, yeah." What you gave me was a *class,* and that's a different game. Give me an *example* of the class you were talking about.

Man: Let's take someone who has never had a satisfying sexual experience.

OK. What are you going to build a part to do? Do you want a part to make them feel OK about that, so that every time that they're sexually dissatisfied, they say to themselves "I'm OK, I'm OK"?

Woman: Have them imagine one, build it in the imagination of the person.

That is *how* we are going to go about building parts. You're back to procedure again, instead of outcome. I'm not going to teach you how to build parts until you know *what* you are building. It's an old rule of mine. Give me some examples of what you would build parts for.

Woman: If someone is born with a coordination problem, you could give them a strategy for being coordinated by copying somebody else.

OK. I'll accept everything except the preface about being "born that way." There are many people who could use a hand-eye coordination part who were not "born that way." They just never developed a part that had anything to do with being coordinated. Even if there's a physical impairment, it still might be appropriate to build such a part.

Bill: Let's say I have an army brat who was raised overseas and who has not had the same experiences that most of his peers have had. I want to help the kid acquire certain kinds of social skills. I could build a part to teach him how to listen carefully to people around him and to build a new history from what he hears people talking about.

What's the outcome of the part's behavior?

Bill: The outcome of the part's behavior is to teach him to speak congruently about things that he has never experienced, so that he can build social bridges and not seem different.

That's still behavior. What's the part's function?

Bill: To help him increase his social interaction with other people.

OK. That's the outcome. I can think of situations where that would be very appropriate.

Man: You could build a part that would motivate you to explore new things, risky things.

A part whose job it is to actually instigate behavior in contexts that are risky. We call that a "chutzpah part." I can think of *many* people who need one of those.

Man: It seems like you're building parts into us all the time. For instance, you build parts in us to observe sensory experience and translate it, and to understand reframing.

Of course. Sure.

Woman: I'd like a part to hear pitch. The outcome would be to be able to sing on pitch.

Hear, hear. Give me some more examples of where you would use this model as opposed to the other reframing model.

Man: Build a part to learn how to do any physical activity, like roller skating or ice skating or any other sport.

Sure. It sounds like strategies, doesn't it? All right, let's go back to therapy now; we're drifting off into the land of generativity. I think it's nice that your tendency is to become generative; however, this seminar is about therapy. The question is "What problems do people bring you as therapists that this model is going to be appropriate for?" If you can't think of anything, there's no reason to teach it to you.

Woman: You could use it working with a child of a missionary who's never had a stable home environment and doesn't feel like he belongs anywhere.

What would that part do?

Woman: It would allow him to feel at home wherever he is.

Sure, OK.

Woman: How about building a part to stand up and be assertive?

Sure. What do you think assertiveness training is all about? "Now we're all going to build the same part here together."

Man: A part to know when to get out of unproductive relationships.

Hear, hear!

Woman: A part to tell people what need their present operation enhances. And they would know why—

Wait a minute. "Operation" is an anchor for me for something other than what I think you are talking about. That was a "cutting" remark, so please rephrase it.

Woman: A part to tell someone why the activity he is involved in is satisfying to him.

A psychotherapist part? "You are happy now *because* . . ."

Woman: Then they would know why they are eating, what need the eating is satisfying, and then they could substitute a preferential activity.

Let me question you on this a little bit, because this is something that therapy has been trying to do for years, and I don't agree that it's a useful outcome. What's the *outcome* of installing a part that tells people about their ongoing behavior while they are doing it? There's one outcome of that that I think is absolutely disastrous: there are always *two* of you there at all times—one of you doing something, and one of you talking about it. That is called dissociation.

Above and beyond that, there's an even worse outcome of that kind of awareness, which is that you don't have very much external sensory experience. The outcome of having a part that constantly monitors your behavior is that you will always be on the inside, monitoring your behavior. You won't know how the world is responding to you. You will be there talking to yourself about why you are having this conversation and why you feel bad. But you'll never see the external behavior; you'll be too caught up internally. That kind of part has important limitations which should be considered.

You can build a part to do that, and in fact, many therapists already have one. They come to my groups and I say "Now, I'm going to put this person up here, and I'm going to touch him on the shoulder and his skin color is going to change." The people with these parts go inside and say "Well, I'm feeling threatened by this. Why am I threatened right now?" Then I ask "What color did he change to?" They come back out and say "I didn't see anything." The problem is you can't see or hear much externally if your attention is inside monitoring your behavior—whether you do it visually, auditorily, or kinesthetically.

When you're caught in a loop, you might want to have what we call a meta-part that temporarily dissociates and takes an observer position and says "Hey, what's going on here right now?" That part's function would be to get you out of loops. But the only time it would engage itself is when you are in a mess; it would not analyze at all times. If you put that constraint on it, then you begin to get a more useful outcome. The importance of thinking very carefully about outcomes is that you can succeed very well at installing parts that will completely drive people bananas in unuseful ways. So when you consider installing something, I want you to ask yourself "Well, what's the logical outcome of building this part? Is this *really* what I want to do, or is there something else that I have in mind? How can I be more specific about my description, so that when I build it, I get something that approximates what I want?"

Let me generalize the idea of a meta-part. A meta-part is only operational at certain times, and the contextual cue that triggers its functioning is usually based on how other parts are functioning. For example, it could be a part that comes into play only when you feel stuck, dissatisfied, or doubtful. Its functioning could also be cued to an external stimulus like a time of day, but if you do that, it may interfere with whatever else you happen to be doing at that time. So it's usually better to have it triggered off by an internal state—a feeling of being in conflict, indecision, or something like that. You can specify that whenever two parts get into a conflict, then the meta-part goes into action.

A meta-part is kind of like an amnesia state waiting in the wings to be fired off. Within the meta-part is a program, a formal set of procedures, that comes out linearly. It's like a computer sub-routine more than anything else. "If parts disagree, then do X." The meta-part operates and modifies the disagreeing parts. It operates on the other parts, but is only functional in response to a cue. The procedure that it uses is usually formal: it could do six-step reframing, it could do content reframing, or it could just give you amnesia. There are lots and lots of possibilities for what a meta-part can do. It's a part that influences other parts to keep them from being in conflict with each other, or keep them from doing something that makes you get arrested, or whatever.

One way of thinking about a meta-part is that it is a mechanism to *build* a response. Another way to think about a well-functioning meta-part is that if you go into a calibrated internal loop that is not useful, that state becomes an anchor for a procedure that elicits a response that will get you out of the loop. That is closer to how I think about it than as a part. The notion of parts is a good pace for most people's experience, but for me there is a bit too much anthropomorphism in the notion of parts. You can think of a meta-part as a part that makes a distinction and then kicks into a procedure that can take you somewhere else.

With a couple, you can build a part in one of them that operates only when they argue. This part recognizes that the reason they argue is because they want things to be better. Rather than going in and negotiating with all the parts that feel right about things and argue, you can build a part that recognizes that they are now making themselves feel bad *because* they want to feel good. What they want is fine, but the way they are going about it stinks. Rather than reframing all the other parts yourself, you can build a meta-part that recognizes this and says "Hey, you are doing this because you love this guy. Do you remember the first time you fell in love with him? Do you recall what that was like? The *way* you are trying to get him to treat you well isn't working. Do you remember what you did then? What else could you do? What does Janie do with her husband that works?" The meta-part goes into some way of generating alternatives: it provides ways for them to get what they really want. At specific times it says "Go in and change your behavior and get out of this loop; you've been here before and it has never worked. Arguing is not going to get you what you hope it will, and in order for you to argue, it must be really important. It must be *important enough* to change what you are doing."

Man: I'm struck by that phrase "important enough." I know it's important intuitively, and it has already been emphasized a couple of times, but can you explain what makes it so powerful?

It's a presupposition. It presupposes that this is more important than the other. If I go "Look, you are tall enough to reach that glass," the implication is that you are taller than I am. If I say to a kid "You are strong enough to stand up for yourself now," that presupposes that there was a time when he wasn't, but he is now. If I say "You are old enough to pay your own way," it presupposes that she wasn't at some time, but now she is and she hasn't recognized it. "You want this because it's important. And that means it must be important *enough* for you to do these other things."

This is a great pattern to use in couple therapy. The couple is arguing and shouting "I'm right!" So you say "You're arguing because X, Y, and Z is very important to you. But is it important *enough* for you to consider other ways of communicating that might work better than arguing?" It's a great double-bind. If it's not really important, then they wouldn't argue in the first place, and they can stop now. If it is important, then it's important enough to try something else that might work, since what they're doing now isn't working. All the power behind being "right" gets channeled into new behavior.

In one couple I worked with, every time her husband would give her what she asked for, she would want *more.* She knew that she shouldn't, but she was dissatisfied and that made him crazy. He used to offer her things, but he didn't much anymore. She had a part whose primary intention was to get him to reassure her that he still loved her. What that part was doing wasn't working very well. I decided to build a part to help it: an ally. Any time she began to have doubts, this new part would come into action. This ally reframed the reassurance part on an ongoing basis. Whenever she had doubts, the ally said "Look, is it important to be reassured?" "Yes." "Well, good. Is it important enough for you to find out what you can do to reassure him that you love him?"

This will result in a much broader behavioral change than simply giving her other ways to feel reassured. The ally will get her to do many things with her husband that don't get reassurance at the moment, but *will* result in her being reassured *spontaneously* at other times, which is what she really wants. You can't directly get somebody to reassure you spontaneously. But you can behave in ways that will eventually get it for you spontaneously at other times. A meta-part can be a good way of doing that.

Woman: I'm trying to relate this to the six-step model, which would say "Find out what need the present behavior that you don't like is satisfying, and find a new behavior that would better satisfy the need."

Yes, that's the six-step model. One way to think about such "problems" is as if every behavior serves a need. Or you can assume that a problem behavior has nothing to do with their needs; it's just a *by-product* of achieving some other outcome. That would also lead you to use the six-step model.

The difference between when the six-step model is particularly useful and when building parts is particularly useful is the difference between building parts that *stop* things and building parts that *do* things. With the six-step model you usually start out with some behavior you don't like and get new choices so that you no longer use the unwanted behavior. That's using reframing in order to stop something. The situations where building a part is most appropriate are those in which a person wants a part that *does* something: he wants to generate certain desired behaviors, and he is not doing it. When people ask for a part that *stops* something, then the six-step model, the secondary gain model, is going to be much more appropriate.

Man: How about building a part that differentiates between professional relationships and personal friendships? College professors who lecture at you when you are chatting could use a part like that.

Yeah, I can think of some people who could use that.

Man: How about a part that will give more flexibility to a person who has a lot of polarities?

Well, you have to be more specific about what you mean. You're being very general. What you're *thinking* of may be really groovy, but you have to be careful about how you describe it, because we've got this other human that we're going to install it in. Does this mean that he is going to become tolerant of having his parts fight with one another? What do you mean?

Man: Let's say the person has a polarity response to situations involving groups of people; you develop a part that will allow the flexibility for that person to listen.

Oh, you mean the ability not to have the polarity response. If you do that, you have to consider the possible secondary gain. If he *always* has a polarity response, is there some positive function? There may or may not be. The nice thing about your example is that if something is that overgeneralized in behavior, very often you can just build a part that listens to *lectures* and no other part in him will object to that, because there is no secondary gain to not listening *in that context.*

No matter what the difficulty is, you can act as if there is secondary gain and fix it. That will always work. If you pretend well enough, you can get anything to be real. But it may turn out that there is no secondary gain. There may only be secondary gain in a polarity response when you are being lectured by parents as a teenager. The polarity response allows you to rebel. However, you overgeneralized that response to all situations.

You become one of the people who sit at the back of one of our seminars. Afterwards, you say "Well, but what about insomniacs? It works well for phobias, but what do you do with depressives?" That person will leave the lecture not knowing anything about how to work with phobias because of his polarity response.

The point I'm making is that not listening may have no secondary gain in one context; it may in another. So if you just build a part for that particular context it may work great, but to avoid objections you have to be *very* specific about what it's going to do.

Man: A part that will get a person to show up on time for therapy sessions, or a part to do homework on time.

Which of the three models is going to be most appropriate for the example he just gave? "People are late." What does that sound like? . . . It sounds like two parts tripping over each other's toes. So you'd use the negotiation model for that.

Woman: A part to discriminate between a dangerous situation and a safe one.

A part to discriminate between what's dangerous and what's safe. What do you think about that? What does that sound like? Does that sound like a situation in which you've got to 1) reframe one part, or 2) build a part, or 3) negotiate between parts?

Man: You could do any of those.

Well, you can always use any of these models, but which one sounds *most* appropriate?

Woman: Build a new part.

Bill: Rebuild an old part. Take the part that has kept him safe enough to get here, that kept him from getting hit by cars or anything, and—

How do you know that? She didn't say anything about that. What happens if you have someone who's always stepping in front of trains? She didn't specify any of that.

Man: He must be getting missed by trains or he wouldn't be here.

That's a pretty big assumption. You can verify that with sensory experience, but I can think of examples of people who need to have parts that distinguish between situations which are dangerous and those which are not, because they get them mixed up.

Woman: That's particularly true of children.

Right. Your parents all built one of those in you. It's part of how you got here. Think of all the people who didn't make it to this seminar.

Let me back up and run through the whole thing again quickly. I made a statement at the beginning that one thing I noticed about therapy is that most of what people are doing is building parts. That's about eighty percent of what many therapists actually do. If that's true, then why is building parts so prevalent? Building parts is often inappropriate. I don't think everybody needs a "parent," a "child," and an "adult," but I think some people do. The question is "Who's going to need a part?" and then "What, specifically are they going to need?" What kinds of familiar contexts occur where people need parts? (Someone walks very noisily across the room.)

How about a part that gets someone to pay attention to sensory experience when they walk across the room, and to notice that they are making a tremendous amount of noise? We just had a demonstration of that need. That would be an exquisite part for some people to have. Perhaps in some situations lacking that part won't be detrimental. However, if you don't have a part that pays attention to how people are responding to you, there may be a lot of people who act as if they don't like your behavior, and you won't have any way of noticing that or changing that. There are many, many people in therapy who have that particular problem. They don't have any friends, and they don't deserve any. How many of you have had clients like that? You may tell them that somebody out there is going to like them, but deep down inside *you* don't like them. Often the problem is that they really have no way of knowing how people respond to them. That would be a really prime example of where it's appropriate to build a part. Where else are you going to need to build a part?

Woman: In couple relationships, you might need a part that would negotiate with your partner.

You get on the borderline there when you talk about having a part that carries on the negotiations. What are the rest of the parts doing in the meantime? I want to know what the outcome of installing this part would be.

Let me give you an example. A couple came to see me because they both had stupid behaviors that fired off automatically and prevented them from talking about what they wanted to discuss. I just picked one of them and installed an interrupter part. The new part did something that captured the attention of both of them, and interrupted the stupid behavior long enough that they could go back and talk about what they wanted to talk about. I don't know what you have in mind, but that's one thing that I've done.

Woman: You could install a part to tell reality from hallucination.

Now that would be a hell of a good part! Someday I may try building one of those. Later on this year I'm going to a state mental hospital to train the staff. This hospital's main function is to "warehouse" the patients that nobody really knows what to do with. A very interesting person has just taken over control of this hospital through an odd set of circumstances. The *only* thing that I intend to teach when I go back there is how to use this model to build a part that makes distinctions between what is shared reality and what isn't. Many psychotics do not have a part to do that.

Man: Many psychiatrists do not have a part to do that when working with those people.

Many do not have it at all, as far as I can tell! The only difference is that they have other psychiatrists who share their reality, so they at least have *a* shared reality. I make lots of jokes about the way humanistic psychologists treat each other when they get together. They have many social rituals that did not exist when I worked at the Rand Corporation. People at Rand didn't come into the office in the morning, hold each other's hands, and look meaningfully into each other's eyes for five and a half minutes.

When somebody at Rand sees somebody else do that, they go "Urrrhhh! Weird." The people in humanistic psychology circles think the people at Rand are cold and insensitive and inhuman. Well, those are *both* psychotic realities, and I'm not sure which one is crazier. And if you start talking about *shared* realities, the people at Rand have more people to share theirs with.

You *really* have a choice only if you can go from one reality to another, and you can also have a perspective on the process of what's going on. It's really absurd that a humanistic psychologist who is hired to teach at Rand Corporation doesn't alter his behavior. Think about how often that happens. If someone who has all the TA jargon goes to a gestalt institute, he'll get wiped out by the gestalt therapist, because gestalt people can yell, and most TA people can't. In that context, as far as I'm concerned, the inability to adjust to the shared reality is a demonstration of psychosis. Qualitatively it's not different. You just don't get put away.

Let's say you're a gestalt therapist or a TA therapist or an analyst or whatever your gig is—even a Neuro-Linguistic Programmer. Tomorrow morning you wake up and go down to some bar where all the guys are. You say "You know, I was working on strategies this morning with a client, and I was watching his accessing cues—" They say "What?" So you say "Well, you know, I studied with Bandler and Grinder. We watch the movement of people's eyes and we know how they are thinking." They say "Sure you do." "Oh, yeah, and then I elicited a response and I touched him, and then I associated it with this other memory simply by touching him." They would think you're pretty weird.

What you have to remember is that reality is contextual. *Here* we can talk about that and everyone nods meaningfully. You have all become a part of *my* psychotic reality. I have built a part in you so that I am no longer crazy.

If we had a psychotic, one of the things we could do is get the psychotic to have everybody else see his hallucination, and then we could call it "religion" or "politics." The point is that realities are defined structures.

In some situations you need to build a part, and you can build a part in any situation. Who in here needs a part? Does anybody in here need a part? What do you want? What is the part going to do?

Teri: It would keep me at a certain weight.

You want a part to keep you at a certain weight. That certainly is a well-defined one. Who else?

Man: I want a part that enables me to see clearly with binocularity, without glasses.

It's a possibility.

Woman: I'd like a part that would be creative with metaphors.

I want you all to notice something. I'm now going to comment on group process. I asked people to define an outcome, and people were having lots of trouble. Just now I said "Who in here wants a part?" and listen to how well-defined the outcomes are! Remember that when you work with people.

Man: I want a part to remind me at regular and frequent intervals that I know what I'm doing most of the time.

All right. If you have to have one like that.

Jill: I want a part to let me know what I *do* know how to do.

What's the outcome of that? That's not an outcome. That's a process. This is the first slip-up we've had here. I want to know exactly what this part is supposed to do. You might get yourself a part to remind you of a catalog of your therapeutic skills, or to remind you to have variety in your behavior. That would be specific. What do you want?

Jill: I want a part that will move me on to something different after I'm convinced that I've already done one thing successfully.

OK. You could have a part that says "OK. You've done reframing; you know the standard model. You're hot at that and that would work here, but let's do it differently this time and have some fun." Do you want that one? Or do you want a part that after you have successfully done reframing says "OK, it worked" so that you don't go ahead and use another model to cure the same problem that's already been cured?

Woman: I'll take both.

Man: I'd like a part that would allow me to relax when I'm sitting in a chair listening to a lecture, or when I'm talking.

Is that appropriate for this model? . . . It *could* be. The key question is "Are you relaxed at other times?"

Man: Yes.

So it's only when you come into a context like this that you get tense. Then the six-step model is more appropriate. If you built a new part to relax you, that would conflict with some other part that is making you tense.

Man: I'd like a part that permits me to retain the content of a lecture without taping the lecture.

Woman: I want an assertive part, but assertive only in certain contexts. Would I use this model, though, if I *had* an assertive part and the unassertive problem was contextually related? In other words, I *have* an assertive part . . . but it doesn't work all the time.

Well, I'm not willing to agree with that description. I would say what you are describing is that you have an assertive part, because you are capable of being assertive in some situations. This could be described in two ways. One is that you go into some specific situation and that part goes "Not me!" The other possibility is that the assertive part says "Get 'em now!" and some other part goes "Shhhh!" The question is

"Which of those two possibilities occurs?" When you know that, *then* you can decide which kind of reframing to use—but either way, it's not building a part.

Harvey: I'd like a part to enable me to make lots of money.

OK. You want a greedy or clever part, depending upon how you think about it. Again, there are still lots of questions about your outcome. If the outcome is to get a lot of money, there have to be some well-formedness conditions about how you'll do this. Otherwise you might just take a gun and rob the first bank you see. This is the same thing I was talking about earlier. I want a *specific* description of what this part is going to do. Otherwise if I install this part, it may just go out and rob a bank.

Harvey: I want a part that will build referrals and find new markets for my skills.

OK, good. If you build the part that's going to generate referrals, then it knows *how* to go about getting money. That's a very specific kind of outcome.

Ray: I'd like a part that would enable me to improvise on the piano.

Woman: I'd like a part that allows me conscious access to visual images from the past.

You can't make eidetic images? How do you spell "greenwood"? . . . OK. You can make pictures; the emphasis is on the word "conscious."

Woman: I'd like a part that would allow me to create hilarious humor whenever I wish. I want a part to just blow people apart into a humorous state.

Man: I want a part that will . . . allow me to . . . pause.

Do you want *another* one? You'd better be a little more specific, because you just demonstrated that you have a part that can allow you to pause. That's a mild incongruity in your communication, but my guess is that you have something more specific in mind.

Kit: I'd like a part to deal with "passive-aggressive" behaviors.

You will have to define that for me. "Passive-aggressive" is a *double* nominalization.

Kit: OK. I feel an incongruity in a set of behaviors that I experience with people and in myself—

We're going off into the "Land of Nominalization" here. We have to be careful. What is this part going to *do?*

Kit: Well, the part is going to serve a need—

All parts are going to serve a need. What is it going to *do?*

Kit: It will be like a periscope.

You can't specify outcome with that kind of metaphor. You've *got* to be very specific, or you'll go home at night and you'll lie down, and your body may come up like a periscope. If you say it's going to be a periscope, what exactly is it going to do for you? You've got to really tie it down to the world of experience.

Kit: I want balance between polarities.

Of? . . .

Man: You could build Kit a part to be more specific.

There you go. Beautiful. If you installed a part in her that was in charge of the Meta-Model, and then she Meta-Modeled her own internal dialogue, think what a gift that would be. Most of my students from the old days have a Meta-Model part.

Kit: I want a part to bring the stuff in me—

Wait a minute. Never mind. You need a part that knows the first four distinctions in the Meta-Model. In the exercise, someone is going to install a part in you that does that on the inside, so that before you speak, you can have the choice of using specific language or not.

Kit: I'd like a part that is . . . I feel that I . . . I've got a new statement to create it . . . since yesterday.

OK. Hold on for a few minutes. Go inside. . . .

Kit: I feel like I am.

Yes, that's right. This is called "pacing observable behavior." Go inside and figure it out. I want you to make a visual image of what it is that would be occurring either in your mind *or* in the world of experience, that would allow *me* to know that this part that you want was operating. I *don't* want your image to be metaphorical. In other words, if you had a part that did this, what would I see that would be different? Take some time and do that on your own.

Lucy: I want a part to increase the frequency and intensity of orgasm with my husband. That would fit into this model.

True. Why not? Go for something worthwhile, I always say.

Woman: Is that building a new part, or is it just . . .

Well, the task of the part that she wants to build is not to make her have orgasms. Its job is to get another part to do it more often. The part she wants is what we call an "elbow part." It gets other parts to go to work. It's like the difference between a motivation strategy and a learning strategy. One gets you to do it, and the other actually does the work. For instance, with a weight problem, it's one thing to build a part whose job is to diet, and it's another one to build a part whose job is to get you to go back on diets. There are different ways of thinking about how you are going to build parts and what you are going to build them for.

What we have been doing so far is step one: determining what specific outcome you want, and making sure that it is appropriate to build a part for that outcome. Before you build a part, I want you always to check to find out if another reframing model is more appropriate to get what you want. . . .

* * * * *

For those of you who have chosen a part that you want and specified the outcome, I want to take you through step two. This is a fairly complex procedure, and we're going to do it methodically—not metaphorically. As a therapist you can dance around a little bit if you want to, but we're going to go through it step by step. I recommend *highly* that you have a piece of paper and a pencil during this procedure, because later there are going to be some things that you're going to have to keep track of, and there may be a lot of them.

I want all of you who are going to play this game with me to go inside and find out if you have any reference structures for the behavior that you want. Access any historical experiences that you can find of doing what you want to be able to do more methodically, more often, or whatever it is. Let's say somebody wanted to have a creative part. Perhaps they were only creative once ten years ago, or maybe they once thought of a new way to write a shopping list. Whatever it is, I want you to find whatever relevant examples exist. When you find those memories, I want you to step inside them, and get back *all* of the experience that goes with those memories. This is a very essential piece of what we are going to do. Take whatever amount of time you need to do that. Isolate specific instances of what you want, and be thorough about it. Make sure that you get at least one, two, or three experiences—if you have them—of what it is that you want this part to be able to do.

If what you want is a part that's going to make you have orgasms more often, don't remember an orgasm, remember a time when you got yourself to have one that you didn't expect. If you are going to build a part whose job is to get you to maintain a certain weight, you don't want to remember a time that you weighed that much, you want to remember a time when you *maintained* a specific weight.

Access those memories as intensely as possible. You don't need a long duration. The intensity of what you access will be the important part.

Woman: And if there are no examples?

If there are no examples, then wait. But be very careful, because there probably are examples of everything in your experience, whether you know it or not. If you can't find any examples, then just hold on, because step three is going to take care of that anyway. . . .

* * * * *

For those of you who could not find any examples *and* for those of you who are finished, I want to go on to step three, which has two parts. First I would like you to create for yourself a dissociated visual and auditory constructed image of how you would behave if you were actually demonstrating whatever it is that this part is going to have you do. So with the weight maintenance, you're not going to see yourself weighing a specific weight. You're going to see yourself engaging in the behaviors that would happen as you were at that weight, and as you gained some, and as you lost some—in other words, whatever behaviors would be operating as you *maintained* that weight. Most people are adept at losing and gaining weight. The problem is that when they get down, they go right back up. That new part's job is not to lose the weight, but to do things that result in maintaining the weight. You need to see yourself in that context: what you would look like, what you would be doing, and what you would sound like.

Next, when you see a whole sequence that you're satisfied with, step inside the image and go through the whole sequence again from the *inside.* Make sure that you like the feelings that you have as you do this, and do a good job. You will go through it twice: once from the outside, and once from the inside. First you visualize a good example of what you would look like and sound like doing the behavior. Then the second time through you find out what it would feel like from the inside. If you're satisfied after you have watched the whole movie from the outside, then step inside the movie and do it from the beginning all over again. If you're not satisfied with the feelings, go back and change the images as you look at them from the outside, and then go through it again from the inside. . . .

* * * * *

Bill: When I go inside, there is an internal auditory which is not apparent to me when I'm looking at it from the outside. I don't know how to get rid of that. I can look at the image outside and see myself writing a manuscript. But as soon as I go inside, I'm sitting there at the typewriter and I'm starting to write out the first sentences, and a voice comes up that has all kinds of objections to what I'm doing. I don't believe that continuing that loop of going out and then back in is going to handle that.

OK, ask that auditory part if—for the purposes of your fantasy at this time—it would be quiet just for a few moments, because what you want to do is to find out *if* this is something you do want. If it turns out that it is something that you do want, you're not going to be able to get it unless this part agrees. That's the next step. So if it has an objection to your having the internal experience that you fantasized that you want, then it will have a chance to object, and rightfully so. But first it should allow you the opportunity of finding out if you want the new behavior. When it allows you to have that experience, you may discover that if you don't have that internal voice, you have nothing to write. If so, you would then have to construct another fantasy.

Woman: Are you asking for one fantasy or several fantasies?

You just want *one* fantasy which is an example of the way you would look from the outside, behaving as if you had this part. And then *if* you like it from the outside and it looks safe—no one strikes you, you don't fall off a cliff or anything—then go through the same sequence from the inside, and find out if you like the internal experience as well. Sometimes you think that you want a part, but when you try it out, you don't like it.

If you're not done, just go ahead and take the time you need to finish the third step. It will do you no good to jump ahead. I'm going to go ahead and give the instructions for the next step. If you miss them, don't worry. I'll probably end up giving them several times, because this step is a little complicated. Make sure you finish the step that you're on first. Take all the time you need. I'll go over it as many times as you need.

* * * * *

When you have the well-formed example of how you would behave if you actually had this part, and you are satisfied with that fantasy from the inside as well as from the outside, then the next thing I want you to do is an ecological check. This is step four. I want you to go inside and ask—and it is very important how you do this—*"Does any part object to my having a part which will be in charge of making that fantasy a reality?"* That is a yes or no question. If you get a verbal "yes," fine. If you get a feeling, you have it intensify for "yes" and diminish for "no." You can use all the methods from the other reframing models for this.

If a part objects, I want you to ask *"What is your function for me?"* This time you don't care what the objection is. That's not the important part. You want to find out what it is that the objecting part does, what its job is, its function.

When you get that information, if it doesn't make sense to you that it would object to your having the new part, go ahead and ask it what, specifically, its objection is. Ask it how it thinks this new part is going to get in its way.

Let's say you decide "I'm going to install a part that teaches me how to hold my breath for an hour and a half." Then you go inside and ask the question "Does any part object?" You get a "yes" so then you ask "What is your function for me? What do you do for me? What's your job?" The objecting part says "Well, I'm the part that keeps your heart beating." If you can't consciously tie together how holding your breath for an hour and a half is going to interfere with the heart-beating part, then I suggest you ask. My guess is most of those connections will be obvious. But if they aren't, then ask.

The pencil and paper are for this step. So far each time I've used this model there have been at least eight or nine parts that object. Depending upon what part you are building, some of you may not have very many objections. When you go about installing a new part, the potential for it to get in another part's way is a lot greater than when you're just altering one part's behavior a little bit. There may be many, many parts that object to creating a new part. The more the merrier, because they are all going to become allies in the design process. Just make a complete list of the parts that object, and each one's function. You want to know if there are parts that object, and if so, what do they do? What's their job? Be thorough. Make sure you get *all* of them. Check each representational system for objections, to find out about all the parts that object in any way. The objections will be the essence of making sure that the part you build is really graceful and works well. They will be the talents of the part that you are going to build. . . .

* * * * *

Lucy: I got six parts down.

OK, you've got six parts down. And you got all of their functions?

Lucy: Oh, no, I've just got the parts listed.

OK, I want you to find out what each one's function is. You say "Part number one, you objected? What do you do for me?" You don't ask "What is your objection?"; you ask "What's your function?" You want to know what each objecting part is in charge of. It's not that you have a part that says "All right, we're going to limit the orgasms here." It's just that the objecting part is doing something *else*. When it considers the possibility that you would have a part that gets you to have orgasms more often, it says "Hey, I'm not so sure I want a part that does that." Now, you might be able to install the new part anyway, and perhaps the part that objected wouldn't interfere with it at all. However, if we find out what its concern is, then we can build an even better part, and be sure that other parts won't object to it.

Lucy: So you want me to find out what each part's concern is?

Secondly. First I want you to know what its *function* is, what it's in charge of. If that doesn't give you an understanding of what its concern is about having this new part, then ask.

Lucy: I'm not sure if I understand. For instance, there is a part that doesn't want me to put pressure on my husband, and a part that doesn't want to give me what I want. Now would those be two parts?

OK, now, what's the function of the part that "doesn't want to give you what you want?" I'm sure that you don't have a part that just sits around and says "What can I keep from Lucy today?" It's got to be in charge of some other task. The question is "What is its job?" It may be a part that doesn't want you to have unrealistic expectations. All I want to know is what its function is, and what its concern is. If you do have a part that doesn't want you to have "unrealistic expectations," then you already know what its concern is. Its concern is that the new part isn't going to work and that you'll be disappointed. You don't have to worry about that one, because what we build will work. You want to know the function of each part that objects, and a little bit about what concerns it about having this new part around.

This new part that you want to build is going to influence your behavior. You want to know if there are other parts of you that object to it having existence in you. We want to know about *every* part that objects to the idea of having this new part. And we also want to know specifically what it is about having this part that concerns the other parts. That is very, very valuable information. We need to know that so that when we build the part, we can build one that is going to be satisfying to the total person, rather than just ramming something in and letting conflicts evolve. There are usually plenty of conflicts already; we don't need to build in more.

I've said nothing yet about actually installing these parts. So far we're just *designing.* The fifth step is what we call "satisfying well-formedness conditions." The well-formedness condition of our design is going to be that no other parts object. We are going to take *all* of their concerns into account and modify the new part accordingly. We don't want to step on anybody's toes here except the conscious mind's. It's the only one who deserves it.

The fantasy that you had last time is the basis upon which those parts made their objections. You made up a fantasy, and a certain part went "Ugghh, boy, that's going to be hard." Another part said "I don't want that!" Some other part said "If we do that, we won't be able to do this." All the parts that had concerns based their objections on that fantasy. So now you're going to make a *new* fantasy. We now have a list of well-formedness conditions to use to modify the last fantasy and take into account *all* of the concerns of those other parts. Before you build the new fantasy I would like you to *redefine* your part so that it takes into account all of those concerns. This is the importance of the amount of time I spent on definition. For example, what were the functions of some of the parts that objected?

Teri: There was a part of me that said that if I maintained the weight I wanted, I might not be a therapist. I wouldn't want to do therapy; I'd want to be outside doing other things.

That was an objection?

Teri: Well, if I stay overweight, I'm comfortable doing what I do now, because I don't feel like doing much outside.

But what is that part's function?

Teri: To keep me the way I am.

No, that's not its function. If there's a part that says "Look, if you lose all this weight and maintain it, you're not going to want to do therapy," then you say "Well, OK, that's a possibility. What's your function?" If it says "Well, my function is to keep you the same" that's called "jive." In this group we know that that's not a function, that's a *behavior.* What we're looking for is a positive function. You don't have a part whose function it is to keep you the same. You have a part that wants to keep you the same *so that* X, Y and Z won't happen, or will happen. If you don't get functions, you're not going to be able to come up with a good set of well-formedness conditions.

Teri: For example, I wouldn't have much time alone with my husband.

OK, so there's a part whose function is to make sure that you spend time with your husband. And one way of carrying out that function is to do therapy, so you can hang out with him at work.

Teri: Right.

Now, that's a concern that makes sense. However, there are lots of ways to build in spending time with your husband. So the part of you that is going to maintain your weight is going to make sure that this part is very satisfied. It will build spending lots of time with your husband into the maintenance program. This now becomes part of the fantasy that you have to build. You don't become thin and run off, because this part isn't going to go for that.

OK, now I want another example of a function.

Pat: The function of my new part is to let me know when I know something. The concern is that it will defeat my motivation to learn more.

OK, so if you had a part that let you know when you know something, then you would be less motivated to learn. So now you have to build a desire to know what's over the next horizon into the new part that you are going to build. That's got to be an integral part of having a sense of what you know. "I really know reframing; I wonder what else there is to learn?" That's got to be built into the new fantasy part.

For *each* objection, you're going to have to modify the fantasy until it satisfies each of those conditions.

Bill: I've got one, the function of which is to keep me honest.

That is not a function. That is a behavior. That is an example of what we do *not* want. What is it trying to do by keeping you honest?

Bill: Protect me from being accused of lying . . . or to be honored if a person tells me I'm honest.

Well, make sure which it wants. There's a real difference between being honored and—

Bill: It feels more aversive than it does—

All right, but be persnickety. Go in, set up a yes/no signal, and find out which it is. Check it out and be thorough.

Teri: I came up with the main thing behind all this. The only time that I've ever been thin, I was crazy. There is a part that's not willing to let me become thin, because I don't want to be crazy.

Well, I certainly think that you could build strict controls on your mental health into a part that was going to put you on a weight maintenance program. Think about it this way, Teri. Poundage and sanity have no relationship to one another, other than anchoring. Whatever weight you weighed when you were whatever you are calling "crazy" had nothing intrinsically to do with being crazy. That time it was a coincidence. There's no causal relationship between losing weight and your being crazy again.

It's the same as when we did the lying exercise last week. I said "OK, it's time to lie." Everybody else said "Yay, we're going to lie!" but you said "If I lie, I'll be crazy. I lied before and I was crazy, so if I lie now and I can't tell the difference, I'll be crazy, because that's how I was crazy before. If you want to make *them* crazy, that's all right, but *I'm* going outside!" . . . And the rest of the people were muttering "Well, we have to stay in here and be crazy."

When I came outside I said to you "Look, lying, and not knowing whether you were lying or not, was an anchor for being crazy for you. The rest of the people in the room haven't done that—as far as they know. When you do it *this* time, we're going to give you a new anchor. We're going to make some black lines around your pictures when you lie, and they are really important black lines. Now you can lie, and know you are lying, so you won't be crazy this time."

All I really did was to put a literal meta-reframe around what was going on. It's a very small change in your strategy. You're still making constructed visual images. We're just separating the constructed images from the others with those black lines, and it's that separation that allowed you to have new feelings about what you were doing. When I said "OK, now make up a lie" you made up a lie. I asked "Are you crazy?" and you said "No." I asked "Which one is the lie?" "Well, the one with black lines around it is a lie. Anybody can see that."

The point is this: if you are going to lose weight and go back to a weight that is associated with being crazy, you also have to put a new frame around it. That has got to be a function of this new part. If you are going to go back to the weight you had when you were crazy, then of course there's the implication that you are going to be crazy again. However, since *you* are not the person who went crazy, *you* can't possibly go back.

That distinction has got to be built into the part that you are building now. It's very essential that it's capable of distinguishing all the differences between *this* Teri and the one that went nuts. This Teri is a different age, and has a lot more information about the world of experience. You know how to do a lot of things that the other one didn't know how to do before. *That* Teri didn't know anything about NLP. She didn't know how to anchor psychiatrists. There are lots of tools that you have explicitly now, that you didn't have then—not only the things you've learned here, but in TA, and lots and lots of things that have nothing to do with psychotherapy. So this new part has got to be able to point out, now and then, how you are different.

Are there any other questions about how you utilize objections to redesign the part you want to build? This is a very important part of this process. This is the crux of building parts that will be functional, so that you don't end up being an anorexic or something like that.

Bill: I want a part to allow me to write papers comfortably, without agonizing. There's a part that objects. When I ask "Well, what's your function?" it says "My function is to make you aware of all the possible objections to, or criticisms of, what you are writing."

OK. The contradiction I'm hearing is that that part *wants* you to write. Its job is to help you with your writing. Is it objecting to your being comfortable?

Bill: I like to write; the problem is that I sweat blood doing it.

That's impossible. That's the same contradiction. You're saying "I *love* to write; it's *so painful.*"

Bill: A friend of mine once said "I don't like to write; I like to *have written.*"

Well, that's different.

Bill: What I'm aware of is that I sit down at the typewriter all fired up. "Gee, this is some great stuff I'm going to put out here." And then I go *"Ughhh!"*

Yeah, I agree. And do you know what you need to do in order to satisfy this part? One simple solution might be to ask it to read your papers at the *end* of each page.

Bill: Well, I was considering asking it to save its objections until I have a finished first draft. There's this other part that says "When you sit down, you write the first draft."

OK, but you don't need to deal with the specific objections. You want to find *solutions* that preserve the *functions* of the parts that object. The important thing is that it objects. It's saying "Look, if you write this stuff, you're not going to consider all the objections people would have." What if you had made a fantasy where you sat down and wrote comfortably, and then at the end picked up your work and let this part go to work with a red pencil to revise it? Would it be satisfied then? This is what I do with other people's writing. I have a part that does that really well, especially if it's somebody else's work. They call that "editorial work." That can be a very valuable part.

Lucy: I'm hung up on a part that doesn't want me to give up control—

Of . . . ?

Lucy: —which I've taken to the part that will—

Wait a minute! These forms are very important. You have a part that objects, right? What is its function?

Lucy: Its function is to keep me from feeling helpless.

That is not a function; that is a behavior.

Lucy: It protects me from hurt.

That is a behavior. That is not a function. What will happen if you feel helpless? What is it trying to do for you by keeping you from feeling helpless? So what if you feel helpless?

Lucy: It's a needless function.

No, it's not. It's just that you don't know what it is yet. What is it trying to do for you by protecting you from feeling helpless? That's the first part. The second part is how does having orgasms more frequently have anything to do with feeling helpless or not? I don't need a verbal response to that. The point is to get the function clear so that you can understand how you have to modify your fantasy so that *that* part can be satisfied as well.

Ray: I was very surprised that any part objected to my improvising on the piano. The first objection was that I may end up playing the piano more at gatherings and interacting with people less.

OK. I didn't ask you to ask that question. This is important. I said if there is a part that objects, do *not* ask it what its objection is. Ask it what its *function* is, so you know what that part is in charge of doing. *Then* if you don't understand how it would end up being concerned, ask it what it's concerned about.

Ray: And I asked it the other way around.

Right. It is very important that when you're in my group you ask it my way. When you go home you can build parts your own way. If you don't know what an objecting part's function is, it's very, very hard to please it.

Bill: I asked the question "What do you think will happen if you get critical feedback?" And the answer that I got was "If I get that, then I'll feel lonely and inadequate." So it's keeping me from feeling lonely, and inadequate.

Well, in one sense that's the same answer. It's just a rephrasing. "Well, you know, it's my job to keep you from feeling lonely and inadequate." "Well, what would happen if I felt lonely and inadequate?" "Well, you would feel bad. My job is to keep you from feeling bad." "Well, what would happen if I felt bad?" "Well, if you felt bad, then you would feel like people don't like you." What it's doing is just redefining the same thing that it doesn't want: for you to feel bad. But the redefinition does give you some more information. One of the things that you can do is to build into the construction of the part *either* protection against people criticizing you, *or* a way of enjoying criticism. You could build in the understanding that when people are criticizing you, it offers you the unprecedented opportunity to do a lot of things. One is to demonstrate how loudly you can yell. Another is to utilize their behavior. When people are angry at you, it's an *unprecedented* opportunity to test your utilization skills. There are so many opportunities out there. So you don't have to feel lonely; you can make criticism the basis for a lasting relationship.

I'll tell you one of the odd things that I noticed growing up. Everybody that beat me up became my friend, and vice versa. Growing up as a teenager in a very rough place, I discovered that one of the best ways to make a permanent, lasting friendship was to beat the snot out of somebody. I became conscious of this sometime around the eighth grade. If there was somebody I wanted to hang out with, one of the fastest ways to become friends was to go beat the snot out of him. I don't know how that works, but it's an interesting phenomenon.

Man: Haven't you found some contexts where that behavior is not appropriate?

No, I haven't yet, actually. My whole professional relationship is built on it. I go around the country insulting people, and they pay me money. It's weird!

Harvey: I want to give you some more of my list of functions to see if I understand this. To keep me from failing is one. Giving me play time is another. Those are functions, aren't they?

Sure.

Harvey: To get love from others.

To elicit a particular response, yes. Hopefully that part knows what it means by the nominalization "love." You might have it be a little more specific. That's important.

Harvey: OK. I've got another one: To be a caring person.

That is a behavior, not a function. I'm going to teach all of you this information yet. You may not learn to build parts, but you're going to learn what a function is by the time you leave here! "To be" is a description. Listen to the phrase "to be or not to be." When you make a statement ". . . to be something or other" it's a description of a behavior. ". . . to be angry. I want a part to make me be angry." That isn't a function; that's just a description of a behavior. The part wants you to care about what or whom, where and why, and for what purpose? What is it going to get by having you be caring? What would happen if you weren't?

Harvey: The idea behind it is that I don't want to become like a machine.

That's the ultimate in humanistic psychology. "I don't want to be an android; therefore I'm going to act like this *all the time.* I'll hug *everyone;* that way I will not be a robot." The point is that this part wants you to do something that constitutes "caring." I have no idea what that means. Does that mean that you tell people honestly what they really ought to hear? Or does that mean that you touch everyone? What does it mean? Don't answer, because I don't care what the content is. I want *you* to know, and I want you to know what the function of that specific behavior is. It may be that that part wants you not to be an android, in which case all of this has nothing to do with being caring or not. You may go back inside and say "Have you ever thought about how much being 'caring' can be androidal? Let's have caring and not-caring; we'll alternate days. At least I'll be a *different* android."

The question is "What is the part's function?" If the part's function is to keep you from being an android, then the question is "What does that mean?" Does it mean not having repetition in your behavior? Does it mean *not* doing all the things that Maslow said were bad? It's essential to find out what the part's function is.

Ray: This time I asked the question about function and the response was "I'm here to take care of you so you won't become like your father."

Only a psychologist would say that.

Ray: My father improvises on the piano.

Right. But that still isn't a function. You have to go a little bit further than that. If you were to be like your father was, improvising on the piano, then you would be what? There was something about the way your father improvised that some part of you thinks is negative in some fashion. He either made a fool of himself, or he did something else that some part of you didn't like, right? Now, what was that?

Ray: He avoided interacting with people.

OK, so there's a part that wants you to have personal interaction with people. Good. Now all you have to do is build some way to have personal relationships with people into the way that you improvise on the piano. You have to define what "personal" means, because obviously it isn't singing songs. Maybe it means that you have to be able to play background music and have meaningful psychological conversations.

Woman: Is "to be taken care of" a function or a behavior?

That is neither. It's so unspecified, it's nothing. "To be taken care of"—how, specifically, . . . in what way? . . . by whom? . . .

Woman: Way back then is what I'm after, when I was in my original family.

You're going to build this part that's going to do something, right? What is it going to do?

Woman: It's going to let me be comfortable dancing in front of groups of people.

Let you dance? You've used the wrong reframing model, because there's obviously a part that stops you from doing this.

Woman: Yeah, I know. I knew that to begin with and—

But you thought you'd slide it in anyway. The point is that obviously there's going to be a part that isn't going to like this, because its job is to keep you from dancing in front of people. That part will have a very strong objection. So there's a part of you that objects, and its function is to have you "be taken care of." Go inside and tell it "I don't have any idea what 'to be taken care of' means. What specifically does that mean in experience?"

Woman: In my original family I had to do X, Y and Z to be taken care of.

OK. You had to take out the garbage in order to get a Twinkie, but I'm asking "What does that mean in your experience *now*?" What you've got now is so unspecified that I can't help you. It's like looking at somebody and saying "Noun, verb, adjective, noun." There's no content in your sentence, so I can't even respond to it. It's just a little *too* formal. What you want to know from this part is "What do you do for me as a person *now*?" You have to go back to it and say "Look, I need to know *in experiential terms* what it is that you do for me as a person. You are obviously a part of me. I do not live with my parents anymore. I want to know what it is that you do for me, and how you are concerned about my dancing. If I dance around, what's going to happen that's so bad?"

You want both those questions answered. You want to know what that part's job is. "What do you do for me?" "I get you to be taken care of." "How do you do it? What is it that you do?" You see, "being taken care of" might mean that people hug you. Or it might mean that people feed you. Or perhaps it means that people are nice to you. You need to find out what that means in the land of experience. That is what counts in the end.

Dan: I want a part to fully access visual and auditory information that I take in. A part objects to reaccessing totally all visual and auditory information.

And I agree with it. What's its function, though? What does it do for you? What would happen if Dan actually had a part that could recall *all* visual and auditory information? People like that are called *idiot savants,* and they get put into mental hospitals. *Idiot savants* are completely dysfunctional; they can't operate at all as human beings. They are constantly aware of everything that ever happened to them. They can multiply great. They are whizzes at mathematics, but they can't function in the world of experience, because they have so much internal "downtime."

When a part has a concern, take it into account and then redefine what the new part is going to do. Dan might redefine it as "I want to build a part that is going to make available some information about all the anchors that are occurring in a particular environment," or "I want to be able to visualize specific pages in a book I read once." Whatever it is that you want to be able to do, specify it in *experiential terms* so that you know exactly what is going to happen, and so that the other parts of you know whether they are going to object or not. Then if they have objections, they'll be good ones.

Bill: I've got a function that I'm having a lot of trouble phrasing. The stuff that I'm getting says "Look, I want you to minimize the probability of being laughed at and treated with disdain. And I want to maximize the probability that you will at least be treated with respect, and hopefully even honored."

OK. Well, that certainly is a rather extensive function. It doesn't want you to make a fool of yourself.

Bill: OK. Is that a function?

Yeah, that's a function. However, the question is what would happen if you made a fool of yourself?

Bill: That's not my question. My question is "Are those words which convey function as opposed to words which convey behavior?"

Well, those words mainly convey behavior, but the functional implications are tied to the behavior pretty well.

Bill: What are some words that do convey functions?

OK. For example: "*If* I made a fool of myself, then I would lose income because my clients would go away." The part's behavior is protecting you from making a fool of yourself *because* it's afraid that you will lose your friends and your business associates and your clients. The function is to keep your friends.

Bill: So it's the "then" part of an "if, . . . then" statement?

That's one way to think about it. There are many ways of getting the function. It's just not as simple as you want it to be. The function is *what* you get; behavior is *how* you get it.

Lucy: I'm on my list again. A part that rationalizes objected and then said "It doesn't matter."

Ask it if its objection is really important. . . .

Lucy: Nah. I've got another part that doesn't want to give me what I want, because I've already got so much it isn't fair. That is its reason.

I didn't ask you to find out reasons. What is the *function* of your having a part like that? That's the important question. We don't want to know the part's reasons.

Lucy: OK. I'll have to look at it again.

What kind of part is it?

Lucy: A bad part; I don't want it.

No, No, NO! There are no bad parts. We have *all* good parts. The only question is, "*What kind* of good are they doing?"

Lucy: It's making sure that I deserve the things that I get.

And rightfully so. OK. So that's its function, and its concern is that if you get this too easily, you won't appreciate it. Then you build in having to do certain things that make you deserving of the outcome you want to have.

Nancy: I can take care of all the objections and concerns, but then I'm getting a message that I need another new part—an ally—to help do all that.

Fine. However, I think it probably would be better if you found an ally that's already in there. You don't need to build a whole new ally. Just go in and find some other part that can already do what you need.

It's too much work to build two new parts in the same day.

Nancy: One part's concern is to be sure that I would be able to notice other people's disapproval.

What is the function of the part that wants you to do this?

Nancy: Well, it would be the part that is concerned with my failing.

It's not concerned with whether you fail or not; it's concerned about whether people disapprove of you or not.

Nancy: Well, yeah. The two are connected.

Certainly. If you fail, people may disapprove of you. But what it's concerned with is people's opinion of you.

Nancy: Yeah, and it's also related to getting some things that I want.

OK. That part is concerned that if they disapprove of you, then they won't give you a job, or they won't give you something else. Are you telling me that you don't believe you have the sensory experience to tell when you are behaving in a way that people disapprove of? I want a literal answer to that question. Do you, or do you not, have that much sensory experience? . . .

Nancy: I guess I do.

OK. Just go and get the part that does that, and say "Hey, part, I need your help over here. We're building George, a part who's going to do X, but George needs to have sensory experience about this, and you know how to have sensory experience. I want you to connect with this new part *if* we decide to build it." The new part doesn't have to have every quality. If you already have parts with certain qualities, you just get those parts to help out.

When you have all the functions and concerns of all the parts that object, then go on to *redesign* the fantasy so that *all* those concerns are satisfied. *Check with every single part* to make sure that each one is satisfied that this is a representation of an outcome that includes all the things they are concerned about *and* whatever it is that you want the new part to do. You make a new fantasy in which all the objections don't need to exist.

So in Teri's case the new fantasy must include the new part having responsibility for making sure she distinguishes between the way she is now and the way she was when she was "crazy" so that she can tell the difference. As long as she can tell the difference, the part that doesn't want her to go crazy won't object.

If there's a part that's afraid you are going to make a fool of yourself, then you have to build in the ability to have the sensory experience to notice when that happens. Without that you won't know, and those other parts are always going to be afraid that if you do certain things, you'll make a fool of yourself. You have to have feedback loops to satisfy those parts. If Bill writes, then he's got to be able to have ways of becoming somebody else and reading his writing in order to find out whether his response is "That's stupid!" or "Hey, that's pretty interesting."

Whatever concerns your parts have, you build safeguards into the fantasy so that you have a representation of what the world of experience would be like if you had a new part that functioned to get the outcome that includes all the concerns the other parts have. We not only want to build a good part, we want to build a *graceful* part as well, a part that can do what it does and not step on any other part's toes.

Now, if you have all the objections and outcomes, go ahead and build the new fantasy. First do it dissociated, and then do the whole thing again from the inside. Revise that fantasy until no part objects. . . .

* * * * *

If it's possible for you to make up a fantasy of yourself doing something and then step inside it and have the experience of doing it, you have already made all of the necessary adjustments at the unconscious level—in terms of strategies, in terms of representational systems, in terms of everything relevant—for that part to know how to generate the behavior and behave in accordance with what you want to accomplish.

A music teacher once told me "If you can hear something inside, then you can play it outside. The trouble is learning how true that is." Another person that I took music lessons from said "When you can hear it on the inside, then do it with your mouth. And if you can do it with your mouth, then you can do it with your hands." What was behind that is the understanding that in order to make a fantasy, you have to do everything mental that needs to be done in order to actually do it in experience. For instance, in a detailed fantasy you see somebody and tell him a joke and he laughs. As you did that, you had to go through all the necessary strategies to develop the joke: the creativity, the gestures, the talking—all of those behaviors are functioning in a detailed fantasy.

Step six is much more metaphorical than we usually are, and it demands some congruence on your part. You ask your unconscious resources to analyze that fantasy and to pull from it the essential ingredients. What you want your unconscious to do is something it does all the time anyway. You want it to take those first memories that you started with—the times in your past when you had actually done the behavior or something similar—and the fantasy that worked, and all the underlying structures, and you want it to give all that *entity*. That is how you randomly got all your parts anyway. Your unconscious can do that for you; it does it all the time. Those of you who are TA therapists and have TA parts, who do you think made them? You made them.

So you go inside and you say "Look, either one of two things is the case: either my unconscious mind is in charge of building parts, or I have some part in there that builds parts. Whichever it is, I want you to build this one and to give it *entity*. You don't do this step until you have a well-formed fantasy that no part objects to. When you've modified the fantasy so that *every* part is satisfied, then you do this step. You have your unconscious or some part of you give it entity so that it will function on its own.

Man: Could you go over that again?

You want to get some part of you, or your unconscious, however you think about it, to analyze the fantasy. What I'm saying is "Look, in the fantasy you used a strategy that worked. You want the part that you are building to use the experience of that fantasy as a foundation, and to operate out of that strategy." This is not what you would tell a client, by the way. You use whatever metaphors you need to with a client. Whichever way you think about it, whether you call it a strategy or a part, you say "Look, go in there and get what you need to know." This is what I would tell a client. "Get what you need to know from that fantasy to be able to build a part of you that can do this exquisitely and easily, and at every moment that it needs to be done."

I want you to go ahead and run through the rest of the steps. If you get stuck, let me know. Then I want to demonstrate to you some ways of testing. . . .

*　*　*　*　*

Are you done with that step? OK, now we get to the most important step of all: step seven. We have to *test* the part to make sure it's there. There are several things you can do. You can go inside and ask "Are you in there?" That's always a good first step. You can also do things behaviorally that would engage that part and find out what happens. You should also add lots and lots of future-pacing activities to your testing phase, especially when you do it with other people.

Now, how is your part going to work? Tell me something about what it would do. When would it be apt to do something?

Teri: Well, if I were to get on the scales and weigh two pounds more than what I want to weigh, it would let me know that I need to stop eating so that I can get back down.

So it would put you on a diet. Will it design the diet for you, or is there another part that does the dieting?

Teri: I already have a part that does that.

OK. You have another part for that. This part's job is to say "The time is now." What else would it do?

Teri: When I get to the weight that I want, it will give me a picture different than what I looked like when I was crazy.

What would it be apt to do right here?

Teri: Ah, it would allow me to go into the dining room and be with people while they are having dinner, and only eat what I really want to eat, and not allow me to eat everything.

It will disconnect the automatic hand-arm-mouth sequence? OK. How would I know if that part were active, Teri? If I walked into the dining room, what would I see?

Teri: You'd probably see some food left on my plate, depending upon whether it's something that I like or not. Visually, I'm not too sure that it would show for a while.

Is this part in a hurry to lose weight or does it do it slowly?

Teri: Slowly. I'd only agree to doing it slowly. I've already worked it out with my husband. If he wants to eat, he can eat, and I don't have to.

All right. Who else is done?

Bill: My part is going to wait until at least—

Shhhh! (with disdain) I didn't call on you. . . . Well, what happened? I was just testing the part. You built a part to help you respond to criticism, right?

Bill: Well, I'm recalling what . . . I was amused . . . and responded in a way that . . . helped me.

As opposed to?

Bill: Feeling that I have just done something awful, and I should be embarrassed, or ashamed of myself, or coming back with an angry response.

OK. Anybody else?

Pat: I have a new part, and I even made it grow, so that it is now about twenty-five years old.

Ah. I like that. OK, you built a part. What's it going to do?

Pat: It lets me know what I know, and to act on it when I know it. And my test is now to tell you that I have this part, and I also know that I know—

Give me an example of an outcome. If you were going to build another part, what would be an example of a function that—

Pat: I am going back home and I am going to use it everywhere. I am going to teach it; I'm going to—

That's what *this* one does. Now, give me another one. If you were going to build *another* part, what function would it have? If I were going to bring you up and have you demonstrate building a whole new part in another area of your life, what would you build? What would its function be?

Pat: Its function would be to utilize my unconscious mind as much as it can, as it did just now.

OK. Now, is that a function or is that a behavior?

Pat: Its function is to extract everything of value from my unconscious.

OK. Is that a function or a behavior?

Pat: I think it's a function.

OK. Are you sure, though?

Pat: It has to do it in action.

Yeah. I'm just asking you if you are *sure,* if you want to commit yourself to this.

Pat: I am sure. It's a function.

OK. Are you all learning how to test these things, by the way? . . . Anybody else?

Man: I think I got it.

What was the part you built? What does it do?

Man: It's a part that says "Go out and try something that you think you know. Try to do it, and see what happens."

So that part will get you to do it, to find out whether you really know it or not. That sounds like a good idea. That's what you built the part for, and you finished, right? OK, what do you think you know but you're not sure if you know it?

Man: Just now I wasn't sure I could tell you that I thought I had succeeded in building that part without getting in trouble.

Did you?

Man: Yes.

OK. Well, what else did you learn to do that you are not quite sure you can do?

Man: I learned to elicit a strategy completely enough so that I know that one step of the strategy moves logically to the next step.

Good. I'd like you to teach a group about that tonight for people who don't understand it, here in this room at 7:30.

Man: All right.

OK. Anybody else?

Man: I have a part that allows me to speak in a group situation.

This is the first time I've heard from *him!* How did it feel to talk?

Man: Fine.

I recommend that each of you try building a part for someone *else* at least once before you leave this seminar, to find out what happens. There are a lot of people in the seminar who weren't here in this session. Go and test this model on somebody during lunch and find out how it works.

Creating a New Part: Outline

1) Identify the desired outcome, the function of the part. "I want a part that will achieve X."
2) Access any historical experiences of doing X, or anything similar. Step inside each experience and access all aspects of doing X or parts of X. Go through each memory in all representational systems.
3) Create a detailed set of images of how you would behave if you were actually demonstrating whatever this part of you is going to have you do to achieve the outcome X:
   a) First create a dissociated visual and auditory constructed movie.
   b) When you see a whole sequence that you're satisfied with, step inside the image and go through the whole sequence again from the inside, feeling what it is like to do these behaviors.
   c) If you are not satisfied, go back to 3a and change the movie. Do this until you are satisfied with that fantasy from the inside as well as from the outside.
4) Ecological check. "Does any part object to my having a part which will be in charge of making that fantasy a reality?" Make sure you check in all representational systems to find all objecting parts. For each objecting part:

a) Ask that part to intensify the signal for "yes" and decrease for "no."
b) Ask "What is your *function* for me?" "What do you do for me?"
c) If the function doesn't tell you what the part's objection is, ask "What specifically is your objection or concern?"
d) Make a complete written list of all the parts that object and their functions.

5) Satisfy all the objecting parts:
   a) Redefine the part you are creating to take into account all the functions and concerns of the objecting parts.
   b) Go back to step 3 and make a new or modified fantasy that will satisfy the concerns of each part that objected.
   c) Check with every part to make sure that each one is satisfied that this new representation of the new part's behavior will not interfere with its function.
6) Ask your unconscious resources to analyze that fantasy and to pull from it the essential ingredients. Your unconscious is to use this information to build a part and give it *entity*.

   "Get what you need to know from that fantasy to be able to build a part of you that can do this exquisitely and easily, and at every moment that it needs to be done."
7) Test the part to make sure it is there:
   a) Go inside and ask.
   b) Future-pace, repeatedly.
   c) Behaviorally engage the part to find out if it responds appropriately.

IV

Advanced Six-Step Reframing

Now that you've all had some practice using other reframing models, we're going to return to the basic six-step reframing model in such a way that you learn to have more finesse with it. Lots of things happen when you reframe your clients, and we want you to have many behavioral choices for dealing with a wide range of responses. I want you all to pretend that you have me as a client, and I want you to reframe me. I'll role-play a truck driver named Ken.

Woman: What do you want?

Ken: I'm not sure what I want, but I can tell you I don't want Y. Y is a real mess, I'll tell you.

Man: What do you need so that you don't have to Y?

Ken: I wish I knew!

Woman: Who has it?

Ken: Y? I have it. I don't want it.

Woman: No, who has what you need?

Ken: I really don't know.

Man: Is Y ever useful to you? (Ken shakes his head "no.") Never ever?

Ken: Never. It's sure gotten me into an awful lot of trouble.

Woman: What is it that you would rather do? What would you like to do instead?

Ken: Well, I've tried to do a lot of other things, but every time I try to do anything else, Y still happens. It's like I don't even have control over my own behavior. I know that sounds silly.

Woman: If you had the choice, what would you like to do instead?

Ken: Well, I don't have the feeling that I've made myself clear to you. I'm here because of what I *don't* want to do.

Woman: OK. Pick something you'd rather do instead. Make it up.

Ken: OK. I'd rather do Z.

Woman: You think Z would be useful to you in those situations?

Ken: Yeah. It would sure be a hell of a lot better than Y.

Man: Have you ever Z'd?

Ken: No.

Man: Do you know somebody who can?

Ken: Don Juan, I guess. I really don't know that he does these things, but I read some books by Carlos Castenada.

Man: What do you see Don Juan doing that makes you think he is able to Z?

Ken: I've never seen him. That's what I was saying. I read about him in a book, and he could apparently do anything he chose to do. I'm sure that if I had that kind of power—it's called personal power in the book—I'd be able to do anything. I'm not talking about my whole life, you know. I do pretty good. Don't get the wrong idea. I'm just talking about this one area.

Dick: So Don Juan does it? And how would you know if you were doing it? (Ken changes his posture, breathing, etc., as he accesses what it would be like if he had "personal power," so that he can answer the question.)

Let me step out of role for a moment. I hope you appreciate that Dick just accessed the desired state in me. That's the point at which you want to anchor my response so that you can use it later. What he is doing now—going for an access of the desired state—is definitely a useful thing to do. You could try anchoring in the state you've just elicited or having me use Don Juan as a model and taking me through the procedure for building a new part. However, you haven't yet gotten enough information to know if that would be appropriate.

Rather than going in one of those directions, I want you to assume a six-step reframing format. That means you don't even need to know what the desired state is. You know that I don't want Y, and that's all you need to know to begin. That's step one of six-step reframing. You've identified the behavior to be changed. I'm going to give you practice at dealing with some of the difficulties that could come up when doing six-step reframing. I'll do this from the position of the client, so that you can try out different ways of dealing with these difficulties. Now I'm going to step back into role again.

Woman: Will you ask yourself if Y is willing to communicate with you, the part that is responsible for Y?

Ken: "The part that is responsible for Y?" Look, I'm just a truck driver. I—you know—

George: What is it like when you are doing Y?

(Ken accesses Y behaviorally in order to answer the question.) Well, I don't . . . you know, I feel sort of like I'm out of control.

George: Where do you feel that in your body?

Ken: Uh . . . here. (Ken touches his belly.)

George: You feel something in your stomach? (Ken: Yeah.) Now I could anchor that, and use that as a specific access to the part responsible for Y.

Right. George just did one of the maneuvers you can use to get access. That's step two of the six-step reframing model: establishing communication with the part responsible for Y. Once he's got access, he would anchor it. As the therapist, I would simultaneously anchor it kinesthetically and also visually and auditorily, so that I could reaccess the part from a distance. This would enable me to reaccess that part whether or not the client is capable of reaccessing the appropriate state intentionally.

You could also get me to do self-anchoring by saying, "And as you feel that, touch the part of your body where you feel it." I spontaneously touched my stomach a moment ago. Without explaining anything to me, you can notice how I touch myself, and then have me redo that movement later as an access. In addition, my body posture, breathing pattern, and facial expression are all self-anchors.

All those nonverbal analogues you just saw are the visual signs that will let you know exactly when I'm accessing the part responsible for Y. George asked me what it was like when I did Y. From this point on, you should know whether I'm actually getting access to that part of me or not.

That was one good maneuver. Now let's go back and do it again. Let's go back to the point where I said "Well, I'm just a truck driver. What do you mean 'Go inside and ask some part of me'?" How else could you get access? We want you to have lots of choices at every step.

Joe: Did you watch the football game last Sunday?

Ken: Yeah, that was a really exciting game!

Joe: I was watching, too, and there was no question that the losing team wanted to win that game. They had all the determination in the world, but they just didn't have the plays.

Ken: Yeah. It seemed like the winning team had a lot more things they could do.

Joe: Exactly.

Ken: Yeah. It was a good game. Do you watch football much? I used to play in school. . . .

OK. That maneuver didn't get me to access the part. Try something else.

Bill: You know, I've been interested in truck driving for a long time, and one thing that I don't know much about is how to shift gears.

Ken: Oh, hey! That's what distinguishes a pro from an amateur.

Bill: Would you tell me how? You have to "double shift" or something, don't you?

Ken: Yeah. Well, we have a special way of talking. And I don't think you'd understand, you know, "double-clutching" and all those—

Bill: Well, would you try telling me about that?

Ken: Well, no. But I could show you.

Bill: Good, good. Go ahead.

OK, now I show him. And at the end of my showing you, Bill, what do you do next? . . . I think that Bill is going for the same access that Joe was trying to get, but he didn't use what he got. The metaphor he used accessed experiences that I know could be used to answer the truck driver's question "What do you mean by a part of me?" Bill, how could you go on to use what you've gotten so far?

Bill: Well, the reason I'm asking is that sometimes I grind the gears when I drive my car, and I need to know—

Ken: Well, you've only got four or five gears at the most to deal with. If you were a truck driver, you'd know how to do thirteen-gear boxes and stuff. You don't need to know that. The thing I'd suggest when you shift gears is that you remember your timing. Your timing's got to be right. In fact, it will save you gas. When you get ready to shift down, you've got to make sure that you coordinate so that you hit that clutch and then the gas and let out the clutch, "double-clutch" it, and then you are ready to go.

Rose: I rode across the country with a truck driver once, and as we were driving along, I realized that he was listening to his tires, and to the sound of his load shifting, and to music on a tape, and he was talking to me—all at once.

Ken: Yeah, you get real automatic when you've driven a truck for a while. After a while you don't even have to think about it. . . .

Now I'm going to come out of quotes again. Rose is going for exactly the portion of this metaphor that I would go for in your position. Don't let this opportunity go by. Rose can now say to me, "I want you to notice that there are parts of you that do things automatically. When I say 'parts,' that's just a way of talking. Of course it doesn't mean anything. There are parts of you that know how to shift gears and listen for load shifts and listen for the tone of the engine, so *you* don't have to consciously think about those things. It's *as if* a part of you drives the truck automatically, leaving the rest of you free to do things like enjoying talking to your passenger or your partner. It's *as if* there are parts of you that can be assigned certain responsibilities, but now the part of you that makes you do Y is out of control. We've got to reestablish some contact, because it's doing things that you don't like."

If you do that, you've relativized your model to the world of a truck driver, without spending twenty-four days teaching him to be an NLP practitioner. You've simply accessed an experience of his that is a counterpart to the notion of "parts." I'm not saying that this maneuver is the one you "should" make next. It is *one* way for you to use what Rose did to overcome the difficulty that I presented.

Accessing an experience of doing something well and automatically is also useful in another way. You've accessed a state in which I am resourceful, and you can use that state later on. In addition, this particular auditory resource state involves a representational system shift from the kinesthetic way that I described the problem state Y.

Woman: So how do we anchor that?

At the point that I said "Yeah, it becomes automatic after a while," you say "Good" and slap your hands together lightly, or anchor in some other way.

Woman: What are you anchoring there?

You are anchoring my understanding that there are unconscious parts of me that are useful, and that I don't know much about.

Man: In this case would it be more elegant to anchor auditorily, since you were talking about auditory resources?

I anchor in all systems. When we teach tactile anchoring, we claim we do so because tactile anchors are so obvious. Actually we teach it because if you anchor with a touch, you are likely to anchor simultaneously in all other systems as well. When I'm anchoring, I change my body posture so that I can touch the client. That's a visual anchor if his eyes are open. At the same time, I'm talking in a certain tone of voice; that becomes an auditory anchor. I recommend anchoring in all systems simultaneously, unless you want to be sure that your anchoring stays outside the person's awareness.

Another advantage of tactile anchoring is that it is irresistible. There are survival programs that will interrupt any other sensory input in favor of a tactile input. If you are inside talking to yourself and I use a tonal shift, you may not even register it, and you may not respond to it. If your pupils are dilated and I use a visual anchor, you may not be responsive. But if you are touched, you will respond.

Strictly speaking, you only need an anchor in one system. In general, anchoring in the system that is accessed will be more streamlined. In this case it's auditory. However, unless you have some special considerations, why not use all systems?

Now let's go back to what we just did with reframing: accessing an understanding of the notion of unconscious parts. If someone doesn't think he has "parts," there are lots of approaches you can take. I once worked with a woman who believed that she didn't have an unconscious mind. She came in with every hair meticulously in place, and she thought that everything she did was under conscious control. The idea of "parts" didn't make any sense to her. I first got rapport at the unconscious level by using mirroring, crossover mirroring, embedded commands, metaphors, and other maneuvers. She was puzzled by what I was doing, but I continued until I was getting really good unconscious responses from her.

Then I said "Now I'm going to demonstrate that you are a fool." That got her attention. "There are parts of you that are very powerful allies, and until you appreciate them, you are going to have lots of difficulties. I want to demonstrate their presence. You have congruently stated to me that you do not believe you have an unconscious mind. You think you are in control of your behavior. It's obvious to me that you are not in control of your problem behavior, but I assume that you run your own body. That is, I assume that you know what your body temperature is, and that you can control it to some degree." She said "Of course." She couldn't make any other answer, because she thought she didn't have an unconscious mind.

So I said "In a moment I'm going to reach over and touch your left arm from the shoulder to the elbow, and when I do, that arm will turn ice cold. And I request that you resist me with all the conscious force you have." I waited until I got an unconscious signal "OK, I'm ready." Then I reached over and touched her arm, and she got chills. Then I said "But notice how warm the other arm is." The other arm instantly became warmer.

I demonstrated to her that I could actually change the temperature of her body, and that she could not resist. In fact, the more she attempted to resist, the more dramatic the changes were. At that point I had convinced her of the reality of at least one other part of herself.

Man: Why was it necessary to do anything with what she consciously thought was true?

It wasn't. The only value in throwing a bone to the conscious mind every once in a while is to keep the person from raising too many objections. It keeps her from saying "This isn't working. You don't understand what you are doing."

Now let's go back to reframing. Assume that you've got access to the part of me that makes me do Y. Now continue.

Bill: You know, as you are driving along the highway, you've got a whole bunch of dials in front of you that tell you lots of things. The water gauge is kind of a way for the engine to tell you "Hey, I need water" when the water level is too low and the temperature is getting too high.

Ken: That's a funny way to talk about it!

Bill: Yeah, I know, but just imagine it. You have an oil pressure gauge that lets you know whether or not the engine needs oil. (Ken: Yeah.) And I know it's kind of silly to think about, but I'm wondering, if the part of you that runs Y were a part of an engine, what type of gauge would you need for that part to let you know what it wants? Would it be a visual gauge? Would it be a sound? Would it be some feeling?

Ken: Well, I can't see anything. I suppose it would have to be a feeling.

Bill: I'm sure that you can tell when your tires need air by feeling the way the truck rides. You know how you can tell whether the tires on your rig are full or not just by the sluggishness of the truck, right?

Ken: Yeah, you've got to be able to! Yeah, I know what you are talking about.

I hope you all understand what Bill is doing. He's using *my* perceptual reality to make all the points that he wants to make. If you have this kind of flexibility to shift your words and examples so as to make sense in my reality, then you can communicate artistically.

Bill: Do you think that after all the years you've been driving truck, you could tell the slightest difference in tire pressure?

Ken: Yeah, I'm good at it.

Bill: Are you good enough to tell a slight difference in this feeling (Bill gestures towards Ken's stomach.) that you get from the part that runs Y?

Ken: Oh, yeah! I know when that's happening. There's no doubt about it.

Bill: Well, I'd like you to tell me what type of difference you feel when it changes?

Ken: Well, when I'm doing Y . . . Do you want me to just go ahead and tell you about this, or do you want me to still use this Y and Z routine?

Bill: You're out front. You're a truck driver. You can just tell me.

Ken: Yeah. OK. When I get home from a trip, I'm really tired. (His shoulders sag.) I've been on the road for fourteen to sixteen hours sometimes. The first thing that happens when I walk in the door is that my wife comes up to me and goes "Hi, honey, tell me about your trip." (He stiffens up.) But all I want to do right then is fall into bed and relax. And the more I try to just do what I need to do to fall into bed and relax, the more she wants to talk . . . you know . . . because she's *interested,* if you know what I mean. . . . You know what happened? She went back to school. I mean, education is important—

Bill: Let's hold it for a second. I would really like to find out all about what she's been doing, but—

Ken: Well, I'll tell you. I don't—

Bill: But I have one question before that.

Ken: Yeah? What's that?

Bill: When she comes up to you and says "Hi, honey . . ." what is she trying to do? What does she want from you? Do you think she wants your attention, your love?

Ken: Yeah, she wants my attention, my love. Yeah. I've been away sixteen hours, you know! (He leans back into a position of pride and self-satisfaction.)

Bill: Do you think you have the ability to show her your love before she even asks for it? Is that a challenge you are man enough to meet?

Ken: Hey! Of course! (He straightens up and his body shifts to a more "confident" posture.)

Good. That's content reframing. Bill didn't bother to go through the official six-step reframing model; he simply used my beliefs about myself to get leverage to induce a change. The thing that is very elegant about the sequence that just occurred is that Bill had the flexibility to find the things in my reality that he could use as leverage to get me to use some new behavior. I've given him several indications, both analogically and verbally, "Well, I've been away sixteen hours, you know," that I take pride in being a real "man." So he says "Are you man enough to take control of the situation?" And that would work. Bill also had the finesse to be able to stop me from talking about my wife going back to school, which was irrelevant to what Bill wanted to accomplish.

Man: Isn't this hypothetical truck driver asking you to change his wife's behavior, though?

As a therapist, the perceptual frame you can use is "Of course you want her to be different, and the *way* that's going to happen is that *you'll* be different: your being different will make her different." Of course you won't tell the client that. You are going to use leverage the way Bill just did, in order to force the truck driver into new behavior. That will have the effect of changing *her* behavior.

OK. Do you have any comments about the sequence that we just role-played here? Notice that this was not a standard six-step reframing. However, most of the steps were there; they were just externalized. After Bill made the content reframe, I *became* the part that was the new behavior. I didn't look the way I looked when I talked about Y. When I *became* the new behavior, I actually accessed the situation in all systems. I saw my wife, heard the sound of her voice, and had the kinesthetic sensations of being at home. That takes care of the future-pace, so Bill doesn't need to ask "Will that part take responsibility for the new behavior occurring in that same context?"

The ecological check hasn't come up yet, but I assume that he would go there next. Alternatively, he could use a second session with me as an ecological check. You don't *have* to do all of the steps in the same session, although it's much better if you do.

Woman: How about testing?

That's a good question. How would you test?

Woman: Are you going home after this, or are you going on a trip somewhere?

Ken: No, I'm going straight home after this. (Ken analogically accesses the new behavior.)

Woman: What are you going to do when you get home?

Ken: None of your business! As a matter of fact, are we about done? I'm ready to go.

Fred: There's just one quick thing before you go.

Ken: What's that?

Fred: Your wife's at home, and you have children, right?

Ken: Yeah, but they're at school right now.

Fred is checking for ecological considerations now.

Fred: When you walk in the door and see your wife, I want you to "put the hammer down and convoy."

Exercise

Now I want you to write down three situations that you frequently encounter in six-step reframing that you want more choices about coping with. It might be that you are unable to get access to a signal system. It might be that you don't know what to do when the client gets confused in the middle of the reframing process and says "I don't know what I'm doing anymore." It might be that the person says she can't access her creative part. Or perhaps the part says it won't take responsibility for implementing the new choices, because it's not certain whether they'll work. Here is an outline of six-step reframing to help you identify the points at which you would like to have more choices.

Six-Step Reframing Outline

1) Identify the pattern (X) to be changed. "I want to stop X'ing but I can't," or "I want to Y, but something stops me."
2) Establish communication with the part responsible for the pattern.
   a) "Will the part of me that makes me X communicate with me in consciousness?" Pay attention to any feelings, images, or sounds that occur in response to asking that question internally.
   b) Establish the "yes/no" meaning of the signal. Have it increase in brightness, volume, or intensity for "yes," and decrease for "no."
3) Separate the *behavior,* pattern X, from the *positive intention* of the part that is responsible for X. The unwanted behavior is only a way to achieve some positive function.
   a) Ask the part that runs X "Would you be willing to let me know in consciousness what you are trying to do for me by Pattern X?"
   b) If you get a "yes" response, ask the part to go ahead and communicate its intention. If you get a "no" response, proceed with unconscious reframing, presupposing positive intention.
   c) Is that intention acceptable to consciousness? Do you want to have a part of you which fulfills that function?
   d) Ask the part that runs X "If there were ways to accomplish

your positive function that would work as well as, or better than X, would you be interested in trying them out?"

4) Access a creative part, and generate new behaviors to accomplish the positive function.
   a) Access experiences of creativity and anchor them, or ask "Are you aware of a creative part of yourself?"
   b) Have the part that runs X communicate its positive function to the creative part, allow the creative part to generate more choices to accomplish that function, and have the part that used to run X select three choices that are at least as good or better than X. Have it give a "yes" signal each time it selects such an alternative.
5) Ask the part "Are you willing to take responsibility for using the three new alternatives in the appropriate context?" This provides a future-pace. In addition you can ask the part at the unconscious level to identify the sensory cues that will trigger the new choices, and to experience fully what it's like to have those sensory cues effortlessly and automatically bring on one of the new choices.
6) Ecological Check. "Is there any part of me that objects to any of the three new alternatives?" If there is a "yes" response, recycle to step 2 above.

Whatever "obstacles" you have encountered in doing reframing, I want you to select three that you'd really like to have more choices in dealing with. Then I want you to do an exercise in groups of three. Person A is going to look at his or her list of "obstacles" and role-play one of them as a client. B will then role-play an NLP programmer and try out ways to cope with the situation. Person C will be a consultant to keep B from falling into content and to keep B oriented.

For instance, if you are A, you will say something like "You've established rapport with me and set up a signal system with the part that runs X. We're on step three: you just asked the part if it will communicate its positive intention to me consciously. The response I've gotten is that I don't experience the old signal at all, but I have two different signals." So A will set the stage at exactly the point in reframing where A wants more choices.

B will then try out one method of responding to the situation that might move A toward the next step of reframing. C will be an observer, or meta-person, and notice whether B's maneuver is effective or not.

Then I want C to ask B to think of *two* other responses to make to that situation, and then try out each of them.

Let me give you an example of the way I'd like to have you do this exercise. Let's say Beth is going to play client, Scott is going to play programmer, and Irv, you are going to be the meta-person, the consultant. Part of your job, Irv, is to observe and listen to the relationship between Scott's behavior and Beth's. At any point in time, I should be able to walk up to you and say "Tell me something about the relationship between the programmer's tonality and the client's tonality" or "Where are they in the reframing format?" So your job is to know everything that's going on—which is impossible, so just do your best.

The second thing that Irv is responsible for as meta-person is more specific. Any time the programmer hesitates or begins to be confused, you interrupt and say "Hold on. Which step of reframing are you on?" "Step two." "What specific outcome are you attempting to get? What's the next small chunk of outcome you are going to get?"

Scott should be able to respond specifically, for example: "I want to establish a robust involuntary unconscious signal system with the part responsible for the behavior." Then Irv will say "How, specifically, are you going to do that?" Scott will respond "I'm going to access it behaviorally by pretending to do behavior X myself and thereby induce it in her. Or I can ask her to do behavior X. Or I could ask her to go inside and ask the part if it will communicate, and make sure that the signal system that comes back is involuntary."

Every time the meta-person interrupts, I want him to get not just one choice, but *three* options for proceeding. First you'll find out what specific outcome the programmer is going for, and then you'll get three ways he can attain it. These ways won't necessarily all work, but building in at least three options at every choice point will make you much more effective in your work. If you've got only one choice, you are a robot. If you've got only two, you are in a dilemma. However, if you've got three, you begin to have behavioral flexibility.

This is what I was asking you to do earlier when I was role-playing a client. You got access to the part in one way, so I said "Now go back to the choice point and do it some other way."

Meta-person, the third thing I want you to do is to interrupt if you don't understand what's going on. If Scott is the programmer, and under stress he goes back to some old program like "How do you feel about that?" then you can interrupt and ask the same three questions: 1) "What step are you on?" 2) "What is the specific outcome you are going for?" 3) "How is what you just did going to achieve that outcome?"

If, in fact, that behavior wouldn't get the outcome, then as meta-person you ask "How could you get that outcome?" When he gives you one way, ask "How else could you get it?" When the programmer has three ways, have him go ahead and pick one to try out.

If the programmer is incongruent in delivering the method, you interrupt again. This time give specific feedback about what the programmer could do to be more congruent. "Change your voice tone and tempo in this way," or "Change your body posture and gestures in this way." You are all here to become more graceful communicators than you already are. If there is any incongruity in your behavior, I believe that you'll want to know about it, because being incongruent is self-defeating. When you are the programmer, your 7 ± 2 chunks of conscious attention will be involved in communicating with the client and getting responses. The meta-person will have more attention free to notice what's going on, so use the information that the meta-person communicates to you.

As a meta-person the finest thing that you can do to assist the programmer is to interrupt at any time that you don't understand what's going on, the programmer hesitates, or the programmer is incongruent in his behavior.

Rose: So when my meta-person interrupts, rather than treating him like a mosquito and swatting him, I'm to treat my meta-person as a generator of new behaviors especially built in for me?

He will be a generator of new behavior *only* in the sense that he will challenge you by asking you the questions. You need to come up with your own solutions. He is not there to provide you with solutions directly.

Woman: Earlier when we were doing an exercise, the meta-person kept jumping in and interrupting what the programmer was doing. It seemed like the programmer was ready to go along to the next step, but the meta-person would jump in before the programmer could move on. Should I ask the meta-person to slow down?

Negotiate with your meta-person about the interventions that are appropriate for you. Keep in mind that it's difficult to interrupt too much in an artificial situation like this one that is set up solely for the sake of learning to have more choices. However, you are a human being with your own needs. If there are so many interruptions that it disorients you, say "Hey! I need at least a minute and a half at a time before you jump in again, unless there's something really important." So negotiate that with your meta-person. And you can also reframe yourself so that you think of every interruption in terms of what you may be able to learn from it.

When you are the role-player, I want you to role-play your most difficult clients. Don't get into your own personal change goals. You'll get changes anyway, by metaphor. You don't have to worry about that.

I'll role-play this exercise again, to make it really clear. Doris, you be the programmer. What I'm going to do is think to myself "Oh yeah. I have one client who is really tough for me to reframe. Every time I do reframing, it starts out really nicely, but by the time I get to step three or four, the signals start shifting all over the place and I don't know what's happening. I don't know what to do with that." So I tell Doris "You've got good rapport with me. You've helped me identify a behavior to reframe and you've established communication with the part. The signal I'm getting is an increase in heat in my hand for 'yes' and a decrease for 'no.' Now you're on step three and you're about to have me ask the part if it will let me know in consciousness what it's doing for me that's positive. It's there that the difficulties come up, so let's start there."

I don't want you to go through the whole reframing format and practice the pieces that you don't need any practice with. You're not doing complete pieces of therapy; you're just doing some small chunk that the person playing the client wants to have more choices about. That person will use you as a resource by having you respond to the difficulty.

OK. Doris, you're the programmer. Do you know where we are?

Doris: The temperature in your hand increases for "yes"?

Yes ma'am. It just did.

Doris: So let's try that again and ask it if it's really sure it's "yes." Check again and see if that increases.

Check again? Do you want me to say something to myself, or what?

Doris: Yeah. Go inside. Ask that part if it is "yes."

The part that makes X happen?

Doris: Yes.

OK. So what should I ask it now?

Doris: Tell it if it is "yes," to say "yes" in a stronger way, to let you know really, for sure.

You mean to just go in and tell it that? . . .

You see, by acting confused I'm making Doris be very explicit in her verbal behavior. Being sloppy in your verbalizations is one of the best ways to mess up any of our techniques and get stuck. Doris said "Let's try that again," but didn't tell me exactly what to try. She told me to "check and *see* if that increases," when I have to *feel* the signal of hand warmth. She said "Ask that part if *it* is 'yes,'" without specifying what "it" is. If you use those kinds of sloppy verbalizations with your clients, either they will be confused, or they may go inside and do something *very* different than what you intend.

My questions require her to clean up her instructions. The finest thing you can do for your colleagues is to demand high-quality performance. If the programmer is sloppy in her verbalizations, be confused. Let *her* sort it out, with the help of her consultant. If Doris hesitates at that point, then her meta-person should ask "What step are you on, and what specifically are you trying to accomplish?" "I'm trying to validate how robust and strong the involuntary signal system is. Specifically I'm trying to validate that a rise in temperature of the right hand means 'yes.'" Then the meta-person says "How are you going to do it, Doris?" She says to me "OK. Go inside. Thank the part for the response. Tell it to heat up your hand again if in fact the warming of your hand is a 'yes' response." So I close my eyes and do it. Then I come back and say "Yeah, it did the same thing again. That is really weird!"

OK. Doris, what do you do next?

Doris: Now you have a very strong "yes." Isn't that nice to have something say "yes" to you? Probably when you were a little boy—

This is where the meta-person steps in again and says "Wait a minute! Hypnotic age-regression is an important tool, but it is inappropriate now."

Doris: I think I need to check to see what the next step is.

Fine. This is training, so you can say "Hold on a minute!" Or you can turn to the meta-person and ask "What is the next step, anyway?" Then the meta-person says "To make a distinction between the behavior and the intention."

OK. Here I am on step three. Anybody else can play the programmer.

Joe: Does that part of you know what the intent of X is?

I don't know.

Joe: Ask it and see what happens to your hand.

See what happens to my hand? OK. I'll look at it. What exactly do you want me to ask it?

Joe: No, feel it.

(He reaches over and feels it with his other hand.) Again, if you insist upon clarity, your colleagues will be forced to make the best use of this situation. So the programmer says "Ask the part that runs X if it knows what its positive intent is. If the answer is 'yes,' it will warm your hand. If the answer is 'no,' the heat will decrease. So notice the feeling in your hand." Now I'm going to go back to role-playing.

Uh, I think it heated up, but what was really strange was that when I asked the question there was a movement in my shoulder almost as if someone pushed me. I don't know what that's about! And also there was suddenly a loud buzzing in my ears. . . . I don't know about this stuff!

Joe: And did you feel a change in temperature in your hand?

Yeah, there was a change.

Joe: What was the change?

It's warmer than it was before. But I don't understand these other things that are happening.

Joe: I would like you to ask the part that pushed your left shoulder if it would increase that feeling if it means "Yes, I have some input to this process." (His left shoulder jerks again.) Thank you.

OK. Good. Remember, I'm the guy who wants choices to cope with multiple-signal responses. He's just given me one choice, namely to ask for a direct response from the part that gave one of the other signals. What other way could you deal with these other signals?

Al: There seems to be another part of you that wants to communicate.

Is that what's going on?

Al: That could be it. Wouldn't you like to find out? Let's ask it. It seems to me that you are reporting two other things in there. Is the part that pushes your shoulder willing to make the pushing of your shoulder a signal? If it is, would it push your shoulder again? (His shoulder jerks again.) Yes, thank you.

That's really weird.

Al: Yes. And there's a part of you that . . .

What?

Al: There may be another part of you that may be causing that buzzing sound you were hearing.

What?

Al: As the buzzing becomes quieter, you can—

OK. Now he's dealing with the other internal event. Does anybody know what you can do with these things once you've turned them into signals?

Jan: Go inside and ask those two parts if they would be willing to step aside for just a moment, knowing that I will get back to them later, and that we will not make any changes until they are consulted.

Excellent. One choice is to put them off until the ecological check.

Rick: How about forgetting about the hand warming and just using one of these new signals for the yes/no.

If you do that you would be running a risk. At this point, you don't know if the part responsible for the new signals is the same part that gave the hand-warming signal earlier. Your suggestion presupposes that they are one and the same. The part that buzzed and the part that jerked the shoulder might be some other parts that object to what you're doing. You don't know what parts are making the new signals, and you don't know what functions they have. What's another choice?

Sue: You could have the two parts that are objecting get a spokes-part to represent them for the time being.

OK. And I'm sitting here looking confused, because I don't know anything about anybody objecting. All I know is that my shoulder moved and that I heard a buzzing. Are you telling me those are objections?

Sue: I guess we don't know that.

That's absolutely right. You don't know that.

Rick: Could we establish a yes/no signal at the shoulder, and then ask the shoulder if it would be willing to allow the hand to continue as the yes/no signal?

That's very close to what Jan suggested a moment ago.

Let me play the meta-person for a moment and ask you what step this is, and what specific outcome you are trying to get.

Rick: I'm trying to find out whether these signals are all from the same part or not and what their purposes are.

Good. Notice, however, that if you use Jan's maneuver, you don't need to find that out until the ecological check, and you may not need to at all. If you get the buzzing and shoulder jerk to go "on hold" until the ecological check, you can find out at that point if they still have some objection. If those signals come up as objections at that point, you know they are different parts. If they don't, you know that either they are signals from the same part, or that the choices that satisfy the part that warms my hands also satisfy the other parts.

The uncertainty is "Are these simply other signals from the same part, or are these other parts that have to be taken into consideration?" You can find that out by saying "If the shoulder jerk is another signal from the same part that's making your hand warm up, would your shoulder again make that movement?" If you get the movement, you say "Good. Now if the buzzing is also a signal from the same part that's making your hand warm up, would the buzzing increase in volume?" If you get an increase, you say "Excellent. I would like you to thank this part of you that is so powerful that it can use multiple signals. For the purposes of your being calm and our understanding what is going on here, I would ask that it inhibit those signals in favor of continuing to use temperature change in your right hand."

In that maneuver I turn the shoulder jerk and the buzzing into yes/no signals, and then ask if they are the same part or not. If I get a "no" response, I can go to the maneuver that Jan suggested.

Jan's suggestion is a good one in terms of efficiency. She suggested that you first have the person thank the shoulder jerk and the buzzing in order to validate the responses. That's always a good pacing maneuver. Then you reassure those parts that no behavioral change will occur until they have been consulted at the end of the procedure to make sure that they agree with what has occurred. If they have disagreements or additional needs at that point, they will be attended to with the same respect that's presently being paid to the part that's warming the hand.

Woman: If all the signals come from the same part, would it be appropriate for me to use the shoulder jerk as the signal system since it's easier for me to see than the hand-warming?

Certainly. If both signals are equally involuntary, but one is easier for you to read, ask for a shift. In general, you can make reframing an opportunity to meta-tune yourself to notice the many subtle changes that accompany the yes/no signals. If I don't see anything that goes along with my client's report of a signal, that's not an ecologically sound situation. I want to have an observable signal so that I have a check on the client's report. The client may lie to me, because he wants a change really badly.

One thing I will do is say "My apologies to your unconscious mind. Given the state of acuity that my eyes have at this moment, I was unable to notice the response. I would like to have direct access to a signal, in order to be absolutely sure that I am communicating with the appropriate unconscious part. I am going to ask you to return inside. I thank the part for having given you the signal, and that's all that is really required. But I ask, for my own behalf, so that I may be usefully instructed by your unconscious mind, that it show me something that is exaggerated enough that I can notice it. I would appreciate that very much." I ally myself with the part, and then ask for a more observable signal.

Man: Could you ask the shoulder part "Would you be willing to work with the other part and make changes?"

The problem with that choice is that it presupposes that the shoulder movement is a signal from a different part, and you have no basis on which to make that presupposition. If you ask that, you may cause a total confusion state. If the signals were all manifestations of the same part, how could it respond to such a question? You've only set up yes/no signals, so the part has no way to indicate "presupposition failure," and you will get a state of confusion. There are times when you want to exclude possibilities by using presuppositions, but this is not one of those times.

Play around with this for about an hour, rotating positions after each role-play. Do as many situations as you have time for. Playing recalcitrant, difficult clients will provide you with live experience in coping with those kinds of situations.

This is an excellent format to gain finesse with *any* technique. Have someone role-play the most difficult client she can think of, and then try out different ways of getting the responses you want. If at any point you are unable to generate three choices for proceeding, and your meta-person can't provide you with additional choices, be sure to call one of us over.

* * * * *

Discussion

You have all been practicing the format called six-step reframing, with variations and with feedback from the observer. I want to be sure that you practice reframing with an understanding of our long-term goal. Our final outcome is for these formats to disappear from your behavior. Any format is a crutch, and is no substitute for 1) having full flexibility of behavior, 2) sensory experience, and 3) knowing what outcome you are going after. If you have those three characteristics of the professional communicator, that's all you need. All the patterning we've done on people such as Milton Erickson, Virginia Satir, or successful business people, have enabled us to develop specific teaching formats. Formats are crutches, or excuses, or tricks, to get you to notice what's going on at the sensory level and to vary your behavior in order to achieve a specific outcome.

At this point, I don't do reframing as a separate chunk except for demonstration purposes in seminars. It's integrated into everything else that I do; I don't do any work without reframing. Every piece of work I do has reframing as a component part. It's only in seminars that I sort what I do into categories.

You will know that you are a pro when you go through a session, and at the end of it you discover that there's no uncertainty: you know that you got the changes that you went after. However, you don't know *how* you did it until you stop and ask yourself what you did systematically. That will be a natural outcome of taking the time and effort to use these formats explicitly until they become so smooth and practiced that they will be as automatic as shaking hands or driving a car; they will have become reflex responses to appropriate contextual cues, so that your behavior will always be appropriate and lead effectively toward the outcomes you want.

Do you have any questions?

Man: Let's say you ask a client to go inside and ask if the part of her that runs behavior X will communicate with her in awareness. She goes inside and comes back saying "Nothing happened." What do you do?

One possibility is to say "Describe what your feelings are right now—how you sense yourself kinesthetically." After she offers a description, you can say "Now begin to do behavior X. She'll either get up and begin to do it or she'll begin to feel what she feels like when she does X. As soon as you see a change that you can detect, you say "Stop. Now describe your sensations again." There will be differences between the two descriptions. Any one of those differences can be used as a signal system.

The reframing format differs radically from the usual techniques in psychotherapy, because in this format I am a consultant; the client is her own therapist and hypnotist. Under normal circumstances I am the therapist and hypnotist and I take responsibility for accessing and eliciting responses. In this case, the client takes responsibility for doing that. I operate as her conscious consultant. If she cannot detect any communication, I ask her to begin to become the part of herself that does X. The physiological differences between her usual state and her beginning to do X will involve exactly the physiological changes that she can use as a signal system. When people engage in behavior they don't like, they usually experience major changes in muscle tone, skin temperature, etc. Any one of those changes will serve you well as a signal system, and will be experienced when you ask the person to do X behavior.

Sometimes you simply have to teach the person how to make distinctions in her internal experience. You ask her to describe her present internal state. Then you ask her to jump up and down for two minutes and ask her to notice the details of how her internal experience changes.

Sometimes a person is so self-anchored into a particular state that it's hard to get any changes. Jumping up and down, or doing any other behavior that is significantly different from her present state can loosen her up a bit.

Herb: When I first learned reframing in seminars, we would do each pattern in a half-hour or at most an hour. I have found in my practice that going through a pattern with a client sometimes takes several sessions.

Fine. That's not an unusual piece of feedback. I've heard that from others. Taking longer is a function of your familiarity and fluency with the sequencing, and also has a lot to do with your sensitivity to the needs of your clients. Sometimes reframing is such a major reorganization of the person that it appropriately takes three or four sessions to accomplish.

I claim that I can run through reframing with anybody in three minutes, but not if I involve her consciousness. So I assume that you asked the client's consciousness to detect the signals and offer reports. Without involving the person's consciousness, it takes me about one-tenth of the time to get the same changes. However, I do think that involving the client's consciousness is a desirable characteristic of this model, because it teaches your client to become autonomous after some period of time. She's been involved in a positive, participatory way at the conscious level in making these changes occur, so it will be easier for her to use the same process later on her own.

Reframing yourself is a fairly complex task. Reframing already involves a dissociation between the client's conscious mind and the part responsible for the problem behavior. If you reframe yourself, a third part of you has to be a programmer who keeps track of the process, which makes it a three-level task. If you successfully do reframing externally with others first, you can make the *process* of reframing automatic. Then reframing yourself is reduced to a two-level task, something that most people can cope with.

If you are a good hallucinator, you can also make it easier for yourself by seeing yourself over in the other chair. Then you ask yourself the questions and notice the responses that you get. That kind of explicit visual dissociation between the part of you that is client and the part of you that is acting as programmer can help you keep your behavior sorted.

Reframing yourself can also involve another problem. You will be using your own limitations to deal with those same limitations, which can lead to some blind alleys. As they say in *Catch 22,* "If you've got flies in your eyes, you can't see the flies in your eyes." By reframing a number of other people who have *different* limitations than you do, you will gain flexibility in dealing with their limitations, and become better equipped to deal with your own.

In spite of the problems I've mentioned, I know a number of people who have reframed themselves and gotten very pervasive changes. If you do reframing successfully with other people for a month or so, you'll probably find yourself doing it for yourself anyway. If you are really eager for some personal changes, it will work for you.

Man: One of my clients is very verbal and conceptual, and he really wanted to follow the procedure, so I did it totally nonverbally and unconsciously with him.

Excellent. That is a really fine choice.

Man: Should the minimal cues that we get when we ask for a signal always be consistent throughout the whole procedure?

Yes. The only exception I can think of is when the signal you get at the beginning is very unpleasant. Then you want to adjust or change the signal right away, but keep the new signal consistent.

Jim: With one of my clients I didn't get anywhere with the first signal he detected—a kinesthetic feeling in his leg. I looked for another signal and got a very, very strong facial response.

My guess is that both signals were there to begin with, and that you could have used either one of them as a signal. You have to take into account your own degree of acuity, and also that your client may have idiosyncratic ways of approaching the process of reframing. Certain kinds of signals may seem more appropriate to a particular client, or to his parts.

Woman: Do you ever run into somebody who says "I can't come up with any new alternatives"?

Yes. In that case you can employ all of the "I don't know" techniques. "Well, good, if you did know, what would they be?" "Guess what they might be." "Dream it tonight and let me know tomorrow." "Think of someone who does behave effectively in that context. Now watch and listen to what she does."

Most of you live under real time-space constraints; you only have an hour or so to see each client. If you get to the point where you are about to run out of time, and you are still at this step, then you can do several things. Send the client out in the world to find a real model. "Go find someone who knows how to behave effectively in this area. Watch and listen to what she does." Milton Erickson used to do this a lot with his clients. If you know of a particular relevant book or movie that has an isomorphic situation, you can give her a homework assignment. Or you can have her ask some friend what she would do.

Programmed dreaming is another choice. "Go inside and ask the part of you that has been trying to come up with creative solutions if it will be responsible during dreaming tonight to develop alternative behaviors and display them in your dreams." Get a "yes" response and then ask "Will the part of you that used to run pattern X take responsibility for selecting from those alternatives three or more ways that are better, and for employing them in the context where they belong?" Then the person goes off with programmed dreaming, has the dreams, and incorporates the behaviors. When she comes back in two weeks, she will be able to tell you what specific adjustments have occurred.

Jill: I've found that many people respond negatively to the word "responsibility" in step five. But if I say "Ask that part if it is *willing* to select from the alternatives?" then everything goes smoothly.

Excellent. Keep your outcome in mind, and use whatever words get you that outcome.

Skip: When you get to the ecological check and there is a signal, you check to find out if it's an objection. If it is truly an objection, I'm puzzled about why you don't just go back to step four instead of going all the way back to step two.

You can do that. Skip is proposing that if you get an ecological check objection, rather than giving the part that's objecting new ways to do what it is trying to do, you go back and find other alternatives for the first part which the second part won't object to. That's an excellent variation, and sometimes it will be better to do that—for instance, if the first part chooses alternatives such as suicide.

Man: A woman I was working with wanted to evaluate each of the three alternatives separately. It seemed OK to me, so she did that.

Fine. It's actually a bit more precise and explicit to do each alternative in turn, than it is to lump them together. Some people require a lot of precision when they process information. You've got to be very explicit with those people, and the chunks have to be smaller than the ones we typically use. In that case, the variation you used would be not only desirable, but perhaps necessary to accommodate that person's personal style.

Woman: I've always done the ecological check *before* the future-pace. Why do you have the future-pace first, when you may have changes or revisions in the new behaviors, and have to future-pace all over again?

You can do it that way, and often you can get by with it. But there is an important reason why we future-pace first. Future-pacing contextualizes the behavior, testing it out in imagination. Parts may only realize that they have an objection when you future-pace and contextualize the new behaviors. If you future-pace last, objections may emerge then, and you won't know that unless you're alert for signs of incongruence at that point.

Woman: What do you do if a client says, "No, that's not what I want" (She nods her head up and down.)?

How you deal with incongruence is a whole subject in itself. My typical response to that is "Yes, I really think it is" (He shakes his head side to side.) At that point, he will "short circuit" and go into an utter confusion state, and I can do pretty much anything I want.

Alternatively, I can simply utilize his response and feed it back. "I didn't think so" (nodding "yes"). "However, let's pretend that it is." By doing this, I have validated both the conscious and unconscious communication, as if saying "I recognize both of you are there."

Then I go on to install the behavior that the unconscious agrees to. The overall strategy I have when I receive conflicting messages like that is to always go with the ones outside of awareness, because I'll always win that way. It's his unconscious that's running the show, anyway. He's just not able to acknowledge it, and there's no need for him to.

This is a problem that the Simontons have run into in doing their work with cancer patients. They will only accept clients who are consciously willing to accept the belief that they are creating their own cancer. That eliminates a large percentage of the population who have cancer. In fact, most cancer patients have a belief system that *precludes* taking conscious responsibility for their disease. Most cancer patients believe that they should not overtly ask for help or attention or whatever secondary gain they derive from having cancer. That belief is what made the disease itself necessary.

Both insanity and disease in this culture are considered to be "involuntary responses," so you are not responsible for them. So one way to get help and attention is to have something happen that is involuntary and that you can't be held responsible for. Insanity and disease are both very powerful ways to get other people to respond to you without taking responsibility for it.

The Simontons insist that their clients take full conscious responsibility for creating their own cancers, which is a remarkable way to approach it. The one big disadvantage of that approach is that it makes their way of working with cancer patients available only to a very small percentage of the population.

Woman: But you could work with the population that consciously believes that they aren't responsible, and ask them to suspend their disbelief for a period of time.

Right. Ask them to pretend. You can even agree that they *aren't* responsible, but you've discovered that by going through certain "psychological" steps, people are often able to have a healing impact on problems that are clearly physical in their origin. Then you go ahead and do six-step reframing in the same way you would with someone who says "I believe I caused this."

I don't even *know* who is "correct" in their belief system. I do know that reframing can have an impact on physical symptoms.

Man: Are you suggesting that one could use the Simontons' system—their whole approach—at the unconscious level?

Yes. All you would need to do is use six-step reframing entirely at the unconscious level. The positive intention and the new choices can all be left unconscious.

When the unconscious mind refuses to inform consciousness of the positive intention, I typically turn to the person and say "Are you willing to trust that your unconscious is well-intentioned, even though it won't tell you what it is trying to do for you by this pattern of behavior?" If I have rapport, they agree. "OK, I'm willing to try that out." If I get a "no" response, I ask if they are willing to pretend. Or you can say "Look, do you really have a choice? You've already done the best that you know how to do, consciously, to change this behavior. When you made the assumption that this was a bad part, you failed utterly. Let's try the reverse assumption for a two-week period, and you tell me at the end of two weeks whether this is a more effective way to pretend."

Woman: At a conference recently I heard the Simontons mention how much they learned from you. They gave the example of adding representational system overlap to their visualization techniques.

Yes. They get good results just by having patients visualize the white blood cells eating up the cancer cells. If you overlap from that visualization into congruent sounds and feelings, it becomes much more powerful. Did they mention anything about the difference between conscious and unconscious belief systems?

Woman: They mentioned that they realize the difference, but they don't know how to deal with it.

That's exactly where we left off. I was with them long enough to feel that they had a good, clear, solid, resonant understanding of the notion of representational systems and overlap. They found it easy to do, and they were delighted by it.

They also recognized that reframing has advantages, just in terms of requisite variety, but they didn't have enough experience with it to incorporate it into their system. If they used unconscious six-step reframing, they would be able to work with the large numbers of cancer patients who are not willing to consciously adopt the belief that they are responsible for their disease.

Woman: Can you work simultaneously with more than two parts in reframing?

Yes. I have worked with as many as twelve or fifteen at the same time.

Woman: So you might have six objecting parts talking to each other, and to the part that is responsible for the behavior?

Yeah, I get them all together in a conference. But I never talk with more than one at any moment, unless I have first gotten them all together to elect a spokespart that will communicate for all of them.

I say "Now, all you other guys hold; we're going to go over here to part A and find out blah blah blah." And then after that "Now, do any of the other five of you blah blah." Time is never a real limitation because you can always say "All right, we're going to pause now. We'll meet here again at eight o'clock tomorrow." The only real limitation is how many parts you the programmer can keep track of. I'm pretty good at keeping track of a large number of things going on at the same time; I've had a lot of practice doing that. You will have to find out how many you can remember. If you start going "Oh, yeah, it wasn't that one, . . . it was ah . . . the other one . . . ah . . . ah . . ." then you are probably going to confuse the person.

Man: I had a client who used to give names to the parts. She had the sex goddess, and she had the lady in white gloves who had a congenital malformation—her legs were permanently crossed—and several others that she could identify and talk about and have talk to me.

Yeah, some of them have names, and if they don't, you can always give them names. There are many things you can do to help keep track of them. But you also have to keep track of who said what, and who's talking now. With some people, all the parts have the same voice tonality, while other people's parts all have different voices. It's purely a matter of how many *you* can keep track of well.

Man: How can I use reframing for self-growth?

The first reframe I would make is to use any other predicate but "growth." There are certain dangers in describing evolving as a person as "growth." People in the human potential movement who are really into "growing" have a tendency to get warts and tumors and other things. As a hypnotist you can understand how that happens with organ language.

You can always just do conscious reframing with yourself. But one of the best ways to do it is to build an unconscious part, what we call a "meta-part," whose job it is each night to review the day just as you are dropping off to sleep, to select two important things to reframe out of your behavior, and to do the reframing each night just after you have dropped off to sleep. We used to do this with everybody in our early groups, and the kinds of changes that people made were fantastic.

Woman: You don't even program the two things? You leave that to the unconscious?

Yes. We put the person into a profound trance and taught her unconscious mind—or some unconscious part—the reframing model. We'd say "OK, unconscious, what we're going to do today is build this part and it's going to do reframing. I want you, the unconscious, to select something that you didn't particularly like about her conscious mind's behavior today. First identify it, and then. . . ." We'd go through all the six steps very systematically. We wouldn't just say "Do it"; we would go through each of the six steps carefully. The person's conscious mind is gone; she is just in a trance, responding. You can do it with finger signals or any other yes/no signal, or you can do it verbally if your client happens to be a good verbal unconscious communicator. I'd go through it once systematically, and then have her unconscious pick something else and try it, and notify me if it gets stuck. I'd literally educate her unconscious in the six-step model until it could do it a couple of times without any problem. Then I'd say "Look, each night just after she's dropped off to sleep, identify and reframe two things that you think are important, given the experiences of the day."

A month later I went back and checked with everybody's unconscious to find out what kind of things they'd done. Those people were changing like crazy. One student's unconscious reported to me that every night he would see himself in front of a blackboard, and he would make a list of all the things that didn't occur the way he wanted them to that day, and then all his parts would describe the possibilities of each one, and they'd have a vote and select two, and then the unconscious would go ahead and reframe those two things. Then his parts would review past reframes, and read the minutes from the last meeting—he was a very organized guy.

It seemed to work very well for about three months with each person, and then each would need another shot of it. People changed so much that the process didn't fire off automatically after about three months.

Woman: Why did you have to teach the unconscious the six steps? If you've been reframing others, the unconscious knows it even more than the conscious, doesn't it?

The important thing is to make sure that the unconscious does it explicitly and methodically. Saying that "the unconscious knows it" is assuming more than I'm willing to assume. Some people's unconscious minds don't know it, and some people's unconscious minds do. But I'm not willing to take that chance. I want to build a part whose job is to jump out every night and say "It's reframing time!" You can always consciously reframe with yourself; however, it's much more convenient to have your unconscious do it after you go to sleep. Let your parts do it. It's hard to install this in yourself; it's better to have somebody else zone you into a trance and do it for you.

Bill: There is a question that keeps bugging me about what kind of signals to use when I'm reframing. Some say to use only signals with definite unconscious yes/no responses. Other people talk about just going inside and asking an open-ended question and seeing what comes up. Yesterday afternoon you were having me go through a negotiation reframe without taking time to set up specific signals—

Oh, *I* had yes/no signals, though. You were responding in ways that I could notice.

Bill: OK, you had the yes/no signals. But in our own experience of reframing ourselves I thought the only thing we could use as a signal was an unconscious response that we were aware of. The response I got was in my favored representational system—that little old internal voice that I always get—which I have learned not to trust in myself or in my clients. How can we trust the signal we get from ourselves, or from our clients, when it is in the most favored representational system?

That's a contradiction. You asked "What signal can come in the most favored system which I can trust to be an unconscious signal?" The most favored representational system is the one that is *in* consciousness. It's best to have a signal that is not under conscious control. If your signal is internal dialogue and you don't trust it, then the only way to have a signal that you will trust is to have an involuntary kinesthetic or visual response that intensifies and diminishes. You get a yes/no involuntary signal which is not finger-lifting or anything you can consciously control.

Bill: I get the same confusion when we talk about finger signals. Everybody talks about hypnotizing people and using finger signals. Most people I work with can do those quite voluntarily. What is the use of having a person give you a signal which can be under conscious voluntary control?

They can consciously move their fingers, but they can't do it with *unconscious movement.* Can you distinguish between conscious movement and unconscious movement?

Bill: Yes. What bothers me is this: the person may be giving me all the signs of being deep in trance, and I'm seeing lots of involuntary changes. And then the finger signal looks like conscious movement. Do I necessarily interpret that as being a conscious movement?

No, not necessarily, but I always do. I would say "NOT *THAT* MIND!" Something subtle like that. I want verification. Personally, I usually do not use finger signals as signals. I use them to distract the client, and as a way of setting up some *other* signal system.

Bill: How, specifically, do you set up those other signals?

One thing I do is calibrate, I say "Your unconscious mind can lift this finger to answer *'yes.'*" Then I watch and find out what *else* occurs naturally. "And it can use this finger to answer *'no.'*" I notice the nonverbal differences between them. If I'm not sure, I do it ten times until I'm sure.

Another thing you can do is this: before the client goes into trance, sometimes you can set up great signals by saying "Look, you are going to go into a trance. What we are going to do is set up a 'yes' (shifts his head left) . . . 'no' (shifts his head right) system of communication." Then when the person goes into trance, you'll often get these great signals—his head will shift left and right. Of course, you can use any movement to install a signal—a raised eyebrow, a flaring nostril, or any other signal that he can detect unconsciously. If he doesn't signal the way you established, then you can do other things. You can say "And when things aren't going the way I want them to, I *lift an eyebrow* in disdain," using embedded commands to make sure the eyebrow lifts. You can do really obvious things, and his conscious mind won't notice. Sometimes I'll set up the yes/no signals with a person's feet using one foot for "yes" and the other foot for "no." I'll say "When you are really positively behind something, you put your best foot forward . . . and you know which foot is the *right* foot to do that with, don't you?" He'll demonstrate nonverbally. The important thing is that I always verify by asking innocuous questions. Rather than going immediately for the material I'm interested in, I start asking questions that I know the answer to, in order to make sure that I have the right signal in the right place. I'll say "Now, your name is Bill, and you know this is to be true, do you not?" If I get a "no" response, then I say "Aha! To *whom* am I speaking?" You can learn about this in detail in *Trance-formations.*

Woman: When you are working with yourself, and there's some part of you that you can't really identify, or there's a part that just refuses to actually come out and say what it is, and you can't really get to that part—

That's just like saying "Well, there's a member of a family I can't really talk to." That's always a function of your communication. Sometimes a person will go inside and he'll say "Well, nothing happens." There are a number of things that you can do. One thing that almost always works is to say "Well, I know that for years now you have not gotten along with this part. You've insulted it and fought with it, and I wouldn't talk to you either if you did that to me. So I recommend that you go inside and *apologize* and tell it that you misunderstood its intentions and now you would sincerely like to communicate with it." After a person goes inside and apologizes, nine times out of ten he'll get a response.

Sometimes a person goes inside to reframe and says "All right, you cruddy stinking part." And of course that part goes "If you want a response, take that! Pachchh! Do you want me to intensify *that?*" Your communication with your own parts has got to be *as* graceful or *more* graceful than what you do with other people.

Woman: Yesterday you mentioned finding a part that didn't seem to have a function. What do you do then?

In principle, what you do is really easy. Since the part doesn't have a function, you just give it a positive function that it will agree to. In practice, doing this can sometimes be a bit confusing.

About four years ago I worked with a woman who told me that when she was alone, she couldn't decide what to do. She became nervous and distraught and paced the floor. When her husband was home, she would sit down and read a magazine, or go outside. But when she was by herself, she couldn't sit down and read a magazine.

I said to her, "Well, it seems like you go to a lot of trouble to get nervous when people aren't around. How do you remember to do it every single time?"

She just stared into space because that was such a weird question. "I don't know. I never thought about that."

"Well, obviously some part of you must be making you do it, and it seems silly to me that the part would do it for no reason at all. It must be trying to do something for you that's useful, and we need to find out what it is."

So we went into six-step reframing. We went through a phase where the signals disappeared and then came back six or seven times. Finally, since I couldn't get to the next step, I had her go inside again. "Ask this part if it knows what it is trying to do for you that is useful." She got no response. So I said "If it doesn't know if what it is doing is useful or not, have it answer yes-no-yes-no." She went in and asked it, and it went "yes-no-yes-no," back and forth like that, repeatedly. She looked kind of confused, because on one level she was getting these nonverbal responses, and on the other, she didn't know what it was about.

Then I said to the part "Would you be willing to tell her the function so that she can tell me? As long as she has to tell me what the function is, and I promise you that I will be the one to decide if what you are doing is useful or not, and not her, would that be all right?" I got an instant and emphatic "yes" to that without her even going inside. Then suddenly she clapped her hands over her ears and got a weird look on her face.

"What did it tell you?"

"Well, I don't really want to say it."

"Well, you have to. I promised, you know. And I keep my promises." The logic in that statement is pretty twisted, but it got her to tell me.

This part said something very metaphoric. "You are always alone with other people, and in a crowd by yourself." I thought about that for a minute, and it didn't make much sense to me, but it seemed like it was trying to get her to do something better with her time when she was with other people. So I asked some questions. "Is it that when she is with other people she doesn't really talk to them, she just sits around and feels secure? And when nobody's there, she spends all her time trying to figure out who she could be with and what she could do? So are you trying to get her to utilize resources when they are more available? Is that it?" Again I got an immediate and emphatic answer: "No." So I had her go inside and ask if it was something else. It said "I don't want to answer that question. What you said just before sounds good. That sounds like something good to do. I get so annoyed when I don't know what to do."

"How is it useful to get annoyed; what is the intention of that?"

"I don't know."

"Well, then, what's the point in getting annoyed?"

"Well, everyone else gets annoyed when I don't know what to do."

"So if there's no one else there, you get annoyed for them?"

"I guess so. I don't know." It still sounded unconvinced, but it sounded agreeable.

"Would you rather do something else?"

"Yeah, that would give me something to do, so that I wouldn't have to be annoyed and anxious."

So I just gave the part some ways of deciding what would be useful to do. That part didn't seem to know what its purpose was. The closest I could come to an understanding was that when she was with other people, they got annoyed if she didn't do something, so she was always doing something. When no one was around, then she got annoyed and anxious but didn't do anything. It was systematic, but there didn't seem to be any useful function that I could detect. It was like a piece of motivation that didn't lead anywhere.

Mary: I'm thinking about someone that about ten of us are working with—

Ten of you are working with someone? *That's* the first thing I would stop. That would make anybody crazy!

Mary: This woman has a lot of nausea, which doesn't have medical causes. I know a number of reasons why she is keeping her nausea—

Well, just think, if she gives up her nausea, she'll lose ten friends. That's the first thing that occurs to me!

Mary: If this woman didn't get nausea, she would have to have sex with her husband, and she gets a lot of other goodies by having the nausea. I tried reframing everything. She keeps coming back again every two months saying "Hey, I have it again" so I'm thinking—

Dealing with the nausea, as far as I'm concerned, is inappropriate. The only thing that makes it possible for her to have the nausea is that she *doesn't* have positive sexual relationships with her husband, and that she *doesn't* have all these other goodies. So I'm not even going to *mess* with the nausea. I'm going to go after all the other stuff that makes the nausea happen. If she had a good sexual relationship, and if she had whatever else is missing in her life now, then the nausea wouldn't happen. That's what reframing is all about: finding out what *else* needs to happen so that the client won't need the symptom anymore.

Mary: She was resistant to all the things we did. We had the husband in with her, and all the time she was resisting. She's not going to leave him—although she hates him—because he provides security.

Clients don't resist, Mary. It is *very* important that you understand that. *Clients demonstrate that you don't understand.*

Mary: The parts resist, I think—

No, parts don't resist. No part of a human being resists a therapist. All they ever do is demonstrate that you are on the wrong track. That's the only thing they do. I have never seen a client who resists. What clients do is say "Hey! Not there! *Over here!*"

You said "I reframed with her." It's impossible for you to reframe with somebody and not deal with the basis for what you are calling resistance. The reframing model has built into it that you don't go after the change, you go after the parts that object. All the reframing models do that.

Man: I have a fourteen-year-old son who gets migraine headaches. Can I use reframing on that problem?

Migraines are quite easy. Those of you who have clinical experience in dealing with migraines, tell me what representational system migraine clients typically specialize in. I want you to think of specific clients who have actually come to you with a complaint about migraines. What representational system do they use primarily? . . .

Migraine sufferers are very visually-oriented. Check your own clinical experience. As with any other physiological symptom, I presuppose that a migraine is a way that a part uses to get a person's attention. The symptom is a way of trying to get him to do something different, to get him to take care of something that is needed.

Think of pain. We all have neurological circuitry in our bodies that allows us to know when there is an injury. If we didn't have that, we could cut ourselves and bleed to death before visually noticing what had happened. Pain is nothing more than a healthy neurological response that says "Hey, pay attention! Something needs to be done here; something needs to be attended to." You can interpret symptoms like migraines as signals, and then use reframing to discover what the migraine is a response to, so that you can offer that part of the person another way of responding. In every case of migraine I've treated, the person has a very highly specialized visual state of consciousness. The only way his body can get information to him that there is something that needs to be attended to is by giving him splitting headaches. Migraines yield quite quickly and easily to reframing.

Woman: I remember something about a time element. I think you said something about testing it out for six weeks, and then if any part is dissatisfied, to renegotiate.

Well, that always happens anyway. That's just to pace.

Woman: Then why do you need to say anything about it, if it automatically happens?

Because if you don't, then when it doesn't work, the person's conscious mind doesn't know that it can renegotiate, and calls it "failure." I look at the client and say "Look, I want your parts to try this for six weeks, and if it works out, then fine, you're on your way. If any one of your parts discovers that it doesn't work, it is to inform you by having you do the behavior you didn't want to do. That's an indication that it's time to sit down and negotiate further." That means that there is no way in the world that the client can fail. I think clients are entitled to that. By the way, that is both a reframe and a future-pace.

One of the disservices that therapists do for their clients is to fail to use that particular reframe in some fashion. I always make the symptom the barometer of change. Then if the symptom recurs, the client doesn't think "Oh, well, another shot of therapy and nothing has happened." Instead, he thinks "Ah, that means I have to reframe again." The stigma of the symptom dissolves over time, because he begins to pay attention to the symptom as being a *message.* It probably always was anyway, but he never thought about it that way. He begins to have a feedback mechanism; even if the reframing doesn't work, he discovers that he only gets the signal at certain times.

For example, somebody comes in with migraine headaches and I reframe and all the parts are happy. The client goes along for two weeks and everything's groovy, and then he suddenly gets a headache in a particular context. That headache triggers off the instruction that the negotiations weren't adequate. So he drops inside and asks "Who's unhappy? What does this mean?" The part says, "You're not standing up for yourself like you promised to." Then he is faced with the choice of having a migraine headache or standing up for himself.

Man: With that man, then, you installed a part that gave him something else to do instead of having a migraine.

Exactly. All the reframing models do the same thing: *they all change an internal response.* Another way of talking about it is that I installed a part whose function is to *remind* him to have a new response. It doesn't matter how you talk about it.

Man: I have a question about reframing and phobias, and the parts that function in phobias. Let's say I'm working with a phobia and do the visual-kinesthetic dissociation technique. How do I know that I'm not interfering with some part that would work in other contexts in the person's life?

You don't. I'm a very practical kind of person. If somebody has a really severe phobia, I figure it's better to go ahead and take a chance on messing her up somewhere else in her life and fix that up later on. I realize that that is not as elegant as I would like to be, but most of the time that's what I'm going to do.

Let me give you an example of what you have to be careful about. We once cured a woman of a phobia of heights. To test it we sent her up to the balcony of the hotel. She came back down with a big smile, and people asked "Well, how did you feel when you went up there?" She said "I felt like I wanted to get up on the railing and dance."

Now, the most significant thing about that comment is that she *didn't* actually dance on the railing! However, that tells you something about how she got overgeneralized in the first place. It's important to understand that a phobia strategy is an example of a strategy which is working to protect the person from something, but it's overgeneralized. When you change the response to the phobic stimulus, make sure that the new response is one that's useful, so the person doesn't go out and dance on the railing or do something else dangerous.

I cured a lady of a phobia of birds—in Chicago, which is the land of pigeons! When I was done, I tested her. I said "Well how would you feel about holding an eagle on your arm right now?" She said "Well, I don't think I'd like that," and I said "Good." The visual-kinesthetic dissociation wipes out the overgeneralization. You want to make sure it doesn't wipe out *all* caution.

Reframing is incorporated into the phobia technique at the beginning when we say something like "I know that the part of you that has been scaring you has been protecting you in important ways." There is always something important gained by having a phobia: what psychiatrists call "secondary gain" or what we call an outcome. That's why you say "You are going to learn something of importance" when you do the visual-kinesthetic dissociation. Hopefully clients will get it on their own. If not, you'll find out about it, especially if you quiz them a little bit.

At the end, I always suggest that some of the energy that has been liberated during the phobia process be used to safeguard them as they explore the new behaviors that are now available to them. Somebody who has been phobic of heights has no experience of what is appropriate and safe behavior in that context. Someone who hasn't involved herself sexually because she was raped or sexually abused as a child has no idea what appropriate sexual behavior is. When you use these change techniques, suddenly all the barriers are lifted, and you have to be sure your clients are protected.

There's a really nice example from Erickson's work with a young woman who wanted to get married. Because of her religious and family background, she had no understanding of sexual behavior. She was very much attracted to her fiance, but she knew that because of her strict and limited background, there would be sexual problems if she got married. Erickson essentially reframed her, and removed all her barriers to full sexual responsiveness and assertiveness. Then he told her that she could only see the young man in the presence of her brother or family until the marriage. Right after she got married she called Erickson and thanked him. She was smart enough to recognize, as she said then, that she was ready to run out of the office and grab the guy and tear his clothes off and get right to it. Given her longer-term relationship with the man and her own appreciation for herself, it was more appropriate that she proceed in a more cautious and respectful manner toward the actual sexual activity.

NLP is a powerful set of tools. Even the simple anchoring techniques are very powerful. Given that power, it's important to frame what you do in such a way that you proceed with caution and respect for yourself and the other individuals involved. If you do this, you won't have wild fluctuations in behavior which are not ecologically sound. This often happens in assertiveness training when "Andy Ant" turns into "Jerry Jerk." Any wild fluctuations like that are indications of failure to contextualize or frame the new behavior.

Man: So essentially when you do the visual-kinesthetic dissociation you are reframing the useful protective intention and keeping that intact.

No matter what you do, you are always reframing, in the sense that you're always changing a response. It's just that when you use the standard reframing model on a phobia, it's very hard to get it to work: when a person contacts the part that gives her the phobia, usually she gets the phobic response as a signal. And when a person has overwhelming unpleasant feelings, she just doesn't function well.

Reframing is a nice model and it works for many problems. However, there are other things that have to be taken into account: overwhelming feelings is one, and another is multiple parts, or sequential incongruities. When you work with a multiple personality, you may cure Susie of a phobia, but Martha over there can still have it. We're going to teach you about that tomorrow afternoon.

In therapy there are certain elements which will always be present. Other things can be involved, but they are not necessary. Secondary gain will always be evident in every therapeutic change somewhere along the line. Manipulation of parts will also be evident in every therapeutic change. You are either going to change a part's behavior, or create one, or negotiate between them. And there will also always be some kind of alteration in the process of generalization. A generalization will either be made or broken, or a pair of them will be combined, or one of them will be split into two. Those three processes—secondary gain, manipulation of parts, and an alteration in generalization—will always be at work in every change.

V

Reframing Systems: Couples, Families, Organizations

The heart of reframing is the recognition that behavior can become detached from the outcome it is supposed to achieve. Psychologists recognized this years ago, and invented the term "functional autonomy" to describe behaviors that continued long after they had any useful function for the person. Psychologists didn't know what to *do* about this, but they did recognize it. They didn't realize that they could directly identify outcomes, and then select or design other behaviors, which they could tie to those outcomes.

The other aspect of reframing that makes it work so easily is that it is explicitly ecological. We make sure that the new behaviors don't interfere with any other aspects of the person's functioning. Any objecting parts become allies in selecting the new behaviors, so that the new behaviors fit in harmoniously with all the person's other needs and behaviors.

This takes care of the person's internal ecology, but it doesn't directly take care of the ecology of the interpersonal system that the person lives in. Sometimes when you change a person, she is fine individually, but the rest of her family suddenly develops problems. When you do reframing, parts will often object because they recognize that certain new behaviors will impact on people around them in ways that are undesirable. However, that presupposes that the person has parts which are able to notice how other people respond to her, and that isn't always true.

The only way to be really sure you are dealing appropriately with the ecology of the larger system is to be able to observe it. This is one of the values of doing couple therapy or family therapy instead of individual therapy. What we want to do next is demonstrate the application of reframing to situations in which you can observe the system that the person is in, and explicitly deal with the ecology of the whole system. Changes that are great for an individual are sometimes disastrous for the family or business organization in which she exists.

One of our students taught the Meta-Model to the nursing staff of a hospital. The immediate result was the patients got well faster, and the average hospital stay was reduced by a little over a day. However, the job of the hospital administration is to keep the hospital as full as possible to maximize income. Soon they had empty beds, and then an empty ward.

When the administration started proposing staffing cuts, the nurses saw the handwriting on the wall, and the average hospital stay went back to what it had been before. The change that was good for the patients was not good for the hospital system as a whole. In order to make it ecological for the hospital, there would have to be some way to maintain the economics of the hospital—generate more patients to fill the empty beds, or slowly reduce the staff by attrition, etc.

Many people go to therapy, start changing, and end up getting divorced. Usually that's because the changes they make don't take their spouses into account. Of course, afterwards you can say that they "outgrew their marriage" or that their spouses "weren't willing to change" if you want to cover up your incompetence. But if you can use reframing with the whole family system, you can do really clean work. It will be much easier to do and it will last longer, because other parts of the family system won't try to undo what you're trying to accomplish.

In order to successfully reframe a system, you have to take into account the needs and wishes of all members of the system. This is the basis for what we have often called "outcome therapy." I think you can do everything you need to do in couple therapy, family therapy, or conference work just using this one pattern. The first thing you do is notice any message that elicits a negative response in someone else—whether in a couple or family interaction, or during a corporate conference or consultation. Then you simply find out from the sender of the message if the response that he managed to elicit was in fact a response that he *intended* to elicit. In other words, it's the old formula "Message intended is not necessarily message received."

Let me demonstrate one example of "outcome therapy"—what we call couple reframing. Beth and Tom, would you come up please? I'd like to have you role-play a couple. I'm going to arbitrarily ask you to interact in the following way: Beth, you say or do anything, and then Tom, you act depressed.

Beth: Hello, Tom, how are you today?

Tom: Oh, I don't know. (He starts to slump and talk in a monotone.)

OK. I don't know exactly what portion of Beth's behavior Tom is reacting to, but whatever it is, I can see that it is getting a response that isn't useful, so I interrupt the interaction and anchor Tom's response. If Beth had asked me that question, I would just answer it, but it seems to have a really profound and over-determined impact on Tom, so I know something important is going on.

My next step is to turn to Tom and say, "Are these feelings familiar?" as I press the anchor I set up a moment ago.

Tom: Oh, yeah.

What's the name of the message you get from Beth when she says "Hello, Tom, how are you today?" in that way?

Tom: "Go away."

"Go away." OK, now hold on a minute here. Beth, was it your intent to give him the message, "Go away"?

Beth: No.

What were you intending?

Beth: I just want to know how he is feeling.

OK. So it was just a straight question. You are interested in finding out how he is.

Now I turn to Tom and say "Did you hear what Beth just said?"

Tom: Yes.

Now, I understand that you got a different message than the one she intended. Do you understand that she didn't intend the one that you got?

Tom: Yes.

OK. Now, Beth, are you really committed to getting across the message that you intended?

Beth: Yes.

This commitment step is really necessary. I'm setting up the leverage that I may need later on if she objects to changing her behavior in order to get the response she wants.

Now I ask Beth, "Have you ever been able to approach this man and ask him how he feels without having that profoundly depressive effect on him?" (Yes.) "Go back into your personal history and recall what you did in the past that worked to get the response you wanted."

If Beth can find an example of when she was successful in getting her intended message across in the past, then I will ask her to do it here, and notice whether or not it works.

Beth reaches out and touches Tom gently as she says softly "How's it going?" Tom responds positively.

In this case it worked fine. If she can't find an example in her own personal history that works, I can have her think of a woman she respects, and ask her how that woman does it. She can use that woman as a model and try that behavior.

If I can't find a new response easily in Beth's experience, then I'll get it from Tom. I'll turn to Tom and say "Have you ever gotten the message 'Hey, how are you?' and understood it simply as a message of interest and concern?"

Tom: Yes.

Would you demonstrate for Beth exactly how that message was given, so that she'll know exactly how to get across this message that she is committed to giving you.

Tom: Well, she came up and put her hand on my shoulder like this, and. . .

Good, thank you. So now I have Beth try that, and I sit back and watch to make sure it works.

If it doesn't work, I can ask Tom how, specifically, she could do this behavior differently to make it work, or ask Tom to go back and search for some other behavior that worked in the past. OK. Thank you, Beth and Tom.

Man: That doesn't seem like a very realistic example. It doesn't seem like Tom would get depressed when all Beth said was "Hello, how are you?"

It's actually quite frequent with real couples, that what seems to be an innocuous behavior triggers a powerful response. The stimulus may not be obvious, but Tom's response *is* obvious, and lets me know that something significant is going on. It may be that Beth's voice tone or the way she glances at Tom is associated with other experiences in their past that I don't know about.

The stimulus that elicits an unpleasant response in someone else may be hard for you to detect because it seems so trivial or innocuous. Once I worked with a schizophrenic teenager and his mother. All that was observable to me was that every time the son started to go berserk it was right after the mother had pointed to her arm. It turned out that the mother had survived the Nazi concentration camps. Every time the mother wanted a certain response from her son, she would point to the part of her arm where the identification number had been tatooed. I don't know how she had built that anchor up to have such an impact on her son, but it was as quick a knee-jerk response as I've ever seen. The kid would immediately start to go really berserk, yet the stimulus was one most people wouldn't have noticed.

When you use this format, you assume that people want to communicate in such a way that they get what they want, *and* that they want to respect the integrity and the interests of the other people involved. That assumption may not be true, but it's a very useful operating assumption, because it gives you something to do that can be very effective. If you make that assumption, it's always possible to find another solution—not a compromise—that satisfies both parties.

Any time there's a difference between the intended message and the response elicited, you first need to train the person who sent the message to recognize that he didn't get the intended response. You make it obvious to the person that the intent of his message was different from the response that he got. "What response did it elicit? Describe it. Did you notice you got it? Good." This builds a perceptual strategy into the person who originally sent the message and makes him more sensitive to the responses he is getting. The next question is "Is this response what you wanted? Is this what you intended?" In ineffective communication I have never yet run into a situation where it is. Then you train the message sender to gather information that will be useful in varying his behavior to get the response he wants.

This is the simplest format for couple reframing. I want you all to try it in groups of four, using the following outline. Two of you will role-play a couple in a problem interaction. One of you will be the programmer, and the fourth person will be a meta-person to keep track of where you are, and to give feedback to the programmer.

Outline

1) Identify and interrupt a stimulus-response (X→Y) loop.
2) Ask the person responding:
   a) "Are these feelings (Y) familiar?"
   b) "What is the message you get when she does X?"
3) Ask the stimulus person:
   a) "Is that (Y) what you intended by doing X?"
   b) "What did you intend?"
4) Ask stimulus person, "Are you committed to getting your intended message across?"

5) Find a way to make message received equal message intended:
   a) Find it in the experience of the stimulus person. "Have you ever gotten the response you want? What did you do then?"
   b) Find it in the experience of the response person. "What behavior would work to get that response in you?"
   c) Select a model, or pretend that you know how to get that response.
6) Have the stimulus person try out the new behavior to find out if it works satisfactorily.

* * * * *

Now that you've all had some experience using this simple format, I'd like to demonstrate some variations. Let's do another role-play. Rita and Joe, play this one for me. It starts like this. Rita, I want you to attack Joe verbally. Joe, you respond by feeling bad.

Rita: "You creep!" (Joe stiffens.)

I interrupt that loop and anchor Joe's response. I ask "Hey, are these feelings familiar, Joe?" (Yes.) "OK, what message did you get?"

Joe: She's angry with me.

Rita, did you intend to let him know that you're angry?

Rita: You're damn right!

So this time message received is message intended. I say, "Well done, congratulations, you are communicating very effectively." This validates that their communications and their intentions are effective, at least at the level they are describing them to me. However, they are both in unpleasant states, and probably those states are not helpful in arriving at a satisfactory solution to their difficulty.

Since the message received is the same as the message intended, but it's not satisfactory, I need to use a variation of the previous format. I can find out Rita's "meta-message," and gain more flexibility. "Rita, what does letting him know that you are angry do for you? What are you trying to accomplish by this?"

Rita: I want him to really hear me, to pay attention to me.

OK. What will having him really paying attention to you do for you?

Rita: Then I'll know he cares about me.

OK. So when you raise your voice and start yelling, you're saying "God damn it. I'm angry because you're not paying attention. If we're in a relationship like this, I want you to pay attention to me because I want to know you care."

So, Joe, this may seem quite contradictory to you, especially when you have these unpleasant feelings, but she is trying to say "Hey, demonstrate to me by being attentive that you care, because it matters to me." Are you interested in this message?

Joe: Yes.

And Rita, you're committed to getting it across, right?

Rita: Yes.

Now I simply search for alternative behaviors that are appropriate and acceptable to both of them.

You can use this variation any time the message intended will not produce productive results. So what if Joe knows that Rita is angry? That in itself is not likely to finish this interaction in a way satisfactory to both Rita and Joe. So I ask, "What is letting him know you are angry going to do for you?" "What are you going to accomplish by it?" "Are you satisfied to stop here, or is there some other goal you are after?" And Rita will find another goal. If she didn't have one originally, she'll make up one for us that will be more useful.

Notice that when I ask these questions, I get the outcome of the outcome, or the intent of the intent. I may have to ask this question four or five times until I find an outcome that *both* of them are interested in. What I'm really searching for is a message or outcome that both parties are interested in achieving. When I've found that, I've got about 75% of the negotiation work done. Once I've got an outcome frame that both parties congruently agree to, it's just a question of varying their behaviors until they find a specific way of getting there together.

OK. So Rita wants to send the message "I want you to demonstrate that you care," and Joe is interested in receiving it. Now I'm at a choice point. I can either get an alternative behavior from her or from him. If I'm using Rita to create a new behavior, I can ask "Rita, out of all the time you've spent together, do you remember a time when you were able to get the kind of attention and caring you want from Joe, that you are not presently getting? Do you remember ever being able to do that?" This is the same as step four of six-step reframing: creating alternatives. She now searches through her personal history and finds an occasion when she has successfully done this. I can have her remember in a specific and detailed way. "See yourself doing this very clearly; listen to the way you do it, etc. When you have seen and heard what you did in detail, try out that behavior with Joe, and we'll find out if it works here and now."

If Rita says "I've never succeeded in the way that I'd like to," I ask for a model. "Who gets attention and caring from Joe? What does she do? Now you try it."

I can even say "Well, make it up. Pretend as if you know how, and try it." If I have an idea, I can coach her. "Why don't you try X, Y, and Z, in the following way?" These are all methods to get her to generate a new piece of behavior and then test it right here to make sure that it works: that the message intended equals the message received.

The one advantage to having Rita search in her own personal history as a way of generating new behaviors is that then you know it has worked in the past, and that it's congruent with her personal style. If you suggest something, it will be congruent with *your* personal style, but it may or may not match *her* style or *his* style.

Janet: When Rita thinks of a new behavior, do you anchor it?

I don't have to, but I usually "overkill" in seminars. Every chance I get to use another anchor, I do. Janet suggested that I could use one here, and she's absolutely right. As Rita searches and finds the example, I can anchor it and then say "OK, now let's try it." I hold the anchor to stabilize the state from which she generates the behavior that worked before.

The other possibility is to use Joe as a creative resource to find alternative ways that Rita can use to satisfy her intention. In either case it is very important to first get a commitment from her that what she wants is important enough that she is willing to alter her behavior in order to get it.

"Rita, are you serious about really getting that message across? You do want his attention? That is important to you?" (Yeah.) It's very important to notice whether her voice tone and analogue behaviors are really congruent. In this case we have a really congruent commitment from her.

Rita, I know you're really serious about this. It's something that's really important to you as a woman. Now, Rita, is this important *enough* to you that you would be willing to change your behavior in order to get the response that you want? (Yes.)

Now I turn to Joe and say "And I take that as a compliment to you, Joe. She does want your attention. Now you know what she intends. She's saying 'Joe, I want your attention!' Do you understand that? That's not the message you got before, but now you can understand what she intends. The question is, can you instruct her in what, specifically, she can do so that you can recognize and respond to her *intention?* What can she do to get your attention in a positive way? Think of times in the past when she has done something that made you *want* to pay attention to her. What did she do then?"

Now I have him specify her behavior to match what he will be able to recognize and respond to. Rita is already committed to adjusting her behavior. She's committed to taking instructions from him about how to get his attention. Who knows better how to get his attention than he himself?

I want to point out that *sequence* is very important. I need to get her commitment *first*. If I don't do that, she will probably have a lot of objections to any change he suggests: "He's controlling me. He just wants to be in charge." First I need to get her commitment that her wants are important—*so* important that she is willing to change her own behavior in order to satisfy them. This frames the changes in terms of *her* desires, so she'll be willing to go along with the changes. To him, I can frame it differently. I'll tell him that his responses are important to her—*so* important that she's willing to adjust her behavior so that it's easy for him to respond in the way she wants.

Woman: Can you say more about sequence? I think that's extremely important, and I want to know more about that.

We are syntacticians. If you were going to describe us as any kind of academician, that would be it. Syntax means "What goes where, and in what order." The thing that makes the visual-kinesthetic dissociation such a good way of working with phobias is the order. One man we taught it to decided to use it "creatively," because he didn't want to be an android. So first he had people go all the way through the trauma, and *then* he had them dissociate. If you do it in that order, the person has to go through lots of pain, and that makes it very hard. If you do the dissociation first, and *then* go through the experience, your clients don't have to go through the discomfort. That makes it much easier and more elegant. The thing that makes NLP work go so quickly is that we make very practical decisions about what order we do things in, rather than saying "Oh, I could do X!" and rushing in and doing it.

Every book we've ever published says "*Gather information!* . . . Evolve system. . . . Solidify change." That is the overall model. The emphasis is on "Gather information" because it's the part almost everybody leaves out. Most communicators go into their trance of doing whatever they do, and when somebody comes in, they just fire off the technique. Often the same technique *would* work if they did something else first.

Woman: That's why I asked the question. Let's say that you have the information. How do you decide what to do and in what sequence? What goes on in your head before you start doing something?

Well, I ask myself a question. I go inside and say "Hey, self. What outcome do I want, and how can I get that outcome?" I work backward from the outcome.

For example: I worked with a family in which the mother was a professional people-helper. She *knew* what was good for her daughter, because she was an expert. Her daughter was saying to the mother "Get off my case!" The mother was saying "Look, I'm the only person in this family who is qualified to know about these things. Even though my daughter won't listen and is freaking out, I know what's best for her." Now, one way to make a change would be to attack her belief that she knows best. However, that would be the hard way to go about it. If you do it that way, you've got to fight with her.

My outcome was to get them communicating again. So I said to the mother "Do you really believe this? I mean this seriously, not sarcastically at all. Do you *really* believe that you have good information that will be helpful to your daughter?" And the mother said *"Absolutely!"*

"I want to believe this, because if you are serious about this, and you're not just saying it, I know there is something really useful that we can do here. Are you really serious?"

"Absolutely. I mean it literally. I'm a very honest person."

"OK. Now if I can find a way that you can communicate this information to her without her freaking out, then she'll have the information. Would you be willing to use a different way of communicating, even though it might not be your natural way of doing it? Is the information you have to give her *important enough* that you would be willing to do something like that?"

"Absolutely."

At that point I had her, because she couldn't back down. The realities that I had built were congruent with the mother's belief system.

Then I turned to the daughter and asked "How does your mother have to talk to you in order to get you to really listen and consider what she says? You may not want to do what your mother wants, but at least you'll be able to hear what she says." The daughter had this cheshire cat grin on her face, and she said "Well, she'd have to treat me like a person."

"How has she been treating you—like a pencil?" That's one way of getting her to specify what "being treated like a person" means. If you give an answer that you know is totally wrong, she will have to correct it.

"Well, she wouldn't be yelling, she wouldn't be—"

"No, no. I don't want to know what she *wouldn't* be doing. What *would* she be doing? What would she look like; what would she sound like?"

Then the daughter demonstrated a particular tone of voice that she wanted her mother to use, and I said "OK, let's try it. And if it doesn't work, do you know what that means? That means you're a liar, and your mother's right that you won't listen!"

So I turned to the mother and said "Pick one of the things that you think is important for your daughter to know, and try to do it in the way she demonstrated." After a couple of sentences I interrupted and asked the daughter "Is she doing it the way you want?"

"Well, her voice is still a little whiny." So we helped the mother adjust her voice and she started in again. The daughter sat there and listened, and then said "I'll do that." The mother was *shocked!* "You *will?*" Previously most of the time the daughter hadn't even heard what the mother was saying because she reacted to her tone of voice.

The important point is that within the context I had created, there was no way for either of them to respond otherwise. The daughter was not going to let the mother be right by not listening. And the mother was certainly not going to say "These things are *so* important, but not important enough that I'll change my tone of voice"—not when she's just sworn on a stack of Bibles that getting the information across is the most important thing in the world. Going after their *willingness* to communicate *before* I went after restructuring the communication was a *very* important syntactic choice. Doing it in the other order would have set up conflict. You do the same thing with the six-step model: you ask the part if it's willing to communicate, and you determine its intention before you go after changes in behavior.

The key question is this: "What is going to make it possible for me to get the change I want?" "What's a prerequisite for the change that I want?" If you go directly after the change itself, two things will happen that are not useful. One, it's going to be like digging ditches. It's going to be hard work, because you're going to have to fight with the person's parts. Two, if you go after it too directly, you may interfere with her strategies.

Teri is a good example of this possible interference. Let's say that I was a well-intentioned therapist who had a belief system that said "Everybody has got to have a way of being able to generate experience." So when I said "Now, it's time for everyone to lie congruently," rather than allowing Teri to go outside the room, I would have said "You must stay and learn this!" If I did that, I would mess with her strategies and make her crazy. She was sitting there saying "If I do this, I'll be crazy!" and her complaint was *completely accurate.* Given the strategies that she had, that was absolutely true. So I had to find out what prerequisites would make it possible for her to do what I asked.

The same thing is true with the rigid know-it-all mother I talked about, or with a guy who has a belief system that women are out to control him. The same thing is true of *every* change that you make. I want to know the *appropriate sequence* to go after what I want, instead of deciding that I'm so all-knowing that I know the right way to do it. There's an elegance in the way people object. Their objections, as far as I'm concerned, are *always* valid, and they tell you exactly what you need to know. There are real dangers for your clients if you ignore their objections. If you can't communicate an idea to someone it's because of the way he is organized. The way he is structured right now doesn't make it possible for him to do certain things, *unless* you do other things first.

As soon as I have a well-formed outcome, I always back up, asking "What would make it possible for them to just fall into that?" If I try something and it doesn't work, I always back up in the process and ask "Well, if they can't do that, what else must be true?" When I answer that question, I have more information to go on.

Woman: I have seen a lot of couples where the woman's outcome, what she wants, is aggravating to the man. How do you deal with that?

Usually it's a specific behavior rather than the outcome that's objectionable. If the outcome is objectionable, then you go to *meta*-outcomes. You find out what the intention is behind the intention that she just stated. Rita, what does it do for you to get his attention?

Rita: It makes me feel good, like a desirable woman.

Good. What other ways do you have to feel good and desirable?

Woman: Let's say her intention is that she wants to get his attention, and he says that the way she could do that is to have sex in weird ways that she's not willing to do.

First I want to point out that this is an example of the specific behavior being unacceptable to her, not the outcome. If that happens, I can say to her "How else could you get his attention? What other ways could you use?"

Woman: I'm not having very much success finding any other ways.

OK. Then try modeling. "Would you think of half a dozen women who seem to be able to get their husbands' attention and notice the ways—publicly, at least—that they seem to succeed in doing that?" If she doesn't know any women who can do that, send her out in the world to find them.

Another alternative is to induce a deep trance and use a technique called "pseudo-orientation in time." You have her jump three months into the future: "Remember three months ago when we first got together? I was just talking to a woman in the same position that you were in three months ago, and I remembered how you really couldn't get your husband's attention at that time except by bizarre, unacceptable sexual activities. Since that was unacceptable to you morally and ethically, I remember that you came up with some alternatives that were so effective that they surprised him as much as they surprised you. But I can't remember exactly what they were. Would you describe in detail what you did?"

There are lots of alternatives at that choice point, but you have to be respectful of the ecology of the system. You could also find out if you could make the bizarre sexual practices acceptable to her. "If you engaged in these bizarre sexual practices, what would happen that is unacceptable to you?" It may be that you could deal with her objections. There are lots of ways you can make a satisfactory change. You have to respect both her integrity and his integrity, find out the intention in both of their communications, and find effective ways for them to get together.

Woman: OK. I thought you were moving toward finding out *his* intention: what *he* would get out of the bizarre sexual activities.

You can do it that way, too. (He turns to Joe.) "If she engaged in these bizarre sexual activities, what would that do for you?"

Joe: It would give me excitement and intensity.

OK. Is there any other way that you have ever been involved that allowed you to feel excited in this intense way?

Joe: In the beginning of our relationship I felt that way.

So now I could access what those experiences were, and what the difference is between those and what's going on now.

You can go for the outcome with either or both members of the couple. Think of the basic reframing model here. There's an imbalance between the conscious and the unconscious, so you always go to the unconscious for the flexibility for the new choices. When you are doing reframing between people, you can make the assumption that they are equally flexible. In that case you can go in either direction at any point. When he's making a demand on her that she refuses, you can discover what that's going to do for him, or you can find out what the refusal is going to do for her.

I've run into cases where the man wants to engage in more sexual behavior. He's not satisfied with their sex life. She's not satisfied with their sexual behavior either, but she's using turning him down as a way to accomplish something else. For example, if she were to be sexually responsive to him, she thinks that would mean he would dominate her in all aspects of her life. She becomes sexually unresponsive in order to assert her autonomy. I've had it go the other way, too. The husband is sometimes the one in this position. Protecting autonomy is the outcome, or what is often called "secondary gain."

The question now becomes "Can she find *other* ways of behaving which insure that she has her autonomy and independence, and that she has his respect?" When she has that, then she can allow what they both want, more satisfying sexual behavior. In order to do this, you have to separate the notion of her independence or autonomy from the sexual behavior itself. She has to have some other way of knowing that she's her own woman and can exercise choice, that is at least as convincing for her personally as being sexually unresponsive. When she has that, you've detached the outcome of independence or autonomy from the specific behavior of being sexually unresponsive. If she wants more sexual behavior and he does too, then they are free to engage in it with her autonomy still protected.

It's always by going to the context, by going to the frame, by going to the outcome, that you get the freedom to move around behaviorally. If you address the behavior directly, it may be ecologically unsound for them as a couple. Once I've gotten the intent and validated that they both agree to it, *then* I can begin to vary the behavior.

Let me give you another example. Let's say a father has just said to his daughter "If you don't listen to me and don't come home by ten o'clock, I'll ground you for a week, and blah, blah, blah . . ."

"Sam, did you notice what happened as you said that to your daughter?" "And, Martha, what were you feeling at that moment?"

"Oh, I feel like a little kid, you know, having to be told exactly what to do, and blah, blah, blah."

"Now, was it your intention, Sam, to deliver the message to Martha that she's still a little kid and you have to take full control over her life with an iron fist?"

"Well, no. That's not what I intended."

"What was your intention?"

"Well, I care. I don't want her hanging out with hoods. I don't want her out in the street. There's dope out there. I want her to be in the house, safe and sound. She's my girl, and I want to make sure that she has the kind of experiences that she needs to grow up like I want her to grow up." The daughter says "But it's *my* life!"

"OK, Sam. Is part of that image that you have of your daughter growing up for her to be independent? Do you want her to be a woman who knows her own mind, who can stand on her own two feet and make decisions for herself based on the realities of the world? Or do you want her to be pushed around by other people's opinions?"

What I've done with this is relate his complaint about his daughter—that she doesn't do what he tells her to do—to his outcome of wanting her to grow up to be independent.

Woman: It's like having interchangeable lenses on a camera: you just put on a wide angle lens to get it into a wider frame.

OK, that's a nice visual metaphor for reframing. A behavior which in isolation seems to be a problem, or inappropriate, makes sense when placed in a larger context. This is really an example of a context reframe. I shift the behavior that the father complains about to the context of his daughter's growing up and becoming independent.

Exploring the father's intention will loosen up the ways in which he will go about expressing the message he originally intended. "Remember, be in at ten o'clock" is not the message received. How else could he get the message across to her that he wants her to be protected and yet allow her to grow up to be independent? How can he be assured—in a way that doesn't offend the daughter—that she is growing up appropriately? The specific behavior of coming home at ten o'clock may be totally irrelevant to achieving that.

This is the same kind of negotiation situation that you have with a couple of corporate executives who disagree on how to achieve a particular goal. You first remind them of the common general frame in which they are operating and that they will both agree with. You remind them, for example, that whatever specific policies they eventually decide on, their goal is to increase profits and maintain or improve the quality of the services or products they offer. We'll go into the business applications in more detail later this morning.

Woman: If you have not accurately specified the general frame—what the positive intention is—will you get a delayed polarity response?

Yes, typically you will. Whenever you deal with content, you run the risk that it is not appropriate for them. Even when the content is not appropriate, you may get agreement at the time, because of your rapport and personal power. But later you will get a backlash—a polarity flip.

There are three ways to avoid that. One way is to do a pure process reframing using the six-step model, in which there is no opportunity to impose any inappropriate content.

Another way is to take the time to gather lots of information. "Well, what is it specifically that you intend to do by demanding so vehemently that she be in at ten o'clock?" "Well, I want . . . " and you get whatever set of words are the appropriate ones for this particular unique human being. Then if you use that *same* set of nominalizations and unspecified verbs and idioms as you describe the new way for him to transmit the information, you will match what he is trying to do at the unconscious level, as well as at the conscious level. That will avoid the polarity problem.

The third and really indispensable way to be sure that your reframe is appropriate is to have enough sensory experience to notice the responses that you are getting, and observe whether your client is responding congruently.

Man: So far you've covered examples of incongruence between the intention and behavior. Do you ever have a case where a couple's relationship is in conflict because they intend different things? He wants more of this; she wants less of this.

If there's a basis for negotiation, there's always a frame within which they can both agree to a common outcome. Give me an example where you think there probably isn't a common frame.

Man: She wants monogamy and he doesn't.

OK. Let's role-play. Jean, you want an exclusive sexual relationship with him, and George is not willing to commit himself to that. First I ask for the meta-outcome of what each of them wants. I ask Jean "What is your intent in demanding a monogamous sexual exclusivity with this guy? What will that do for you?"

Jean: Oh, it will give me a sense of security that I'm the most desirable woman for this man.

Then I find George's meta-outcome. "What is your refusal to be monogamous based on? What will it do for you if you can be other than monogamous and involve yourself with other women?"

George: It lets me know I'm still desirable to other women, and makes me feel important.

Every time that I ask them an outcome question, I loosen up the context in which the behavior occurs. That gives me more freedom to move. George probably won't object to her having a sense of security, and she won't object to his feeling important and desirable. What they each object to is the specific behavior, not the outcome.

Now I use this information to formulate a common outcome that they can both agree to. "So am I correct that you both would like to find some mutually agreeable arrangement whereby, Jean, you can have a sense of security and desirability, and George, you will also feel important and desirable."

If Jean and George both agree to this, I've got a common agreement frame within which to begin negotiations. Now I can work toward finding a specific solution. I can ask Jean, "What other ways could he unequivocally demonstrate to you that you have this kind of security that you desire?" And I can ask George, "What other ways are there for you to feel desirable and important?"

Man: Suppose that she says "No, that's the only way," and he also says "No, that's the only way."

I have my doubts about that; I believe there is always something else behind the behavior and other ways to accomplish it. But if they both firmly believe that there are no alternatives, I will question the frame around our interaction.

"Look, I don't know of any basis for negotiation right now. Is there a basis for you two to continue together? Let's get explicit about this. I don't want to waste my time, and I don't want to waste your time and money. Are you interested in committing a certain amount of time and energy to finding out if things can be changed in a way that would be exciting and interesting enough for you to be together again? Or have you already committed yourself someplace else?"

If there aren't any positive intentions that they are willing to reveal, it may be that there isn't any basis for negotiation. Suppose she is already madly in love with someone else and carrying on an affair. It's just a question of getting rid of this creep and moving on. That's what's often called a "hidden agenda." Getting explicit about a basis for negotiation and framing the overall process will smoke out hidden agendas, and that does everybody a favor!

Woman: If that's the case, since your investment is not to keep them together, doesn't she still need to work out the separation with you? Wouldn't she need to work out how to leave him and go to the other man?

Yes, if she's ready. And I've got to help him recover whatever parts of himself he has invested in being with her.

Challenging the negotiation frame usually scares them, and motivates them both to put more effort into finding mutually acceptable solutions. Then I can go for outcomes, or meta-outcomes—the outcome of the outcome.

"Jean, what would knowing that you are secure do for you?" "George, what would knowing that you are attractive to other females do for you?" Both will probably say, in effect, "Well, I'd have a sense of self-worth for myself that I don't really have now." Now I've got a further loosening of the frame. In order to loosen the frame I can go to outcomes, or meta-outcomes, or meta-meta-outcomes. "Jean, are there any other ways to get self-worth?" Typically if I go that deep into intentions, there will be *many* behaviors which will satisfy that need. When you get that general, you're going to have to do a lot of experiential testing, because they really won't know at that point if the alternative behaviors will be acceptable.

One of the first things I do is to engage in negotiation to establish a three-month moratorium on sexual activities outside of this relationship during which time he will have a chance to try out some of the new behaviors which will satisfy the needs that he has which monogamy denies at this point. That will also give her three months to engage all her resources in finding ways to discover how she can develop security for herself and in this relationship, so that the notion of his being involved with another woman doesn't threaten her in the way it presently does.

As we mentioned before, I can send them out to find models. I'd ask the wife "Are any of the women that you know and really respect in a *non*-monogamous relationship? How do they take care of their sense of security?" I'd say to the husband "Do you know any men who you really respect and admire, and who are monogamous and perfectly satisfied with their own desirability? Good, I want you to go hang out with them and find out what they do."

The search for alternative behaviors can be carried out internally with all their unconscious resources, and also externally by using models around them. Don't be afraid to give them homework. Have them go out and find appropriate models to watch and listen to.

Woman: You said if there's a basis for negotiation, then there's always a frame in which there is a possibility for change.

Those two things are synonymous. By frame or basis for negotiation I mean "Is there some common outcome which you can both agree to? For instance, are you committed to staying with this woman? Are you committed to staying with this man?" That may be the only frame that they can agree on, and of course each of them may have conditions.

Once they have agreed on an outcome frame, then you can negotiate on the way of achieving it. "George, there is some set of behaviors that will satisfy your needs and still be within the frame of your staying with this woman." "Jean, there are some behaviors that we're going to have to discover for you which will allow you to stay with this man and still have the kind of security that you desire. Our task now is to discover what those behaviors are."

Man: When you ask the framing question, and one of them responds "I don't know if I want to stay together or not" how do you proceed from there?

Then I negotiate for a trial period of trying out new choices. "George, are you willing to spend three months accepting this constraint of being monogamous which you consider artificial?" Or "Jean, are you willing to spend three months not accepting the constraint that you desire for your security, in order to find out whether there are behaviors that can be discovered which will satisfy you within this framework?"

Being very explicit becomes important at this point. Whenever there is a head-on-head disagreement about a certain piece of behavior within the relationship, then jump out to the outcome frame and find out if there is one that is acceptable. If there is one, you can proceed. If there's not, you may as well be explicit about that and save everybody time.

Finding a common outcome or agreement frame between members of a family, couple, or organization is a very important step that many therapists or consultants miss. They usually attempt to find specific solutions too soon, and then there are objections. I'd like to have you do an exercise in which your primary task is to find a common outcome. If you also have time to identify a workable solution, fine.

Do this in four-person groups. A and B are members of a couple or organization. C is the programmer. D will be the meta-person. I want C to specify the context—business or therapy. A and B will then generate some conflict, and C, the programmer will do the following:

Agreement Frame Exercise

1) Ask A and B what, specifically, they want, and then restate it to their satisfaction as a pace.

2) Ask both A and B what their specific outcome will do for them (their meta-outcome) and restate it.

3) Find a common outcome such that when you state it, both A and B agree it is what they want. "So what you both want is . . ."

When you are the programmer, I want you to get as general as you need to in order to find an outcome that both partners will agree to. Sometimes all you will be able to get agreement on will be, "So you are both here in order to find some way to continue your relationship to your mutual benefit and satisfaction."

* * * * *

Determining an agreement frame also gives you a way to sort behaviors for relevance during the negotiation process itself. This is particularly important in business meetings and negotiations. Conservatively speaking, eighty percent of all the time spent in meetings is wasted, because what is said is not relevant to the outcome. It goes like this: we're talking about campaign X for product Y and Jim says "Oh, you know what we could do over here with product Z?" It's a great idea, actually. It's wonderfully creative—and wholly *irrelevant* in the context.

Unless you challenge that first irrelevant remark, you unleash an avalanche of free association which is more appropriate for the psychiatric couch than a board meeting. Later it will take you ten minutes to get people reoriented to the frame within which you are working. If you make the outcome frame explicit at the beginning of the meeting, you have a basis which is explicit and agreed upon for sorting out what's relevant and what's irrelevant. We call this a "relevancy challenge." When someone becomes irrelevant, you can say "Jim, I don't understand your remark relative to what we've already agreed upon to do here at this meeting. Why don't you bring that up Friday at our product development meeting?" The next time he makes an irrelevant remark, I'll say "Well, I'm not sure how that connects with what we're doing here," and point to the flip chart. Then the next time that he starts to make an irrelevant remark, I'll probably just have to glance over at the chart, and that will be enough to anchor him into stopping.

In corporations in which we have installed these programs, after a few meetings the total meeting time drops by about four-fifths. People look forward to the meetings, because the criteria for relevancy are made very explicit and things get done. The relevancy challenge is not part of the organizational behavior of most business organizations, and it ought to be for purposes of efficiency.

You can see the same process more clearly in an arbitration situation. There are two groups head-on-head; they are just locked together, and they've completely forgotten the context. The outcome frame has been completely forgotten and most of their behavior is irrelevant with respect to it. Most negotiators will tell you that they are always brought in at the worst possible time—when there's a deadlock. I personally think it's the *best* possible time, because all the issues have been sharply defined and the differences are known clearly. You know exactly what needs to be done.

My first move is to get the two groups away from each other, and then I loosen the frame. I have to reestablish a broad outcome frame—which is the traditional notion of the basis for negotiation. As soon as the outcome frame is established, then I have a basis for relevancy challenges. I can dismiss certain things as being counterproductive, because both sides have already committed themselves publicly to the outcome frame.

At that point I have enough slippage that I can find ways of balancing the two proposals and coming up with a give-and-take. I will insist that the outcome frame contain what both sides should have put there to begin with: items which are not essential, which are "throwaways" for the purpose of barter. I've got to have an equal amount of those on both sides. I've got to create room to move first. If I don't have maneuvering room, then I'm stuck.

Man: Sometimes in my work I have difficulty setting a very explicit outcome frame with people. When I try, they often resist that.

Well, let me give you my frame for establishing a frame: "Look, I'm a professional. I refuse to engage in random behavior here. I have certain criteria for my own performance, and until we know whether there is a basis for us to proceed here, I'm not willing to spend my time and skill." I have only had that challenged once, when a man said "Well, I ain't doing that!" and I said "Fine. Goodbye." I reserve the right to walk out on any transaction, including psychotherapeutic transactions.

By the way, if there is a category of client that you have trouble with, then seek them out. Working with them will provide you with an opportunity for developing your own flexibility. However, once you have demonstrated to your own satisfaction that you are competent to work with that class of clients, if you still don't like them, don't take them. A professional ought to have the option to engage in a business transaction or not, based on her own personal criteria.

However, in the context of professional psychotherapeutic help, I recommend that if you are going to exercise the option of refusing a patient or a client, you have a list of people to whom you can refer them, so that they do have somewhere to go. That is part of your professional responsibility. But there is no need to torture yourself. I worked with heroin addicts for a while until I satisfied myself that I could succeed with them. I don't work with them any more, because I really don't like being around them.

Woman: I'm interested in tuning myself so I can see and hear the patterns that go on between two or more people at one time. I'm trying to be aware of how a family system is interconnected, but I think it's too big a chunk. I want to broaden my ability to do that. Do you have any helpful hints?

Whenever you are learning about sensory experience, you have to chunk it small enough so that you can cope with it. The place I learn the most about multiple-person systems is in restaurants. Go sit down in a restaurant next to a family, and never look at the person who is talking. That way you can see how the others respond to the speaker.

Woman: My question is about validation. How do I differentiate between when I'm actually seeing and hearing something and when I'm hallucinating? When you think you might be hallucinating, do you use somebody else to check what you see?

No, I can induce any belief system in just about anybody, so that wouldn't work. So what if I can convince somebody else of my hallucination? That is the way that a lot of therapies operate right now. The therapist says, "Well, you know, what I'm feeling right now is X. Are you feeling that now?" The person goes "I hadn't noticed it, but now that you mention it, yeah." So now that we have a shared hallucination, we'll act as if it is a basis for choice. That isn't going to work.

You have to learn to make distinctions, and it's probably best to start doing this with couples. You have to figure out what is going on in terms of the naturally-occurring anchored sequences. Let's say that each time he begins to use one tone of voice, you notice that she starts accessing kinesthetically, but if he uses another tone of voice, she accesses visually. When you notice that this relationship exists, then your job is to be able to test it behaviorally. You can always do that inside quotes, of course. You can say "Well, if Jane here said to you . . ." and then you can become Jane. As you do this, you watch Ralph, and notice whether the predicted response occurs. Then you can be Ralph and test another portion of the calibration. "If Ralph said . . ." So you can always test for calibrations fairly explicitly by using quotes. Or you can just adopt the calibrated analogue behavior covertly, and notice what happens.

A friend of mine is a mime. One of his great skills is mimicking another person, both tonally and visually. When we're talking, Lennie will say "Oh, yeah, I saw Jimmy the other day" . . . and then he will *become* Jimmy If Jimmy's wife is there, she'll begin to respond to Lennie as though she's married to him. All the systems that operate between Jimmy and his wife will then operate between Lennie and her. And then he can become somebody else and she will respond differently.

One of the things that Lennie jokes about is that when my students come in and he wants them to do something, he simply becomes me. They respond immediately, because they are programmed to respond to me.

I do this kind of role-playing with individuals, too. I become one of their parts, and it works just the same way. I find out how they respond to the part. Behavioral testing is the only way I know of that you can count on for validating your sensory experience in systems relationships. You and I and Linda over there may have the same hallucination, but that's no basis on which to make a decision.

Man: Could you give us an illustration of becoming a part?

I've been doing that for two days now!

Man: Could you label one so my conscious mind would know?

I'm capable of it, but I'm not going to do it. I'm going to tell you about a family I worked with, to give you an example of how to determine and utilize the family system. In this family the mother was a matriarch. And *her* mother had been a matriarch. Her grandmother had founded a church, and there were streets named after her in the Midwest. This woman knew her dead grandmother's name, but she couldn't remember her grandfather's name even though *he* was still alive!

The one thing that was really noticeable to me was that *everybody* in the family responded to the mother. All she had to do was to look at them, and everyone would cringe. All the males were freaked out. The husband was an alcoholic, the older son was a hoodlum, and the younger son was failing in school and was starting to follow in the older son's footsteps. It's a typical pattern. However, there was a five-year-old girl in the family who was very cute and very expressive. She could get the mother to respond positively to her every time she did something.

In order to intervene effectively in this family, I needed to find out how the family operated as a system. I wanted to know what the natural sequence of interaction was. The best way to do that is to create a crisis, which is something that most family therapists avoid. If I make everything nice and lovely and warm, then I don't get down to the nitty-gritty. So I usually mention the most taboo things in the world for the family.

Virginia Satir taught me this. A lot of people think Virginia doesn't do it, because she does it in a nice tone of voice, but Virginia talks about everything that the family *doesn't* want to talk about. My style may be a little bit closer to Frank Farrelley's in the way I go about it, but it accomplishes the same thing.

So the family comes in and I say "Well, what are you doing here? What went *wrong*?" Immediately the mother says "This lousy kid over here has been getting out of hand." I might turn around and say to the son "You son-of-a-bitch!" And then I ask the mother "What has he been doing, swearing?" Immediately the family goes into crazy land, and the system begins to operate. I can say "Well, what do you do if he does this? You probably don't scold him or anything." She'll immediately start in quotes "Well, I tell him blah, blah, blah" and then immediately the kid will lose quotes and say "Look, goddamit, get off my back!" Then the father will say "Can I get a drink of water around here?" As soon as the family system starts operating, I sit back and observe, because I want to know how the family system operates without me. If it starts to slow down, then I step in and kick it to get it going again. I find out what the really sensitive areas are, so I can keep mentioning them to keep the family going.

This also wears them out, which is really useful. That's one of the things that makes my job easy. I've tried for a long time to train students to do this, but they get caught up in the content of what the family is doing, rather than stepping back and letting the family fight it out so that they can find out how the system operates.

The program in this particular family was really interesting. When the mother spoke, the husband responded like crazy. He went into what psychologists call "massive denial." He climbed into the back of the chair and hid in the cushions. The oldest son was a carbon copy of the mother, and fought right back at her "RRrrrrhh!" And the more he fought back, the more the mother attacked him. If I interrupted the mother's behavior, the son kept attacking, but the father relaxed. That's important to know: the father was not responding to the son; he was only responding to what the mother did.

Woman: What did you do so that the father relaxed?

I shut the mother off for a while. When the fight got rolling, I just got up and stood in front of the mother, and the son yelled right through me. As soon as I cut off the mother visually, the father sighed and relaxed, even though the son was still screaming at the top of his lungs. When I stepped out of the way, the father immediately tensed up again. You can't do that kind of testing if you are glued to your chair the way many therapists are.

In this family, the younger son responded positively to his older brother. And when the mother went after the older brother, she might as well have gone after the younger one, because he responded as if the mother were going after him. He was a completely vicarious human being. If you talked to him directly, he always looked behind himself, no matter where he was sitting. He actually did that. I asked him "What do you think about this?" and he looked behind himself and said "Ah, well, ah . . . I don't know." It was as if he weren't all there. But he really responded to whatever the mother did, even if the mother did it to the father or to his older brother.

The mother fought it out with me tooth and nail, and she was almost my caliber. She could hold her own against me, and there aren't too many people who can do that. But I have some really underhanded ways of fighting. I can switch logical levels so fast that I kept a little bit ahead of her, but I worked hard to do it. There were two male students and one female student in the room with me, and whenever the female student spoke to the mother, her behavior completely changed. The female student said things like "You are so unfair to your son." The mother turned around and said gently "Well, now, dear, some day you are going to be a little older and you are going to be in my place. . . ." It was a *completely* different program. If a male had said that to her, she'd have boxed his ears off!

The mother's programs for communicating with men and women were totally different. The little girl did weird things in the session—things like getting up and knocking papers off the desk, interrupting, and making noise. If the son even took his eyes off what was going on, she'd shout "Pay attention!" But the little girl was safe from that.

Woman: And you didn't directly comment on that at all? You just watched it?

What good would it do to talk about it? If I tell them all the things I make distinctions about, that would make it easier for them to stay the same.

In order to test what I had observed, all I had to do was switch back and forth between acting like the son, the father, and the little girl, and see what different responses I got from the mother. I could actually get different responses from her by adopting the little girl's analogues. She began to respond to me in a way that mixed how she usually responded to men and to women.

There was just no way in the world to get the mother to attack the little girl. I asked "What's the *worst* thing the little girl's ever done?" She said in a sweet voice "Oh, one time she spilled blah, blah, blah." When the mother talked to the little girl, the entire family *loved* it. They wished the two of them would run away together! They all responded positively, because the little girl got treated the way they all wanted to be treated. If the little girl communicated to the mother, the mother responded positively, but if the little girl communicated to one of the other people, the mother did not respond. That's very important. If she did, I could have made trickier interventions. I could have gotten the little girl and the brother going, and gotten the mother responding to that. But the mother didn't respond positively to anyone in the family *except* the little girl communicating directly to her. Everyone in the family responded to the mother.

So I had to figure out what I could get this little girl to do, to get the mother to respond in a way that would get the rest of the family to make the changes they wanted. When I first learned family therapy, I was told that everything works in triads—that when three people communicate, if person one communicates with person two, person three is always going to respond to that communication. It's not true. You can *get* them to respond to it, but they're not necessarily doing it already.

What I want to know in any family is what they are *already* doing, because then I can *use* what's going on now in order to change the system. This is a very important principle: *How can I introduce a small change that will channel all the interactions in the family system in ways that force the system to change itself?* When you can do that, the family system will do most of your work for you. If I want everybody to change in this particular family system, then I'm going to change the daughter. She will alter the mother's behavior, and ultimately everyone else in the system will change in response to the mother. However, it doesn't work the other way. If I had changed the younger son, it wouldn't have affected anyone else, because no one in the family responded to him. He was about as close to non-existence as it's possible to get. It was "to be or not to be" and he wasn't.

By setting such high standards, the mother made it easy for the men to succeed at failing. I wanted her to lower her standards and to respond in some kind of softer way with them. What I did sounds really direct, but sometimes the direct approach is best. I took the little girl aside, and I told her "Look, I need your help. I want you to play this game with me, and it's going to be *our* secret. If you play this game with me, something *magical* is going to happen when you come back here next time." Previously the little girl had always run away and hidden whenever the mother started to criticize one of the brothers. I told her "You don't need to do that. I want you to test your powers, because I'm giving you powers that you didn't know you had, that you have now. If she's yelling at Billy, I want you to go up to her and simply tug on your mother's hand and ask her the following question: 'Mommie, do you love Billy?' and keep doing it until you are convinced that she is telling you the truth."

Of course, this little girl was great at it. She would say "Mommie, do you love Billy?" And the mother would say (angrily) "YES!" When she asked again "Mommie, do you love Billy?" the mother would say (softly) "Yes, yes I do." "Do you *really,* Mommie?" The girl just went on and on and on like that.

What's going to happen in this system as a result of this intervention? The whole family was convinced that the mother was the Wicked Witch of the North—and you'd probably agree with them! But it's very hard to be the Wicked Witch of the North when a cute little girl is going "Mommie, do you love Billy?" Now, in the middle of "Look, you indifferent slob, you forgot to take out the garbage!" Billy's going to hear things like "Yes, I love him." That's going to change the whole ball game.

Man: So he got both the yucky negative and the "Yes, mother loves me."

Yes. But getting negative messages became an opportunity to then have positive feelings.

Man: "Getting negative messages becomes the opportunity to have good feelings" sounds like the way to program somebody to go through behaviors in order to generate negative messages so that he can feel good.

But *these* people didn't do anything wrong to get criticized. And when the mother answered the little girl's question, she typically went into an explanation of what she was doing. "The only reason I'm telling him this is that I'm afraid that if I can't do something to motivate him to do well in school, then he's going to have to be a hard laborer like his father and work in the coal mines. I don't want him to have to work in the coal mines. I want him to have a job that is clean." She started to communicate what she was trying to do—the intention behind her behavior. Basically, that little girl accomplished a reframing of the mother's behavior.

Man: The girl must have had some way of coping with the mother if the mother turned on the girl and said "Stop asking me these damn questions."

The mother would *never* do that. I knew that before I intervened. The mother *couldn't* yell at her, or at any other woman.

Woman: The little girl anchored something for the mother.

The little girl *became* an anchor. Everybody wanted to hang out with her from then on. It wasn't safe to be anywhere else! This little girl had always been ignored before. Being ignored happens very often to middle children, and to children after about the fourth-born. If you decide that's not useful, find some way to make the child an anchor for all kinds of positive behaviors. That's a very powerful intervention.

When the family came back the next week, the difference in the way they looked and interacted was immense. As this new family system develops, ultimately people are going to respond to the younger son because this little girl is going to demand that they do, and it will happen through the mother. The little girl's job now is to pay attention to all these people because I told her to.

Woman: That's fascinating, because you really used the person who is least troubled. Other therapists would say there is no problem with this girl and the mother.

Well, there isn't a *problem* with anybody. I don't believe in problems. The important point is this: not only do I utilize the system that is there, *I use the existing system to create a new system.* In order to do that, I have to determine who is the one person in the system who will be able to change all the others. Very often it's not the aggressive, boisterous person who will be able to do that. People often think that persuasion comes with noise, and it doesn't. Persuasion comes with *tenacity.* People who are very expressive are also very changeable. Anyone who explodes in anger will also have severe polarity responses the other way.

Too often in family therapy the therapist works with a person who is easy to change, which of course means that the family is going to be able to change him back just as easily. If you change someone who is symptomatic, someone who is flipping out, someone who is already responding massively to the family, that person is going to be *really* easy for the family to change back. The person who has the symptoms will be the *last* one that you want to work with. The very fact that the family system can produce schizophrenia or anorexia or whatever means that the symptomatic person is easy to influence. If you can influence him into being normal, then the family is going to be able to change him right back. So you've got to get at him from another angle. The family member you want to go after is the one who is really *tenacious.* If you make a change in a really tenacious individual, everybody else will bounce around for a while, but eventually they will adjust to the way that person has changed.

Man: Can you recontextualize reframing a family system in terms of the problems that occur in business organizations?

Sure. In many ways, a business is just like an extended family, and much of what we have discussed can be applied directly. However, you have to change some of your verbal and nonverbal behaviors to be acceptable to the business world. For instance, you don't talk about the "unconscious mind," you talk about "habits," and you may need to wear a suit instead of a sport shirt. You also have to change some of your basic presuppositions.

For instance, in NLP we presuppose that choice is always better than non-choice. That is usually not true in business. There are a few business contexts where you want a lot of variability and creativity, but often a lot of effort goes into standardizing and routinizing human beings to make them dependable. You don't want assembly-line workers always trying out new ways of doing their jobs, or doing it blindfolded for variety.

Another thing you have to be aware of in the business context is that there is a certain amount of secrecy and paranoia whenever you deal with anything that business people think gives them a competitive advantage. In the therapeutic context there is no such thing as a "trade secret." As soon as someone has a new idea, he tries to tell *everyone* about it so he can get some recognition. Businesses often spend a lot of money developing new techniques, and when these are successful, they try to hold on to them as long as they can.

There is also a lot of conservatism in business people, which is based on two things: (1) they don't have a good understanding of how a business organization works, and (2) they have found out the hard way that often when they try something new, it fouls up the system.

You often see this happen whenever a major position in the managerial or executive area of a corporation is vacated by promotion, dismissal, or retirement. The organization will almost always decide to search *externally* for a replacement. That's a behavioral statement that says business people have no idea what the qualities are that characterize a good manager or executive. Since they don't know, they have no basis for training or selection except a person's "track record." Typically they don't want to take an employee from another position within their organization. If they had explicit criteria for what an executive position requires, it would be much more cost-effective to train people within the organization.

Even after a successful external search, when the new executive steps into the organization, typically everything in that organization deteriorates for a period of time. If the new executive really is effective, she will ultimately reorganize her departments, and usually she will fire or transfer several personnel in the process.

At least part of what goes on is that each manager tends to have a style of information handling which is unique. Since there isn't any explicit model of information handling, people fly by the seat of their pants *at least* as much in business as they do in therapy. One aspect of a managerial style is the amount of specificity or detail that a manager requires in reporting relationships.

Over a number of years a manager's staff learns what level of detail she is going to insist on, and they adjust their own reporting procedures to take that into account. Soon their reporting is running at just about the level of detail that is required by the manager they are reporting to. After that relationship has been established for any length of time, the staff person reporting will be upset if the manager asks for more or less detail.

To ask for more detail will be perceived by the staff person—particularly at the unconscious level—as being a challenge to his competency. "Why is she asking for more detail than I had to provide before? Does this mean she doesn't trust my judgement in reporting in this area?" The resulting negative interpersonal relationships can be very troublesome.

To ask for less detail can also cause problems. The reporting person offers a certain level of detailed information, but the new manager waves that off and asks for a more global judgement. All she wants is a "go/no-go" decision. Then the reporting person feels incomplete, and as if he and his work are not valued. He feels that the information he has worked so hard to develop is not being utilized. He also becomes concerned that now he has the responsibility for making *decisions,* instead of just the responsibility for gathering and presenting information. He may become quite nervous about keeping information which he traditionally had passed on to the manager and therefore no longer had any responsibility for.

One of the most powerful and immediate interventions is to instruct an incoming manager/executive in the notion of control of the quality of information. This allows you to do for verbal information the same thing that blow-up technology does for aerial photography. It allows you to control the detail of the information. You can have the most detailed, highest quality information possible, or you can reduce it to a simple decision: a "go/no-go" signal.

Once a manager is taught this, then she gains a sense of being able to exercise quality control down that information network that leads from her desk to the point of production or service. If she has no confidence that what she decides and plans can be transmitted—maintaining a high quality representation through the entire network that's going to have to respond to the change—then she doesn't make waves. She leaves things running adequately, and that's why you get the mediocrity and conservatism that is traditional in business. Any change runs a risk of a misrepresentation or misinterpretation somewhere along that chain. Therefore, it makes sense to be quite conservative.

With this understanding, a manager can exercise full control over the quality of the information flow within her network. She can make changes with the assurance that her representations will be communicated with high quality and detail. Then she can set standards of excellence as opposed to standards of mediocrity.

Once a manager has an appreciation of the notion of exercising control over the quality of information, she will be quite sensitive to that when she takes a new position. She will realize that the people who are reporting to her, and her peers, and the people she reports to, all have certain typical quality requirements for the information they process. In many instances we have taught a manager who is stepping into a new position to establish a positive frame by saying to her staff: "My understanding is that this is a well-oiled team that I'm joining, etc." Next she explicitly brings up the notion of quality of information, and that certain adjustments will need to be made.

"You all had important and significant relationships with my predecessor. She had her own personal style, and you all learned—both consciously and deliberately, and by habit—how to present information to her. I'm different. I don't even know how I'm different, specifically, but for the next few weeks or a month, I want you to be particularly sensitive—and I will also—to the fact that there are some occasions on which I'll need very specific, very detailed, high quality information. At other times I'm going to simply ask you for a 'go/no-go' opinion."

That way of framing the transition is both a reframe and a future-pace. It specifies the outcome: developing an adequate level of information flow. It alerts the staff that there will be some adjustments, because there are going to be differences. The new manager is not God and doesn't know what the differences will be specifically, since she was never exposed to the quality control measures that the previous manager used. That allows the staff to take a deep sigh of relief and say "OK. She's saying that she recognizes there are going to be adjustments made, and she wants my cooperation in achieving the outcome: finding an appropriate level of specificity in reporting information."

Man: So a generalization that you could make from that example is that you need to be careful to frame any change in such a way that the people affected by it will respond in a positive way.

Yes, exactly. And that may mean framing changes differently for different levels or departments within an organization. Every maneuver in a business organization has to be done in such a way that it makes sense within the perceptual frame of the people who are affected. A five-year plan, if it were transmitted in its entirety to an assembly-line worker, would make no sense at all. For the assembly-line worker, the five-year plan has to be presented in terms of what happens to him and his job. To talk about the financial background and so forth would simply be confusing to him. It's literally information that he doesn't need to know. The description of a five-year plan at the executive level is not part of the perceptual reality of the assembly-line worker. It has to be relativized to his perceptual frame.

For example, I had a friend who was hired as the chief executive officer of a large firm. He is one of the few really high-quality business communicators that I know of. He has a really fine sensitivity to nonverbal behavior, and so on. One class of employees at the main headquarters of this firm was being operated by a time clock. The workers punched in every morning, punched out at noon, punched back in after lunch, and punched out in the evening. My friend has a philosophy that machines should never supervise or run people. One of the first changes he made after he'd spent a month or so taking over the reins as chief executive officer, was to remove the time clock. He explained to his primary staff his principle about not wanting machines to run people in his organization. He presented a frame to them which was adequate for their understanding, and then ordered all the time clocks removed on a Friday evening.

Now, consider the situation for the employees on Monday morning. They had been punching the time clock for years. No matter what happened on the way to work, or the night before, punching the clock was what hypnotists call a "reinduction signal" for them; it was an anchor that triggered access to all the skills and states of consciousness which were appropriate for effective performance at work. The time clock provided a signal in all representational systems. You see the clock, you push the card in kinesthetically, and you hear that funny sound as it punches the card.

My friend had inadvertently removed the exact anchor that they needed to perform successfully. The efficiency of the organization dropped by half in the first week or so after he had done this. I happened to arrive about a week later, and everyone was really upset. The solution that I came up with turned things around quite nicely. I proposed that he issue a short little statement to the first-line supervisors to pass on to the employees on Friday afternoon. This statement explained his belief that it was inappropriate for people to be run by machines. In his organization he wanted people to run people. Consistent with that, he had removed the time clock which had been there. And when they came to work on Monday morning, they would be interested to notice their supervisor standing in the position where the time clock used to be, and they could feel quite good about the fact that they could see a smile on the face of the supervisor—something they had never seen on the face of the time clock. The supervisors were told to say "good morning" and shake the hand of each employee as he came in. This provided a direct bridging, replacing the time clock by the supervisor in all representational systems. I'm sure that for the majority of employees, when they saw the face of the supervisor, they actually saw a superimposed image of the time clock! That gave them immediate access to the skills and states of consciousness that were required for efficient work.

That reframed the change, and preserved the signal function of the time clock. As a matter of fact, there was a productivity overrun. The employees bounced past previous efficiency levels for the next week. Then things settled down to slightly above previous levels. Business people know that if they let routines develop efficiently, then any change will probably disrupt them. However, if they very explicitly bridge or future-pace the changes to specify the way that they want them to operate, they can reduce the risk of disrupting the organization when they make changes.

Man: So is that reframing, or is it a future-pace?

It's both. You see, if you make a change without establishing an explicit frame around it, that leaves the employees to make up their own frames. So some of them might think "They've taken away my time clock, and that's just a way for them to disrupt my routine so that I don't perform my job well, because they're going to try to get rid of me." It doesn't matter exactly what the workers hallucinate. The point is that the frames they select may be ones in which the change is considered inappropriate or disruptive. The maneuver I described recontextualized the change so that the workers could make a positive response at the appropriate time and place.

Man: For several years I worked as a lab chemist. I took off my white lab coat every Friday afternoon, and I'd have complete amnesia for anything connected with the lab until I put on my coat again the next Monday morning. As I put it on I'd ask myself "Now what was I doing Friday afternoon?"

That's a nice example. Imagine what would have happened if someone had taken away all the lab coats!

All behavior takes place in some context, and that context is the anchor for a certain set of responses. Framing is another word for contextualization, and reframing is recontextualization. Sometimes you do that by changing the actual external context. More often you change the internal context—the way a person internally frames and understands events—so as to get a different response. Whenever you do this in a system, you have to take into account how the entire system operates to be sure that the changes you make are ecological.

VI

Reframing Dissociated States: Alcoholism, Drug Abuse, etc.

There are certain conditions that have to exist in order for six-step reframing to be effective. If you have someone who is severely dissociated, you can't expect reframing to work. Alcoholics, drug addicts, manic-depressives, and multiple personalities are all severely dissociated. Often people who overeat or smoke also fall into the same category. I'm going to talk primarily about alcoholics as an example. But I want you to understand that what I'm saying also applies to all the other examples of extreme dissociation.

If you ask the alcoholic in a sober state about his experiences while he is drunk, he will usually be partly or totally amnesic. Similarly, if you ask him while he is drunk to talk about experiences that he has when he is sober, typically he finds it difficult to offer you any information. That's one of several pieces of evidence you might use to notice that a person is dissociated: the fact that when he is operating out of one model of the world, he does not have access to experiences and resources that he has when he is operating from the other model of the world. He is a multiple personality in the sense that he has two distinct ways of operating in the world which never co-exist in his experience. The two are never in his body or his behavior at the same time.

The thing that really makes reframing work is that you develop a channel to the unconscious. By unconscious I mean the part of the person that is forcing him to do the behavior he consciously wants to change, or preventing him from doing the behavior that he consciously wants to be able to do. Reframing is a two-level communication whereby you talk with whatever part of him is conscious, and use involuntary responses to communicate with the part that is responsible for the behavior that is the focus of the change.

Typically the part of the alcoholic that brings him to your office is the sober part. That's the one who walks in. However, the sober part is already fully committed to being sober, so you don't have to do anything with that part. That's the part that already has lots of appropriate understandings about the disadvantages of drinking, but can't do anything about it. If you work with that part, you can get completely congruent responses about making changes. However, as soon as he goes into a bar, he'll be drinking again. What you need is access to the part of the person that gets him to go on binges, because that's the part of him that is running the show with respect to drinking. Since these two parts of the person are severely dissociated, while he is in one state, you cannot communicate with the other state. So when an alcoholic walks into your office in a sober state, it's extremely difficult to get access to the part that drinks, which is the part you need to change.

Most of the problems people have involve incongruity, or what is often called "conflict." There is a mismatch, an incongruence, between the part of a person that makes him do something, and the part of the person that wants him to stop. Usually this incongruence is *simultaneous:* the person behaviorally expresses both parts simultaneously. For example, someone may say "I want to be assertive" in a very soft voice. The two parts are somewhat dissociated, but they express themselves at the same time.

In alcoholism or substance abuse there is a different kind of dissociation in which the incongruence is expressed *sequentially* over time. The sober part and the drunk part are *so* separate that they don't express themselves at the same time in the person's experience. They manifest themselves in sequence: first one, and later the other.

The six-step reframing format is designed to deal with simultaneous incongruity. Rather than make up an entirely different approach for sequential incongruity, you can just change a sequential incongruity into a simultaneous one, and use what you already know how to do: six-step reframing.

This kind of maneuver is common in other fields. A good mathematician will always attempt to reduce a complex problem to some other simpler problem that she already knows how to solve. If you take a difficult problem and reduce it to some other simpler problem, then you can solve it more easily.

The easiest way to change a sequential incongruity into a simultaneous one is through the use of anchoring. In the case of alcoholism, first I get access to the drunk part and anchor it. Then I anchor the sober part. Finally I collapse the two anchors in order to force the two states to co-exist.

When someone walks into your office, the sober part is right there, so that's easy to anchor. Getting access to the alcoholic part requires a bit more skill. One way to get that access is essentially to do a hypnotic induction in which you regress him to the last time he was drunk, or to some other good example of the alcoholic state, by gathering detailed sensory-grounded information from him about his experience of being alcoholic. "Go back to the last time. What do you feel like just as you are about to take the first drink? What was it like the last time you binged? Where were you sitting? What did you see? What did you hear? What did you say when you ordered the first drink? What was it? What did it look like? You can smell it now. And what exactly did it taste like? And how do you know when you are really drunk?"

If you ask your client these kinds of questions, you will see a definite shift in his behavior. As he gives you this information, he will begin to re-experience the drunk state. You'll see breathing and body posture shifts, and you'll hear a shift in the client's voice tone, tempo, and timbre qualities. You'll see a difference in facial expressions and in body movements. If you feed back those components of his experience that alter his state the most, you will amplify his experience of being alcoholic. When you see a really definitive shift, you can anchor that state.

Usually thinking of the smell and taste will take the person right back to the alcoholic state. Olfactory access is probably the fastest way to regress. Any time you want someone to re-experience some past state, if you can find an odor associated with that state, just having the person smell that smell will immediately take him back to that past state in all systems. Because of the way smells are processed neurologically, they have a much more direct impact on behavior and responses than other sensory inputs do.

Man: You called this method a hypnotic induction. Are you saying that any time you ask someone to go back, you've induced a hypnotic state or begun an induction?

There might be a question of semantics here about whether you want to call it hypnosis or not. I wouldn't call it that overtly; that might elicit resistance from the client. But, in my perceptions, what I've just described is indistinguishable from an "official" trance induction. The depth may vary a bit, but the actual procedure and the internal strategies a person employs are identical. So one way to get access would be this kind of an induction. What's another way to access the alcoholic part?

Man: Overlap. Have him see himself drunk, and then fit himself into his body in the picture.

OK. What's another way to get access to the alcoholic part? You should have half a dozen choices.

Man: Give him a drink.

Then you would have the problem of getting access to the sober part.

Man: Take him to a bar.

Yes. That's using context as an anchor to elicit the state.

Another way you can do it is to pace and lead your client into a drunken state. Mirror your client and then begin to talk, walk, and act like a drunk yourself.

Another possibility is to give him direct instructions. "I want you to pretend to be drunk." He'll probably say "But that's what I'm trying to avoid!" Then you say "Yes, I understand that, and in order to avoid it, you first need to have the choice of pretending." There's no actual logic to that statement, but it sounds meaningful, and will get your client to do it.

Once he's begun to pretend, you can increase the quality of the access with feedback. "Ah, come on. Slur your speech a little more. Let's have a little more body sway—a little more tremor here. Are your eyes really blurred yet?" Give him verbal and behavioral feedback to adjust his behavior until you have a good access to his alcoholic part.

It's important to have a variety of ways to get access when you are dealing with people who have severely dissociated sequential incongruities. If you're not satisfied with the access you get using one maneuver, you can always shift to another.

Once you have access, anchor it so that you can get it back. When you have a good anchor for both his sober part and his alcoholic part, then you are ready to "blow his brains out," technically speaking. You collapse anchors for those two states by firing both anchors simultaneously, making both of those states occur at the same time. I generally use kinesthetic anchors for this, because he cannot get away from my touch.

The visible results of collapsing anchors on two states as different as sober and drunk states are remarkable. It definitely induces an altered state. I've seen a client reeling in states of semi-consciousness or unconsciousness for anywhere from three minutes up to an hour and a half. You will see what looks like total confusion; he will literally be unable to organize any coherent response. Sometimes his body movements are out of control, and he has whole-body convulsions. I've actually had a client go into a psychotic break and attempt to do anything he could to get my hands off him, because he knows that his experience is connected with my touch.

What's going on is that I'm jamming together two physiological states that were absolutely dissociated. He has never had those feelings simultaneously in his body. He has never tried to breathe the drunk way and the sober way at the same time, or had the muscle tone or the internal states of consciousness associated with those two states at the same time. In a sense, he was a multiple personality, and you are slamming those two parts together. This really is a sort of shock treatment, and some people have even spontaneously described it that way. The difference is that it's not externally induced, and it will only attain intensities that people can cope with. It's ecological in that sense.

When you have finished collapsing those two anchors, the integration is in no way complete. It simply allows you to have a bridge, so that the alcoholic and the sober person co-exist in the same body at the same time. The two parts are no longer mutually exclusive and completely dissociated. That makes it possible for you to do reframing. This is a *precondition* for establishing an effective channel of communication through the sober part to the alcoholic part which knows about the drinking problem and what needs it satisfies.

Woman: What do you do while you hold the two anchors and the person is confused for an hour and a half?

I only have to hold the two anchors until the integration is well underway. Then I just make sure he is in a place where he won't hurt himself; that's about all that's necessary. It's also useful to introduce lots of post-hypnotic suggestions while he is in this state of confusion. He will be utterly defenseless at that point. Make sure that your post-hypnotic suggestions are content-free so that you don't impose. You might say "As you continue to thrash around, notice that there's a direct relationship between how intense the feelings are now and how rapidly you'll gain the behavioral choices you want with respect to drinking."

Since he can't defend against suggestions at that point, you have a tremendous responsibility for the way you frame the suggestions. "You will no longer *want to drink*" would be the most disastrous way of approaching it. It would be better to keep your mouth shut than to say something like that. You need to talk in positive terms about what *will* happen in the future, rather than what won't. "You will be able to find alternative ways to *satisfy yourself* in the way that alcohol *used to*" is much better. When you talk about the alcohol, you need to speak in the past tense, presupposing that he will no longer use it. All of the hypnotic language patterns described in *Patterns I* and *Trance-formations* are appropriate here. If he says "But I don't understand you," you can respond "Of course you don't understand me, and the less you understand me consciously, the more you will be able to reorganize unconsciously in positive ways."

Man: When you collapse anchors for being drunk and being sober, don't you run the risk of making the person act drunk all the time?

That is a reasonable concern. Giving hypnotic process instructions such as those I've been describing is a way to make sure that the integration you get from collapsing anchors is useful. You say things about how those two states can begin to blend in such a way that the person incorporates all that is useful and valuable in each state, losing nothing, so that the integration can serve as the foundation for more choice, etc.

Let me remind you that this is only a preliminary step. I'm deliberately breaking down barriers between two dissociated states and inducing confusion. I'm literally violating a discrimination, an internal sorting process, that the alcoholic has unconsciously used to make himself effective in life. After doing this, I'm going to have to clean it up with reframing. All I've done is create the precondition for reframing. I now have access to the drunk part and the sober part at the same time. I have reduced a very difficult situation of sequential incongruity to something I can cope with: simultaneous incongruity.

After he recovers and is relatively coherent, I would simply proceed with six-step reframing to secure specific alternative behaviors, and to future-pace the new behaviors appropriately. At that point you reframe in the same way that you would reframe anything else.

However, one thing is very important. If you're working with something like drinking, smoking, or over-eating, you have to be sure that the new alternatives not only work better than the old choice, but that the new alternatives are *more immediate*. You need to be very sensitive to criteria, and "best" in addictions usually has a lot to do with immediacy. If your new choice for relaxing is taking a vacation, that's not nearly as quick and easy as eating a piece of chocolate cake that's already in the refrigerator. It's a lot *easier* to smoke a cigarette than to meditate or go running on the beach. You can't run on the beach when you're in an elevator, but you can smoke a cigarette.

You can build in immediacy by specifying it at step four. "Go in and find three choices that are more acceptable, more immediate, more available, easier, and faster than the one you are using now." Often people don't do that when they do reframing. Their clients then come up with long-range alternatives that don't work, because they need something really immediate.

Another thing you can do with any addict is to make his actual feeling of desiring the drug an anchor for something else. The person needs to experience the feeling itself as having a different meaning. Right now he has a certain feeling that he interprets as a craving for a drink, and it pumps him into drinking. You can put him in a trance and make that feeling *mean something else.* The feeling of "craving" could now lead to intense curiosity about his surroundings, for instance.

I've used this approach of collapsing anchors and reframing effectively with alcoholics and heroin addicts in one session. I have up to two-year follow-ups now, and it's been successful.

After you've done reframing and found new choices for the secondary gain of the alcohol or the drug, you need to test your work. With an alcoholic, my test is to give him a drink and find out if he can stop after just one. I consider that the only valid test of whether I have done a complete and integrated piece of work. With heroin, I'd find out what anchors used to trigger off shooting up, and then I'd send the client out into that context to test his new choices.

Lou: That's really amazing. I've worked with people in AA, and they think that "Once an alcoholic, always an alcoholic." Are you saying it's possible to cure alcoholics so that they can drink but not get drunk? They can go into a bar and have one drink and then walk away from it?

Definitely. When I work with an alcoholic, three months later I'll go out to some bar with him and have a drink. I watch and listen closely for any of the behavioral shifts that used to be associated with the alcoholic state. That will test whether I've done an integrated piece of work. I want to find out if he can have a drink and have the same response to it that I have; namely, that it's just a drink. I'm going to find out if he can perform the behavior that previously was automatic and compulsive without being compelled to go on and have more. Alcohol is an anchor, and using that old anchor is a good test of my work.

I don't mean to criticize AA, by the way. For decades AA was the only organization around that could assist alcoholics effectively. Historically it was a wonderful thing, and at this point we need to move on to something else. AA has a non-integrative approach, and people in AA are almost always bingers. They believe that "Once an alcoholic, always an alcoholic," and for their people, that's true. If one of them sits down and has one drink, he won't be able to stop; he'll continue on a binge.

The claims I am making would be outrageous to anyone in AA, and also to the belief systems that most therapists have been taught. They are not incredible if you approach addiction from an NLP standpoint. From that standpoint, all you need to do is 1) collapse anchors on the dissociation, 2) get communication with the part that makes him drink, 3) find out what secondary gain—camaraderie, relaxation, or whatever—the alcohol gets for him, and 4) find alternative behaviors that get the secondary outcomes of alcohol but don't produce the damage that alcohol does. A person will always make the best choice available to him. If you offer him better choices than drinking to get all the positive secondary gains of alcohol, he will make good selections.

Lou: How would you deal with someone in AA then? They seem to believe that nothing will work except AA, and they won't listen to anything else.

Yes. AA is a "true believer" system. If you're working with someone who belongs to AA, you just accept that. You say "You're absolutely right." Then you might add "Since you are so convinced that 'Once an alcoholic, always an alcoholic' it won't be any threat to you if we try something different, because it will fail anyway." When someone has a strong belief system, I accept it, and then find ways to work within it. Then I can always induce a covert trance and just program directly.

Your question about belief systems reminds me of something a medical doctor in England tried with heroin addicts. He had a clinic with a large methadone program to keep his clients from experiencing withdrawal. Once he had a new group of addicts coming in, so he did a controlled experiment in which he randomly divided the addicts into two groups. The control group just got methadone as usual. He trained all the subjects in the experimental group to be really good trance subjects. The two groups would come in at the same time for their methadone, but the experimental group would go to his office. There this doctor would put them all into a trance and have them hallucinate shooting up. At the end of six weeks, no one in either group had shown any withdrawal symptoms. At that point he told the experimental group what he had done, and all but two of them immediately went into withdrawal! That is an indication to me that the body is capable of handling the chemical imbalances if the person's belief system is consistent with doing so.

After I've tested for ecology, and to make sure the new choices work, I usually give the person something that he can actually get hold of to use as an anchor for his new choices. It might be a coin, or something else that he can put in his pocket and carry around with him. This will help take care of the old motor programs associated with drinking, smoking, or whatever. Part of the choice of drinking, for example, is actually going through the motions of holding onto a glass and moving it up to the mouth. Having some tangible physical anchor gives the person something else to do with his hands.

People sometimes consider AA members obnoxious because they don't want anyone else around them to drink either. Their reason for this, of course, is that seeing someone else drink stimulates that choice in them by identification. Since the old motor programs haven't been integrated into having new choices, this elicits the old drinking behavior in them. When you don't have this kind of sensitivity in an ex-drinker, that's another good indication that you've got full integration.

Woman: I have a question about the anchoring. Would you anchor the sober state first, when the client walks in, and then access the drunk state?

There are lots of ways you can do this. You don't even need to anchor the sober state in order to get integration. After your client has accessed the drunk state, you can say "Hey! Pay attention here. What do you think you are doing, acting like a drunk in my office?" Then you'll get the sober part back. Your client will say "Oh, I'm sorry! I thought that's what you wanted me to do. I was just trying to follow your instructions." You continue with "What? Pull yourself together here." You then hit the anchor for the alcoholic state at the same time that you are saying "Stay sober; pay attention here."

Woman: Is the sober state a powerful enough anchor to be collapsed with the drunk state?

The sober state does need to be as intense as the drunk state. If you collapse anchors and don't get an integration, but rather something which looks like the drunk state, that indicates that you need to get the sober state anchored more intensely. I would stop doing the integration and say "Hey, wake up! Come on! Hey, wake up!" I would bring him back to a sober state completely. I'd stand him up, move him around, give him a cup of coffee, etc. When he's sober again, I'd ask

"Do you know where you are? Do you know what you are doing here? What's your purpose for being here?" I'd get the sober part back fully, and then I'd anchor it.

Man: Couldn't accessing the alcoholic state be dangerous if the client gets violent when he's drunk?

If that's the case you'll need to take extra precautions. You would use visual or auditory anchors instead of kinesthetic anchors. You might keep six feet and a chair between you and him, with the exit behind you. Or you may be well-trained in martial arts and have full confidence in your ability to protect yourself, as I do. You deserve to be sure that your physical and psychological integrity is always preserved. You are a psychotherapist; you are not being paid to put your body or your psyche on the line.

Woman: Would you be able to interrupt such a violent state if you'd anchored the sober state first? You could then use that anchor to bring the client back out of the alcoholic state.

Sure, but don't use a kinesthetic anchor for that. If you're close enough to touch someone who is acting violent, then he is close enough to hit you. An anchor that interrupts a rage state can be a good choice, as long as you can fire it from a distance. You can use auditory or visual anchors for that. A student of ours is teaching foster parents in halfway houses how to use non-tactile anchors to interrupt rage states. Depending upon the clientele you deal with, you may need that. You can anchor from a safe distance by a clap of your hands or some gesture. Another way to do it is to start talking to him using one voice tone, and as he goes into the alcoholic state, you change to another voice tone. Your voice tone then becomes an anchor. Then if he starts to go into a rage state, you say "Hold on a minute" in the tone of voice you used for his normal state.

Man: I appreciate your comment about giving content-free posthypnotic suggestions to the alcoholic after collapsing anchors. I think that many programs for alcoholics have failed because the therapist or agency has tried to come up with specific alternative behaviors to drinking. They tell the alcoholic "Let's all go bowling" or "Let's all go do leatherwork." That approach is painfully ineffective.

Absolutely. Bowling and leatherwork are *very* unlikely to be able to satisfy the secondary gain in drinking.

Man: It seems as if it would be a good idea to have an indefinite amount of time available if you're going to use this approach with alcoholics. This might be difficult to do in hour-long sessions.

Yes, that would be ideal. However, you live in a world of hourly schedules. I'm not a good model for a practicing psychotherapist in this respect. I don't make my living doing psychotherapy anymore. I don't even do psychotherapy anymore. I did for a while to make sure that I tested all the patterns I'm teaching you with a wide range of presenting problems. So when I offer you something, I know it works, and I can demonstrate to you that it works. However, even when I had a private practice, I wouldn't schedule more than two or three clients a day, and I'd leave huge gaps between them so that I could run the session anywhere from ten seconds, which was the shortest time I've ever worked with a client, up to something like six and a half hours, which was the longest.

Man: You've got to tell us about the ten-second client!

You can easily do a content reframe in ten seconds. But I was thinking of a man whose presenting problem was that he couldn't stand up to people who were aggressive. As soon as he told me that, I threw him out of the office! In those days, a group of us had arrangements with each other and with some of the neighbors that they would interact with our clients in certain ways when we offered certain signals. So as soon as I threw him out, I yelled to my wife "Catch him!" So Judith Ann strolled out on the front porch just as this man walked by almost whimpering "He threw me out." She started talking to him, "Oh, no! Did John do it again? Did he throw you out without any sympathy, without any sensitivity to your needs as a human being?"

At this point, of course, she had perfect rapport. He was saying "Oh, take care of me! Help me!" As a friend who happened to be there, she then told him how to cope with the situation. It took ten seconds for me to access the problem state, and then she picked up the client and programmed him in the next few minutes.

If you work in an agency, you have lots of opportunities to do that kind of thing. You can teach your clients things through role-playing, and the learning will transfer if you future-pace them well. However, it will always work better if you *don't announce that the frame is role-playing;* you just *do* it. You can behave in exactly the way that they can't cope with, thereby accessing that limited state fully and purely. They're not just pretending or thinking about it. Then if you have somebody pick them up on the bounce, you can do really amazing things very quickly.

Woman: From what you've said, we can assume that alcoholics and hard drug abusers have very dissociated states, and also be alert that some people who smoke or overeat have these sequential incongruities. Are there other indicators of sequential incongruity?

I don't know of any fail-safe way of detecting sequential incongruity, but there are some things you can watch for. Sometimes I've done what I thought was really great work and it didn't work at all because I didn't detect sequential incongruity. With these "almost multiple personality" cases, sometimes whatever you do seems to work really well. You get all the appropriate responses; you get new choices for the client, you test and future-pace and everything. Then he leaves, and when he comes back the next week he can barely remember what you did last week, and can't even verify whether it worked or not. However, you can tell that your work hasn't been effective at all. If the problem is something like smoking or overweight, it may be very obvious.

When this happens, you can suspect sequential incongruity. The main guideline I use to identify this is to notice that over some period of time you see really radical shifts in a client's behavior. When people who overeat tell you things like "I find myself staring at a pile of chicken bones, and it's as if I just woke up" that's a good indication of sequential incongruity. Sometimes you can suspect it if their behavior sounds very strange, or if your work goes too easily.

When I suspect sequential incongruity, I sometimes use altered states of consciousness to run tests. For example, I had a lady who had a hysterical paralysis of the leg. She came in and we did reframing, and wham! her leg was unparalyzed. I immediately paralyzed it again and she was furious at me. "My leg was fine, and now it's bad again. Why did you do this to me?" I said "That was just *too* easy. I know there is a part in there that's going to sneak out later on."

Without actually leaving the time-place coordinates of my office, I had her experience different life contexts internally. Her life was fairly limited. She went to the hospital, to the doctor's office, and spent the rest of her time at home. The part that objected to her leg being fine jumped out at home, and I agreed with the part's motivations. The part wanted her husband to do things around the house. Basically her husband was one of those "old-world" men who say "Women should do all the housework. The man's job is to go to work and earn money." It was a rather unique situation: she was rich, so he didn't have to go to work, but he still thought that she should do everything around the house. If she didn't, he beat her up. Of course, when her leg was paralyzed, *he* had to do things for *her*. Before we cured the paralysis, we had to do something about that. Otherwise, if she went home without paralysis, she would have to do all the housework.

Mary: So then what did you do?

I changed the husband. We engaged him in "assisting with his wife's rehabilitation program." I arranged for a limited improvement in her paralysis when I took her home. We told the husband "In order for the rehabilitation program to work, it is going to require perseverance on your part. She can do certain things now, but you should definitely not allow her to do other things, because we would run the risk of a relapse. And of course this program may take *years.*"

To try to get this woman to cope with her husband was too big a piece to do easily. I want you to think of outcomes in terms of chunking. The question I ask is "What's the biggest piece I can do quickly and expediently?" Is that going to be one simple reanchoring, or is it going to be a more complex piece? I start with the smallest piece I can do easily and build on that.

Man: So you make a minimal change in the system, get feedback, and make another minimal change—increasing the chunk size as you go, if you can do that.

Yes. I had one other woman like that who had radical hysterical symptoms. Both were out of the same mold. One had numb feet and the other had a paralyzed leg, and both had Italian husbands. I'm sure not every Italian husband is like that, but these were both Italians from the "old country" and neither was married to an Italian woman. These men both had very strong cultural belief systems which were not congruent with their wives' beliefs, or with American culture.

Let me give you another example of sequential incongruity with which I used a very different approach. I don't always collapse anchors first and then go for a completely integrated outcome. There are other ways to deal with sequential incongruity. A psychiatrist friend of mine had a secretary who was as classic a manic-depressive as you could have. You could even predict the day of the year when she would flip. You got six months of the "up" part where everything was wonderful. She lost weight; she got really attractive and vibrant, and got all the work done. And then, on July 31st, suddenly the other part came out. She gained weight and got depressed and incompetent and so on. This had been going on for twelve years when I met the psychiatrist. He was too fascinated to fire her, even though six months of each year she was totally incompetent. He always knew that at a certain time of year, the whole thing would switch around, and she would take care of all the things that she hadn't done in the previous six months.

The fascinating thing is that when I worked with her, no matter which part of her I worked with, or what I changed, or what she learned to do—even tasks like learning to type on a typewriter that had the keys in a different configuration—when the parts flipped over, none of it transferred. She was almost like two people, although she wasn't a complete multiple personality. In each of her states she had some memory of the other state: she remembered where she lived, and most of what had happened in the other state. But learnings and personal changes never transferred back and forth. So, of course, the one that was "up" would go out and make changes and accomplish things, and the one that was "down" would go hide. One of them kept becoming more and more confident and capable, and the other one more and more depressed and incompetent.

When you have people like this, one of the things that you have to do somehow—no matter what else you do—is to integrate those two parts. But in order to integrate them, you've got to get them together in the same time-place coordinates. That's not very easy, because the one that's not in your office can be very hard to get to. You could anchor one, and wait six months and then anchor the other. And if you had really good anchors, you might be able to pull them together.

One approach that has worked really well for me is "pseudo-orientation in time." That is a hypnotic phenomenon in which you hypnotize the client and you project her into the future in increments. Then you have her arouse from the trance believing, for instance, that this is not her second visit but her sixteenth. It's now three months later, so you can ask her about the past. Pseudo-orientation in time is a neat way to get a client to teach you about therapy. You hypnotize her and tell her you have cured her, and in a moment you are going to arouse her from the trance. It is now August, and she is returning for her last visit, and she has agreed to document some of how all these changes took place.

Then you bring her out of the trance and say "Hi! How have you been?" "Oh, I've been wonderful." Then you say "I have such a bad memory. Will you recall for me exactly what you consider the most essential thing that I did which changed you?" Your client will then tell you really great things to do! A lot of the techniques that we teach people in workshops have come from doing pseudo-orientation in time.

It takes either a fairly good hypnotic subject or rigorous hypnotic training to be able to do this. It's a complicated trance phenomenon. Of course, once you've become used to doing it, it's not complicated anymore.

Another thing I do is to set up a signal for the different states. I try to detect where the polarities lie. If they are temporal, then I set up signals for the different time zones. Some of them are contextual: some people have sequential polarities depending upon whether they are at work or at home, for example. Some people switch between vacation and everyday life. If it has to do with a drug substance, then of course I set up an anchor that induces the substance state.

When I have good anchors for both parts, I can literally carry on conversations with each one sequentially. With the manic-depressive woman I talked about earlier, I had anchors for a July visit, and for a December visit. I set up anchors not only covertly, but also directly hypnotically: "When I touch you on the knee, it will be July" so that I could literally go back and forth between the two parts and work with both of them. So when I did reframing, I'd induce one state and I'd say "Now, you go and ask the part . . ." and then I'd induce the other state and do the same thing. It was like doing reframing with two people at the same time.

I used to run groups where I would bring in ten or fifteen people and just start going around the room, using the six-step reframing model. The first week I would always do it with content, and then the next week when they came back, I could do it purely formally. I would have them pick something that they could talk about the first few times to make sure they could tell the difference between an intention and a behavior and that sort of thing, and I would go around the room and troubleshoot as they all went through the steps at the same time.

Man: But the two parts of the manic-depressive woman are in the same person. How do you reframe them to the same conclusion?

If you have sequential incongruity—somebody diets like crazy and then gains weight like crazy—that's actually only an incongruity at the level of content. At the formal level, the two parts are the same. Both are obsessions, and both of them show a loss of control. One is saying "I'll starve myself"; the other is saying "I'm going to eat everything in sight." At the content level, they are opposite, but at the formal level, they are exactly the same. Those people don't diet intelligently. They don't build up to a maintenance program slowly. It's always either crash diets or "pigging out." If you offered them anorexia, they'd take it! The solution has to take the part that overeats and give it some other way of getting what it wants so that it goes back to eating in moderation. And the part that diets like crazy also has to be reframed, because otherwise when you reframe the eating part, the diet part will go "Ahhhh! Now is my chance!" and go crazy, and then you will get a backlash in the other direction.

After I've worked with the two states in someone with a sequential incongruity, I usually build a part whose job is to integrate these two states, or I set up some kind of unconscious program to lapse together the times when they operate. With the secretary, the times were six months, so I didn't want to do it that way because it would have taken years to get anywhere. I decided to do time distortion: I went into the past and set up a program for integration to begin five years earlier and have the date of integration be the date she was in my office.

It didn't take me long to do this, because anybody who is that dissociated is a great hypnotic subject. She would *have* to be, or she couldn't be so dissociated in the first place. I did a hypnotic induction and arrived in her past as someone else, some shrink she had seen five years ago. As that shrink I installed the integration program in her unconscious, and then had her create all the necessary alterations in her history so that she could conclude the integration spontaneously in my office, five years later. Sometimes in order to be able to work these things out, you have to create a lot of personal history.

Woman: I have a client who became amnesic for everything preceding an incident in which he "came to" and found himself looking down the barrel of a shotgun, with a stick on the trigger to fire it. Now he's totally amnesic for his whole life prior to that time. As you might expect, he comes from a really awful family situation. He also has a lot of experience at dissociation, having been an alcoholic for a long time. Now he's a sober AA person.

I think you're talking about the same formal situation. What has he requested from therapy?

Woman: Well, his stated goal is to get his memory back.

That kind of goal reminds me of a kind of fairy tale from my childhood. When I was a little kid, my folks used to read me fairy tales at bedtime. I was the oldest of nine kids, and we used to have these big family storytimes that were really fun. It was a nice ritual.

One class of stories that my parents told used to drive me crazy. Some character would be walking along through the forest one day and suddenly he would meet a magical creature whose beard had gotten caught in a fallen tree. I could never figure out what kind of a magical creature would be stupid enough to get his beard caught in a fallen tree! The main character would save the magical creature, and the magical creature would say "You now have three wishes." The person would always blow it. He'd immediately say "I want to be immensely wealthy." Then the entire countryside would be destroyed and in ruins, and his family would be wiped out, because everything would be covered with gold.

That kind of story is a good metaphor about the need for the ecological protections we build into reframing. The character doesn't think about the secondary effects of his wish. He doesn't specify context or procedure; he just names a goal. Reaching the goal is much more disastrous than not having reached it at all. Consequently, the character always uses the second wish to reverse the ill effects of the first one. Then he says something like "I wish I had never met this creature." And that uses up his third wish. So he blows all three wishes and ends up back at zero.

Often people's conscious requests in therapy are a lot like that. People ask for things without any appreciation of their own personal context, or the larger family context in which they are embedded. So one of the ways in which I might proceed in your position, would be to act naive. I might act as if I am taking his request seriously, and arrange for him to go back and recall just a few things.

First I would set up a strong amnesia anchor. Then I would induce a trance in which I was guaranteed that I could create amnesia if I requested it. Then I would have him stay dissociated so he could view things from his past externally, and not be kinesthetically involved. Then I would ask his unconscious to pick three incidents from his personal history; one pleasant, one not so pleasant, and one disastrous, to give him some idea of the range of experiences in his personal history. After he has observed those, I would arouse him, and ask him for his response. If he wanted to continue, then I could. If he didn't want to continue, I would re-induce the trance, create amnesia for those recovered pieces of information, and then proceed to setting new goals.

Once a therapist brought in a trainee who wanted me to use hypnosis to discover something about her past. She believed that her older brother and a friend had raped her when she was eleven years old. She wasn't certain this had actually happened, and she wanted to know whether it was true. My response was "What difference would it make to you if you knew?" She had no answer to that question—it had never occurred to her. You might consider asking your client that.

Janet: Well, I have asked him, and he says he wants to remember so that he doesn't have to feel so funny when he runs into somebody that he used to know and doesn't remember. I feel like he's set up a task that is impossible for himself, because he doesn't *really* want to know.

That would be my first guess, too. He has consciously asked to recover a memory, so that's the goal, but he also has good reasons *not* to remember.

Janet: He was also in a VA hospital for awhile. He's very proud that they used sodium pentathol on him and got nothing! They also used hypnosis on him and it was unsuccessful in helping him recover the past. All he can remember are very precise details of the day that he woke up looking into the barrel of the shotgun.

I would probably go for his meta-goals then. "You want to recover memory. For what purpose?" "So that when I meet people from my past I would know how to treat them." "Oh, so what you really want is not to recover memory. You want a way of gracefully dealing with the situation of meeting people who claim to be from your past." One way to get that outcome for him would be to teach him a little "fluff." "Gosh, it's been so long! Where *was* it?" It's quite easy to teach him "fillers" that will gracefully elicit all the information he needs to respond appropriately.

Whenever there is a direct conflict on any level, you just jump up to the next level. You ask for the meta-outcome. "What will you gain from this? What purpose will this achieve for you?" Once you know this, you can offer alternatives that are much more elegant. He will soon give up his original request, because recovering his history will have no function for him anymore.

Janet: As far as I can tell, his family situation continues to be horrendous. I tried saying "Well, you can't remember anything, so why don't I just have your family tell you the good things that happened in your life?" His family couldn't come up with *anything!*

Another alternative would be to make him a good hypnotic subject, with the goal of creating a new personal history for him. Get him to agree to using hypnosis, not for recovery of his memories, but for building him a new personal history. If you got a bad one the first time around, go back and make yourself a better one. Everybody really ought to have several histories.

Janet: How would you do that?

Directly. You can say "Look, you're a talented guy, but you don't know where you came from. Where would you like to have come from?"

Janet: This is an unsophisticated farmer.

That makes it easier. The toughest of all clients to deal with are sophisticated psychotherapists, because they think they have to know every step of what you are doing. They have nosy conscious minds.

In the book *Uncommon Therapy* a case is described in which Milton Erickson built a set of past experiences for a woman. He created a history for her in which he appeared periodically as the "February Man." That case is an excellent source for studying the structure of creating alternate personal histories.

Fred: Is schizophrenia another example of sequential incongruity and dissociation?

People diagnosed as schizophrenic usually have certain aspects of themselves which are severely dissociated. However, the dissociation is generally simultaneous. For example, a schizophrenic may hear voices and think the voices come from outside of himself. The voices are dissociated, but both "parts" of the person are present at the same time.

Fred: OK. I have been working with schizophrenics for a long time. I have been using some of your techniques, but not as efficiently or precisely as I would like. What particular adjustments would you suggest with so-called schizophrenics?

From the way you phrased your question, I take it you've noticed that some people who are classified schizophrenic don't manifest the symptoms which other people with that label have. There are two ways in which working with a schizophrenic is different from working with any of the people here in this room.

One is that people labeled schizophrenic live in a different reality than the one most of us agree upon. The schizophrenic's reality is different enough that it requires a lot of flexibility on the part of the communicator to enter and pace it. That reality differs rather radically from the one that psychotherapists normally operate out of. So the issue of approach and rapport is the first difference between dealing with the so-called schizophrenic, and someone who doesn't have that label. To gain rapport with a schizophrenic you have to use all the techniques of body mirroring and cross-over mirroring, appreciating the metaphors the schizophrenic offers to explain his situation, and noticing his unique nonverbal behavior. That is a very demanding task for any professional communicator.

The second difference is that schizophrenics—particularly those who are institutionalized—are usually medicated. This is really the most difficult difference to deal with, because it's the same situation as trying to work with an alcoholic when he's drunk. There's a direct contradiction between the needs of psychiatric ward management and the needs of psychotherapy. Medication is typically used as a device for ward management. As a precondition to being effective in reframing, I need access to precisely the parts of the person that are responsible for the behaviors I'm attempting to change. Until I engage those parts' assistance in making alterations in behavior, I'm spinning my wheels—I'm talking to the wrong part of the person. The symptoms express the part of the person that I need to work with. However, the medications considered appropriate in a ward situation are just the medications which remove the symptoms and prevent access to that part of the person.

Working effectively with people who are medicated is a difficult and challenging task. I have done it a half-dozen times, but I don't particularly enjoy it. The medication itself is an extremely powerful anchor that is an obstacle to change.

Let me tell you a little horror story. A young man was wandering down the street of a large city after a party. He was a graduate student at the university there. He'd been smoking some dope and drinking a little bit of booze. He was wandering along, not really drunk, but certainly not sober. At about three o'clock in the morning he was picked up by the police and taken in for being drunk in public. They fingerprinted him and ran a check on him, and it turned out that he had been in the nearby state mental institution several years previously. When he was there, he'd been classified as a schizophrenic, and had the good fortune to run into a psychiatrist who is a really fine communicator. After the psychiatrist worked with this young man, he had altered his behavior, was released, and was doing quite nicely in graduate school. He'd been fine for years.

When the police discovered this history of "mental illness," they decided that his behavior wasn't the result of alcohol or drugs, but rather the result of a psychotic lapse. So they sent him back to the state mental hospital. He was put back on exactly the same ward he'd been on before, and given the same medication he'd been on before. Guess what happened? He became schizophrenic again. He was anchored right back into crazy behavior.

This kind of danger is my reason for insisting that the test for effective work with an alcoholic be exposure to the chemical anchor that used to access the dissociated alcoholic state—to have the client take a drink. Then you need to be able to observe whether taking a drink leads to a radical change in state—whether there is a radical shift in breathing and skin coloring, and all the other nonverbal indications of a change in state. If there is such a shift, then you don't yet have an integrated piece of work; you still have more integration to do.

If you take the challenge of working with institutionalized schizophrenics, you can make your work a lot more comfortable and a lot more effective if you make some arrangement with whomever is in charge of drugs on the ward. Being effective in a reasonable amount of time is going to depend upon your ability to work with people while they are *not* on drugs, or upon your ability to establish hypnotic dissociated states in which they are essentially independent of chemicals. Those are very difficult tasks; it's a real challenge.

Janet: I have a client who was diagnosed schizophrenic. She was on medication which she's off of now, but she's beginning to hear voices again. That's scaring her. She's very frightened.

Well, first of all, it doesn't frighten her. She has a physiological kinesthetic response to hearing the voices. At the conscious level she has named that response "being frightened." That may sound like semantics, but it's not. There's a huge difference between the two, and reframing will demonstrate that difference.

My first response to this woman would be to say "Thank God the voices are still there! Otherwise how would you know what to do next? How would you do any planning?" One or two generations earlier, a person who heard voices was characterized as being crazy. That's a statement about how unsophisticated we are in this culture about the organization and processing of the human mind. Voices are one of the three major modes in which we organize our experience to do planning and analysis. That's what distinguishes us from other species. So my first response is "Thank God! And now let's find out what they are trying to communicate to you." I might say "Good! Let me talk to them, too. Maybe they've got some really good information for us. So go inside and ask the voices what they are trying to tell you."

Janet: "How I should kill my mother."

"Good! Now, ask the voices what killing your mother would do for you." You go to the meta-outcome. If an internal part voices a goal which is morally, ethically, or culturally unacceptable, such as "kill my mother," then you immediately go for a frame in which that *is* an appropriate behavior. It may sound bizarre as you hear it, but it's quite appropriate given *some* context. The question is, can you discover the context? "What would killing your mother do for you? Ask the voices what they are trying to get for you by having you kill your mother."

The person is likely to interrupt you and say, "I don't want to kill my mother!" You can respond "I didn't say to kill your mother. I said to ask the voices." You need to maintain the dissociation, and then proceed with the standard format of six-step reframing. "Those voices are allies. You don't know that yet, but I'm going to demonstrate that they are. Now, ask them what they are trying to do for you."

Ben: I'm currently working with a patient who is a chronic schizophrenic. I've discovered that I'm challenging his thirteen-year career as a chronic schizophrenic by working with him. During the last session, he essentially said that he has an investment in maintaining this career. So I applauded his great success at it.

What Ben is saying is really important. He applauds the schizophrenic's thirteen-year-old career. "How well you have done as a schizophrenic for thirteen years."

Ben: He has the same name as a famous person, and I said that he was as talented at being a career schizophrenic as this person was in his field! He has actually had thirty-two years of treatment, but he has never had adequate family therapy before. In the context of family therapy he told me that he believed his mother would die if he resolved these problems and really became himself.

Was his mother present as he was talking about this belief?

Yes. I explained that she would not die if he got better. In fact, I said she would be pleased. Actually, the mother is somewhat incongruent about wanting him to recover. But I don't know where to go from there. My guess is that I should begin working on the mother.

OK. Ben's been working with a schizophrenic, and now he's going to work on the mother. The next step is the specific way in which he hooks them together. In other words, the mother says to the schizophrenic "I won't die if you get better. Go ahead and get better. In fact, I want you to get better." (He shakes his head "No.")

Ben: I didn't read the incongruence that clearly, but I feel that is accurate.

The question is, will the schizophrenic believe that incongruent statement? Definitely not. The schizophrenic is much more sensitive than you and I to those nonverbal signals. He's had a whole lifetime of reading them.

One thing you can do is to get a congruent response from the mother.

You might begin by sorting out the parts of her that do and don't want him to get better. "OK, pretend that you want him to stay sick. Now tell him all the reasons why it's important that he stay sick." She says "But I don't," and you say "Well, that will make it easier for you to pretend." Then later you say "Now pretend you want him to get well." "Well, I do." "Of course; that will make it easier to pretend." The logic of it is flimsy and irrelevant. All that's important is that you make it easy for her to respond. If you want to see something impressive in terms of nonkinesthetic anchors, have the mother alternate between those two behaviors while you watch the schizophrenic. Smoke will come right out of his ears!

Your eventual goal, of course, is to make the schizophrenic independent of whether the mother is congruent or not. In one sense, maturity is reaching a symmetrical relationship that allows a parent to be as incongruent as she wants, and the child can still maintain his own context and momentum in his life.

Whether the schizophrenic believes his mother wants him to stay sick or get well, if you're doing reframing you can say that the purpose the schizophrenic has in staying schizophrenic is to show honor to the mother. His purpose is to demonstrate how much he cares and how concerned he is about her welfare.

This is just standard reframing. I've gone from a piece of behavior, being schizophrenic, to the intent or the purpose of the behavior. I drive a wedge between the behavior "schizophrenia" and the intention or purpose of the behavior, and I validate the outcome. "You're *right!* Don't you mess around, because you care for your mother and you've got to demonstrate that to her as far as I'm concerned. I care for my mom, too." Use whatever analogue is appropriate for this particular guy.

Then you *insist* that he be schizophrenic until he has tested other ways of showing the respect and caring that his mother deserves and that he wants to give her. You insist that he continue to be schizophrenic until he discovers alternative patterns of behavior that lead to the outcome: showing respect and caring for his mother. "She deserves the best. If schizophrenia is the best, then you need to stay with it. If we can find a better way for you to demonstrate caring and respect for your mother, you'll want to do it that way, because she deserves the best." By doing this, you operate entirely within his model of the world. At the same time I would also be working with the mother to sort out her behaviors.

Sometimes when someone has come in with aspects of her experience dissociated, we have chosen *not* to go for an outcome of complete integration. A big Dutch woman who had been in this country for twenty years was brought in by her husband, because she was displaying acute schizophrenic symptoms. She heard voices that were constantly propositioning her sexually, and making lewd and incomprehensible statements. She didn't even understand the meaning of those statements, because she was a "clean woman."

A number of well-intentioned psychiatrists had attempted to deal with this woman. They explained to her that the voices were really *her* voices, and were a result of the fact that she was angry with her husband who had been involved with some other woman ten years earlier. This woman was extremely religious, and she had no way of accepting that explanation in her world-model. Her rage was unacceptable to her, so it was projected into auditory hallucinations. If she believed that those voices were hers, it would have shattered her conscious appreciation of herself. The voices were saying things and proposing activities that were abhorrent to her as a good, clean, religious woman. By trying to get the woman to accept this, the well-intentioned psychiatrists were running up against a stone wall.

This woman refused to go to psychiatrists because they were insulting her. So her husband and daughter brought her to us. The problem was getting serious, because she was slugging people who she thought were making indecent proposals to her. She was hitting and slapping waiters in restaurants, and people on the street—and she was a formidable opponent! Consequently, she was about to be locked up. We decided on a fairly limited therapeutic goal. The family was poor, and didn't have any interest in generative change. Mama just wanted to be comfortable, and the rest of the family just wanted Mama to be all right.

She was obviously already very dissociated. In this case it was a representational system dissociation. She had dissociated both the kinesthetics of the rage and the auditory representation of it. We made use of the dissociation, and simply widened it to get an altered state. Then we appealed directly to the part of her that knew what was going on. In the first session we were content with convincing her unconscious of a spurious piece of logic. We told her unconscious that since it had important things to say to her, it should say those things in her language of origin, so that she could *completely* understand. By doing that, we shifted all the hallucinated voices into Dutch. The consequence of this was that she couldn't beat up anybody here in the U.S., because she was hearing *Dutch* voices, and she knew that the people around her only spoke English. This was very confusing for her, but it was a good way to prevent her from getting into situations in which she'd actually be arrested or committed.

When she came back, we induced an altered state again, and I had a "revelation" on the spot. God spoke to me, and I reported to her what God said. "God said 'It is right and just and proper that blah, blah, blah.'" This revelation gave her instructions to move all the voices into dreams. So every night this woman would drop off to sleep and have violent dreams about taking revenge on her husband who had stepped out on her. During the day she was perfectly comfortable. We built in safeguards, so that the violent dreams didn't spill over into her behavior during the night, or she might actually have beat up her husband.

That's an example of an extremely limited therapeutic goal. It's been five and a half years now since we worked with her. She's happy and everybody in her family is happy. But that's not an integrated approach. She still has two dissociated parts of herself. Using the metaphor of the alcoholic, she is still capable of bingeing.

Man: In her dreams you mean?

Yes, and there's some possibility that it could spill over into her waking behavior, too. My guess is that if her husband got involved with another woman again, that would break down all the barriers that we set up to sort her behavior. You can always use that kind of dissociation to sort someone's behavior, but you should realize the limitations of not achieving full integration.

You need to be able to select and contextualize behavior, so that you can respond differently in different situations. Overcontextualization results in extreme dissociation, and severely limited and inflexible behavior. Extreme dissociation can work adequately in limited and relatively stable environments, but it quickly becomes maladaptive and ineffective in the face of changing conditions.

The ideal situation is to have full integration, so that any behavior can be available in any context. Our goal for you and your clients is to be able to respond to changing conditions in generative and evolutionary ways. In order to do this, it is useful to integrate dissociations fully, so that you have all your resources available to you anytime and anywhere.

Note

It is a common experience with many people when they are introduced to Neuro-linguistic Programming and first begin to learn the techniques, to be cautious and concerned with the possible uses and misuses of the technology. We fully recognize the great power of the information presented in this book and whole-heartedly recommend that you exercise caution as you learn and apply these techniques of a practitioner of NLP, as a protection for you and those around you. It is for this reason that we also urge you to attend only those seminars, workshops and training programs that have been officially designed and certified by *THE SOCIETY OF NEURO-LINGUISTIC PROGRAMMING.* Any training programs that have been approved and endorsed by *THE SOCIETY OF NEURO-LINGUISTIC PROGRAMMING* will display on the cover of the brochure (or on the front page of the literature) a copy of the registered certification mark of *THE SOCIETY OF NEURO-LINGUISTIC PROGRAMMING* shown below:

THE SOCIETY OF NEURO-LINGUISTIC PROGRAMMING is a partnership made up of Not Ltd., a corporation, and Unlimited Ltd., a corporation, set up for the purpose of exerting quality control over

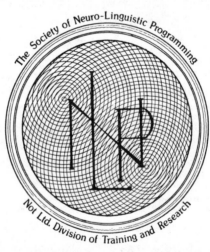

those training programs, services and materials claiming to represent the model of neuro-linguistic programming. Not Ltd.'s Division of Training and Research is the international headquarters and coordinator for all approved training programs in neuro-linguistic programming.

There are three levels of certification granted by *THE SOCIETY OF NEURO-LINGUISTIC PROGRAMMING: Practitioner, Master Practitioner and Trainer.* The certificates are granted with respect to the skill level of the trainee. *Trainer* represents the highest level of ability.

If you are considering seeking the services of a person who is skilled in neuro-linguistic programming we recommend that you find someone that has been appropriately certified. A directory of all certified individuals is maintained and distributed by Not Ltd. D.O.T.A.R.

If you would like further information on training programs, certification, research or publications on topics relating to neuro-linguistic programming please feel free to contact:

Unlimited Ltd.
1077 Smith Grade
Bonny Doon, CA
95060

Not Ltd. D.O.T.A.R.
517 Mission Street
Santa Cruz, California
95060

Bibliography

Bandler, Richard; and Grinder, John. *Frogs into Princes.* Real People Press, 1979 (cloth $9.00, paper $5.50).

Bandler, Richard; and Grinder, John. *The Structure of Magic I.* Science and Behavior Books, 1975 ($8.95).

Bandler, Richard; and Grinder, John. *Patterns of the Hypnotic Techniques of Milton H. Erickson, M.D. I.* Meta Publications, 1975 (paper, $6.95).

Bandler, Richard; Grinder, John; and Satir, Virginia. *Changing with Families.* Science and Behavior Books, 1976 ($9.95).

Cameron-Bandler, Leslie. *They Lived Happily Ever After: A Book About Achieving Happy Endings In Coupling.* Meta Publications, 1978 ($8.95).

Dilts, Robert B.; Grinder, John; Bandler, Richard; DeLozier, Judith; and Cameron-Bandler, Leslie. *Neuro-Linguistic Programming I.* Meta Publications, 1979 ($24.00).

Farrelly, Frank; and Brandsma, Jeff. *Provocative Therapy.* Meta Publications, 1978 ($9.95).

Gordon, David. *Therapeutic Metaphors: Helping Others Through the Looking Glass.* Meta Publications, 1978 ($9.95).

Grinder, John; and Bandler, Richard. *Trance-formations: Neuro-Linguistic Programming and the Structure of Hypnosis.* 1981 (cloth $9.00, paper $5.50).

Grinder, John; and Bandler, Richard. *The Structure of Magic II.* Science and Behavior Books, 1976 ($8.95).

Grinder, John; and Bandler, Richard. *Reframing: Neuro-Linguistic Programming and the Transformation of Meaning.* 1982 (cloth $9.00, paper $5.50).

Grinder, John; DeLozier, Judith; and Bandler, Richard. *Patterns of the Hypnotic Techniques of Milton H. Erickson, M.D. II.* Meta Publications, 1977 ($17.95).

Lankton, Stephen R. *Practical Magic: The Clinical Applications of Neuro-Linguistic Programming.* Meta Publications, 1979 ($12.00).

Trance-formations and *Reframing* can be ordered directly from: Real People Press, Box F, Moab, UT 84532.

All the other books above can be ordered directly from: Meta Publications Inc., P.O. Box 565, Cupertino, CA 95014.

Index